Somali, Muslim, British

Somali, Muslim, British

Striving in Securitized Britain

GIULIA LIBERATORE

BLOOMSBURY ACADEMIC
LONDON • NEW YORK • OXFORD • NEW DELHI • SYDNEY

BLOOMSBURY ACADEMIC
Bloomsbury Publishing Plc
50 Bedford Square, London, WC1B 3DP, UK
1385 Broadway, New York, NY 10018, USA

BLOOMSBURY, BLOOMSBURY ACADEMIC and the Diana logo
are trademarks of Bloomsbury Publishing Plc

First published in Great Britain 2017
Paperback edition published 2018

Cover design: Adriana Brioso
Cover image © Kate Stanworth

ISBN: HB: 978-1-3500-2771-8
PB: 978-1-3500-9462-8
ePDF: 978-1-3500-2773-2
ePub: 978-1-3500-2772-5

Names: Liberatore, Giulia author.
Title: Somali, Muslim, British : striving in securitizedBritain / Giulia Liberatore.
Description: London : Bloomsbury Academic, 2017. |Series: London School of
Economics Monographson Social Anthropology
Identifiers: LCCN 2016052845 (print) | LCCN 2017018804(ebook) | ISBN
9781350027725(ePub) | ISBN 9781350027732 (ePDF) | ISBN 9781350027718
(hardback)
Subjects: LCSH: Somalis–Great Britain–Case studies. |Women, Somali–Great
Britain–Casestudies. | Muslim women–Great Britain–Case studies. |
Muslims–GreatBritain–Case studies. | Immigrants–Great Britain–Case
studies. |Womenimmigrants–Great Britain–Case studies. | Great
Britain–Ethnicrelations–Case studies. | BISAC: SOCIAL SCIENCE /
Anthropology /Cultural. | SOCIAL SCIENCE / Gender Studies. | RELIGION /
Sexuality &Gender Studies.
Classification: LCC DA125.S56 (ebook) | LCC DA125.S56 L532017 (print) | DDC
305.893/54041–dc23
LC record available at https://lccn.loc.gov/2016052845

Series: LSE Monographs on Social Anthropology

Typeset by Deanta Global Publishing Services, Chennai, India

To find out more about our authors and books visit
www.bloomsbury.com and sign up for our newsletters.

To my parents, Grazia and Sergio

CONTENTS

LIST OF FIGURES

ACKNOWLEDGEMENTS

This book was written during a Leverhulme Early Career Fellowship at the Centre on Migration, Policy and Society (COMPAS), and a Bryan Warren Junior Research Fellowship at Linacre College, at the University of Oxford. Initial research was funded by the London School of Economics and Political Science (LSE) PhD Scholarship, the Rosemary and Raymond Firth Award, and additional LSE funds. Additional research was also made possible by the Leverhulme Trust- funded Oxford Diaspora Programme.

Sections of Chapter 8 appear in *Anthropological Quarterly* (volume 89, issue 3), and sections of Chapter 6 have been published in *Bildhaan: An International Journal of Somali Studies* (Volume 16), and in the volume *Religion and the Global City* edited by David Garbin and Anna Strhan and published in 2017 by Bloomsbury Academic. I thank the publishers for allowing me to reproduce this work. I also extend my appreciation to the Poetry Translation Centre, Clare Pollard, Lidwien Kapteijns, John W. Johnson and Hamdi Khalif for allowing me to reproduce extracts from their work, and Michael Walls for allowing me to reproduce his map of the Somali regions.

My deepest gratitude goes to all the Somali women in London who shared their life stories, experiences and knowledge with me throughout the years. Many opened their homes to me, and took precious time out of their day to invite me into their lives. To preserve their anonymity I cannot mention their names here, but I thank them all for their warm hospitality, prayers and enduring friendships. I have learnt so much from them, and I sincerely hope this book is able to do justice to their strength and endurance. Caasha-Kin Duale, Leyla Hussein and Kinsi Abdulleh have asked not to be anonymized, and I can thank them by name. I am also indebted to Zainab Dahir, who continues to support my learning of Somali with patience and enthusiasm. She is a fantastic teacher and I am very grateful that she has not given up on me just yet! Ayan Mahamoud and Jama Musse Jama welcomed me in their home when I visited Hargeysa, Somaliland, and have treated me like family throughout the years. They are also a great source of inspiration, and I am very fortunate to have them in my life. I am also indebted to the numerous Somali organizations that provided me with the opportunity to volunteer and take part in their activities. In particular I thank Kayd Somali Arts and Culture, Ocean Somali Community Association, British Somali Community, Somali Eye Magazine, Newham Somali Development Association Ltd and Kulan Youth Association.

I cannot thank my supervisors and mentors enough for their hard work over the years. Henrietta Moore has been a source of influence and inspiration as well as a caring, supporting and patient mentor. Mathijs Pelkmans has been incredibly thoughtful, supportive and encouraging; his perceptive engagement with my work has often pushed me in new directions. Laura Bear, the editor of the LSE Monographs on Social Anthropology, has been extremely generous with her time and advice to help me complete this book. I am also grateful to Deborah James, Elizabeth Hull, Felix Stein, the committee for the LSE Monographs Competition, as well as Jennifer Schmidt and the editorial and production teams at Bloomsbury Academic. At the LSE I also thank the participants of the Friday Research Seminar on Anthropological Theory, where I presented my work in November 2011, and the convenors and participants of the PhD writing up seminars in 2011–12.

Many friends and colleagues reviewed chapters or versions of this book in its various stages, or engaged in stimulating conversations with me, helping me to refine my writing. In particular, I would like to thank John Bowen, Caroline Osella, Saynab Maxamud Xasan, Anna Tuckett, Agnes Hann, Lidwien Kapteijns, Sertaç Sehlikoglu, Matthew Engelke, Catherine Allerton, Ammara Maqsood, Kaveri Qureshi, Munira Ali, Riccardo Liberatore and Mary Horgan for insightful, critical but constructive feedback on drafts of my work at various stages. I am also indebted to Leyla Hussein, Mulki Al-Sharmani, Fatima Najma, Ismail Einashe, Vanessa Hughes, Daniela Kraemer, Aude Michelet, Tom Boylston and Abdiaziz Ali Adani for our many inspiring exchanges over the years. Thanks also to Michelle Chew and Kay Celtel for their help with copy-editing. Kate Stanworth has kindly provided me with some of the beautiful images featured in this book, including the cover image, for which I am grateful.

In Oxford, I worked with Nick Van Hear on the Diaspora Engagement in War-Torn Societies project as part of the Leverhulme Oxford Diaspora Programme. Some of the research conducted during that project has fed into this book, and I am indebted to Nick who has been such a warm, welcoming and supportive mentor and colleague throughout my time at Oxford. I'd also like to thank Bridget Anderson for our chats in the COMPAS corridors, Morgan Clarke for his mentorship, and the Anthropology of Religion reading group at the Institute of Social and Cultural Anthropology (ISCA) for providing a stimulating and refreshing space to discuss many of the ideas that have fed into the following pages. Writing this book in Oxford would have been a lonely endeavour without the enriching and collaborative support of Ammara Maqsood and Leslie Fesenmyer.

My family, and in particular my parents, Sergio and Grazia, I thank for their unwavering encouragement and faith in my abilities. Last but certainly not least I thank Micheál Ó Floinn, who not only has read an endless number of drafts with his discerning and meticulous eye, but has lived through all the struggles and pleasures of research and writing with all the patience and love I could ever have asked for.

NOTE ON LANGUAGE

For Somali words, including those of pseudonyms and places, I have used the Somali spelling to maintain consistency throughout (with the exception of Mogadishu). Where individuals have asked not to be anonymized, I have used their preferred spelling of their name. In Somali the 'x' is pronounced similarly to the Arabic 'haa', and the 'c' is pronounced similarly to an Arabic ''ayn'. Many Somalis in the UK tend to anglicize their names (e.g. Canab as Anab or Ifraax as Ifrah) often by removing double vowels, the 'c', or using the 'h' instead of the 'x'. Some might retain both names, using the Somali spelling with their family, and the English spelling for general public use. For Modern Standard Arabic words I have adopted a simplified transliteration with no double vowels and diacritical marks.

I have avoided scare quotes as much as possible, particularly around the words culture, tradition, religion, authentic or authenticity in order to ease the flow for the reader.

CHAPTER ONE

Introduction

Firdos Ali's 2015 play *Struggle* features Suuban, a young Somali woman who flees Mogadishu in the 1990s following civil strife and settles in the UK with her maternal uncle. Her initial experience of living in the UK is one of invisibility. This comes to an abrupt end after 9/11. Following incidents of receiving verbal and physical abuse on the streets, Suuban produces a YouTube video about her experience of discrimination as a black Muslim woman. The video goes viral on social media, and she becomes a voice for her community, setting up 'Visible', a charity to support Muslim women in the UK.

Suuban's political involvement has repercussions. She is scrutinized by the media, attacked by anti-immigration advocates and criticized by Somali elders for not engaging with Somali politics. These critical voices, which are read out as Twitter feeds (@ Suuban, #MuslimWomen, and so on) by actors from a corner of the stage, are repeated after every major scene in the play. Everyone has something to say about Suuban, what she should do, and who she should be. Alongside the Twitter supporters, critics and trolls, the UK security agency MI5 also make constant intrusions into her life. They send agents to her home on a recruiting mission and, despite suggestions from her uncle and fiancé that she takes up their offers, she sends away. *Jihad*, she informs the MI5 agent, countering his stereotyped understanding of the term, is the struggle black Muslim women face in the UK on a daily basis; they have the odds stacked against them.

While she struggles with life in the UK, Suuban also uncovers a family history of violence and betrayal. The play shifts between

2013 London and mid-1970s Mogadishu, bringing together Suuban's story with that of her now deceased mother. As Suuban uncovers her past and learns about her mother's criticisms of the Barre regime and the abuse endured at the hands of men, both women emerge as independent, enduring and fervent characters in their struggles and strivings. As the play combines past and present, Somalia and Britain, and mother and daughter, it concludes with Suuban's creation of a hashtag #UncomfortableBrits for those who, like herself, will never quite fit in.

Received with a final standing ovation when performed in October 2015 at the annual Somali Week Festival held in Bethnal Green, East London, to a large audience of young Somalis, the play clearly resonated with the viewers' experiences of life in Britain. Somalis have been among the most publicly stigmatized Muslim groups in Britain. While following their arrival in the late 1980s and early 1990s, Somalis were initially described as an 'invisible', or marginalized community (Harris 2004: 10), they suddenly gained visibility in the post-9/11 context as the 'problem' of Islam emerged in public debate. Over the last two decades, Muslims, and Somalis in particular, have been cast as segregated, underachieving and as a threat to national cohesion and security. Their cultural and religious 'difference', and their integration within Britain, have become a source of contention, and Somali women in particular have symbolically come to stand as signs of this difference.

This book shifts perspective away from these public debates about Somalis, which often conjure up a host of problematic depictions ranging from *jihadi* brides to perpetrators of gang violence and victims of female genital mutilation (FGM). Instead, it demonstrates how Somali women differently engage with publicly problematized questions of what it means to be Muslim, Somali and British, and how they rework and challenge dominant categories and debates in the process. Based on eighteen months' ethnographic fieldwork in London, it privileges the women's everyday interactions and their imagined, embodied, affective and reasoned engagements with a range of texts, projects, debates and forms of public culture. It explores how these are employed in reimagining relations with themselves as well as multiple others, including God, kin, friends, colleagues and the British public. These dynamics are investigated through the lens of aspiration, as they play out in these women's lives and personal projects.

I argue that, despite having the odds stacked against them, the Somali women who feature in this book exhibit a capacity to aspire, and to imagine new ways of being in the world. Their ideas about themselves are shaped by dominant categories, narratives and forms of governance around culture, religion and national identity. However, by drawing on different forms of knowledge, ranging from Islamic reformist texts to British public culture, they are able to reimagine their relations to themselves and others in new ways (Moore 2011; Long and Moore 2013), reworking and unsettling problematized questions around difference and belonging in Britain. Aspiration, therefore, emerges as a human capacity – an element of subjectivity – that is expanded in moments of social or personal change. As Suuban's case illustrates, the sudden visibility around Islam propels her to engage with questions of what it means to be Muslim, black and female in a British context. Her personal engagements with these questions, and her aspiration to imagine and make sense of herself, transform her relations with kin, Twitter supporters and critics, as well as her connections with the past. In the process she transforms what it means for her to be Muslim, black and female.

Like the play, this book also explores changes over time – from post-independence Somalia to contemporary Britain – through the voices of two generations of Somali women. In so doing, it traces the genealogies of contemporary understandings of Somaliness, the increasing dominance of Islamic revivalism in the UK, and the ways in which both have been shaped by past and present forms of governance in Britain. It begins with the memories of nationalist modernity of the first generation of women who were raised in post-independent Mogadishu. Through their narratives, it describes the ways in which a nationalist notion of *Soomaalinimo* (Somaliness) emerged in relation to the modern and to an idea of an authentic traditional culture, which included religion and was also rooted in colonial ideas of Somali ethnic customs. It subsequently describes these women's flight abroad at the end of the 1980s and early 1990s, as civil war spread across the Somali regions. It chronicles their efforts to make sense of life as refugees in Britain, and to raise good Somali daughters by engaging more actively with reformist texts and teachings, which increasingly separate an authentic Islam from traditional culture.

The second part of the book turns to the young women raised in the UK throughout the 1990s and 2000s, educated first under

New Labour's policies of multiculturalism, and more recently in post-9/11 Britain, where Islam has become inseparable from appeals for greater security, cohesion and a stronger national identity. Within this context, these young women are engaged in multiple endeavours. Some negotiate pious projects in relation to public debates about Islam and ideas of culture. Others seek to transform and rejuvenate what it means to be Somali, Muslim, British, modern and progressive without necessarily reproducing restrictive, bounded or essentialized notions of culture and religion.

By prioritizing women's aspirations for new possibilities, the following ethnography challenges homogenous and static accounts of piety, while also presenting a more complex understanding of Muslim subjectivities than that found in the recent anthropological literature on Islam. What is revealed is a rich and nuanced understanding of Somali women's own efforts to fashion new ways of being in the world, which disrupts academic and public debates that emphasize difference and privilege static views of the Muslim subject. Through Somali women's perspectives, it sheds light on the ways in which 'difference' is scrutinized and governed in contemporary Britain. The following section turns to policies and debates around security and national identity, which form the backdrop of this book.

Security, British values and the Muslim 'other'

Security concerns have dominated debates and policies around Islam and multiculturalism in post-9/11 Britain.[1] Most recently, in the wake of the growing ISIS threat and reports that British Muslims were travelling to join the group, the Conservative government under David Cameron passed the Counter-Terrorism and Security Act 2015 (CTSA 2015), which has seen the Prevent policy enshrined into law. Initially launched by Blair's New Labour government in 2003 as part of Contest, Prevent was expanded following the July bombings of 2005, and revised again in 2011 by the Coalition government.[2] Under unprecedented measures, the CTSA 2015 requires local government authorities, the health sector, prisons, schools and universities to adopt 'due regard to the need to prevent people from being drawn into terrorism' (section 26(1)). In line with the 2011 amendments to Prevent, the Act compels these authorities to implement measures to deal with the risk of radicalization, and to tackle 'all forms of terrorism' and 'non-violent extremism'.

The revised Prevent strategy has shifted away from New Labour's 'winning hearts and minds' approach, which focused on engaging Muslim communities, to working with public sector institutions in tackling radicalization and extremism (O'Toole et al. 2012). Specified authorities are required, inter alia, to ensure that front-line staff receive Prevent awareness training, and that systems are put in place to identify and refer persons 'at risk' of radicalization. Higher education institutions are specifically required to adopt IT filtering policies, to implement procedures for the management of external speakers and events, and to monitor the use of prayer rooms and faith-related facilities. The strategy is pre-emptive, intervening in the pre-criminal space by monitoring, referring and reforming individuals deemed to be 'extreme', and hence at risk of radicalization and of potentially committing terrorist activities.

The introduction of this legislation should be seen in light of significant shifts in discourses and policies around the politics of difference in post-9/11 Britain. Throughout the 1990s and early 2000s, the legal and policy framework with respect to minorities in the UK included ethnicity (but not religion) as a defining characteristic of a recognized group. This framework was developed throughout the 1970s, as a consequence of a growing surge of migrants, particularly from South Asia and the former colonies, and followed on from the race-relations paradigm that had dominated previous decades (Modood 2010: 9). Although not universally or uniformly accepted, mainstream politics and public opinion throughout this period increasingly recognized the claims made by minorities to be accepted as 'different', and began to oppose race-based negative discrimination in public services, housing and employment (Grillo 2007: 980). By promoting the recognition of collective goals, advocates of multiculturalism drew on a modern notion of an 'authentic' identity formed dialogically through recognition (Taylor 1994).

Within the multicultural paradigm, ethnicity came to acquire the characteristics of a bounded notion of culture. As Anne Phillips (2007) shows in her book *Multiculturalism without Culture*, in current legislation and policy, culture has been employed to denote fixity and otherness, and to define minorities in totalizing ways, and as determined by their cultural norms and practices (see Chapter 5). In the 2000s, New Labour's increasing recognition of faith – partly a consequence of a policy engagement with grassroots campaigns for the recognition of religion within multicultural frameworks – inherited many of these reifications of culture and ethnicity. The management of Muslim groups has been viewed as an extension of existing legislation aimed at protecting the rights of racial and ethnic minority groups, and as a consequence religion, culture and ethnicity have been treated as interchangeable entities or categories of difference.[3]

Since the early 2000s this shift towards the incorporation of faith within multicultural frameworks has come under attack, as have prevailing liberal ideologies that have dominated policies since the 1970s. Echoing rhetoric that has become widespread across Europe, politicians and media pundits across the political spectrum have begun to promote a 'post-multicultural' approach, and to reassert ideas of integration, cohesion and common values (Vertovec 2010).[4] By developing values at odds with those of Western liberal society, so the dominant argument goes, multiculturalism has been seen as a threat to social cohesion and as having provided the conditions for the growth of extremism (Grillo 2007: 980). As Trevor Phillips, former chair of the Equality and Human Rights Commission (EHRC) infamously alleged, Britain was 'sleep-walking' towards segregation and multiculturalism was fuelling 'separateness'. In a recent book, left-leaning journalist David Goodhart (2014) argues that under New Labour too many people were allowed to settle in the country over too short a period of time. Many were allowed to live separate lives, contributing very little to the mainstream. Muslim communities, particularly Somalis, he states, have struggled to integrate and have tended to rely too heavily on the welfare system. This has made it harder, Goodhart continues, for ordinary British people to feel that they are part of the same 'imagined community' and thus to willingly share resources with these groups.

This type of anti-multiculturalism rhetoric has proliferated in the UK in the speeches of politicians and religious leaders, in reports and discussions in the media, as well as in policy statements and strategies and public and popular opinion. A series of reports and policies published in the early 2000s stressed the need to address economic and social exclusion, and simultaneously emphasized the importance of greater cohesion, common values and a civic notion of Britishness (Grillo 2007).[5] These mainstream debates have also converged and interacted in complex ways with the xenophobic rhetoric of populist minority right-wing movements (ibid.), and more recently, with calls for British citizens to leave the European Union and to 'take back control' of the country. Anti-immigration sentiments (directed both at European Union citizens and at other minorities), and a concern that 'too much diversity' has been detrimental to Britain, have been further intensified by these appeals to national sovereignty.

Islam has come to occupy the centre stage of these anti-multiculturalism debates, as the 'problem' of multiculturalism has become inseparably linked to the 'Muslim problem'. These criticisms and arguments were echoed in the Home Office's (2001) *Community Cohesion* report, which set out to investigate the causes of the riots in the northern towns of Oldham, Burnley and Bradford. It suggested that 'multiculturalism's allegedly divisive character stems from a supposed institutionalization of difference and undermining of "cohesion" [and] "common values"' (Grillo 2007: 986).[6] Cameron's (2011) speech at the Munich security conference, which took place during my fieldwork, further reinforced the associations between Islam, multiculturalism, cohesion and national identity. He blamed 'state multiculturalism' for an increase in segregation, violence, the development of conflicting values and a loss of national identity. Although Cameron made a clear distinction between Islam and extremism, suggesting that only certain isolated Muslim groups were promoting extremism, he argued against the passive tolerance of previous years in favour of 'an active, muscular liberalism' (ibid.). The latter, he claimed, actively promotes certain values such as freedom of speech, freedom of worship, democracy, the rule of law and equality of race, sex and sexuality.

The CTSA 2015 has been introduced amid growing nationalist, anti-immigration and anti-multiculturalism rhetoric and public concern for greater sovereignty, protection and security. The Prevent strategy draws explicitly on the notion of 'muscular liberalism' by broadening the definition of extremism to 'vocal or active opposition to fundamental British values'. Extremist Muslims are positioned in culturalized terms as illiberal, un-free, lacking in choice and as a threat to the nation. The preventative monitoring and reforming of extreme Muslim behaviour to 'fit' within liberal Britain is justified as necessary to ensure the security of the nation.

This securitization of Britain provides the background to this book. My interest throughout, however, is not with understanding multiculturalism, culture or religion as descriptive terms, nor as analytical entities or concepts (Modood 2010, 2005; Parekh 2000; Taylor 1994).[7] Neither am I concerned with issues of diversity, integration or assimilation, or with providing answers to the questions that have emerged in debates around the demise of multiculturalism (Vertovec and Wessendorf 2010; Meer and Modood 2009; Joppke 2004). Following Foucault (2000), I analyse these debates as creating 'distinctive fields of problematization' – areas of knowledge that have come to pose a problem for contemporary politics (Bracke and Fadil 2012: 40). These rhetorical and policy shifts around the retreat of multiculturalism have produced politically charged questions of what constitutes Somali culture, and what it means to be a Muslim and British woman.

Rather than describing or analysing the meaning of culture, religion or nationality per se, I argue that these categories, and the boundaries between them, have become 'problematized' in the contemporary moment – that is, they have emerged as objects of thought that invite reflection and elaboration. As I indicated at the beginning, I investigate the historical legacies to these problematizations, exploring how notions of culture, and its relation to Islam, for example, have changed over time and have been shaped by shifting forms of governance.

Throughout the book I prioritize the solutions offered by different groups of Somali women, and place their voices alongside those of politicians, academics and theorists. While these women's solutions are shaped by dominant debates and forms of power, I argue that they also rework the elements of these problematizations and refract, unsettle and critically intervene in these debates. I pay particular attention to the appropriation of elements of the liberal tradition in these debates, and the political effects of these rhetorical devices on Somali Muslim women. This book, therefore, is not only an ethnography of Somali women, but also a reflection on how liberal democracies such as Britain scrutinize, manage and govern difference.

The Islamic revival in Britain and beyond

Over the last two decades, Europe has witnessed an Islamic revival. This is part of a global phenomenon which first emerged in the 1970s in the Middle East and South Asia, but it is connected to a longer tradition of renewal (*tajdid*) and reform (*islah*) of Islamic faith and practice (Voll 1983). Globally, reformist movements have involved a wide range of traditions and projects, which all share a concern with aligning religious beliefs and practices with core foundations of Islam and with purifying Islam from local customs and innovations (Osella and Osella 2008: 1–2). In the UK, the revival first gained prominence in the late 1980s and early 1990s and, like elsewhere, has been manifest in a surge in 'public piety' (Deeb 2006), the adoption of embodied practices and rituals – most notably the donning of the *hijab* (veil or headscarf) and the implementation of prayer – as well as the embracing of new ethical sensibilities (Dwyer 1999). It has also led to the proliferation of Islamic schools, training centres, institutes, bookshops and pedagogical material, and the growth of Islamic societies on university campuses. Those involved have been predominantly the children of migrants from Bangladesh and Pakistan who came to the country throughout the 1960s and 1970s. Smaller numbers of participants include second-generation Somalis, Turks, Arabs and converts.[8] Muslims involved in the revival have been engaging in new ways with Islamic scholarly texts and modes of reasoning that were previously reserved for those trained at traditional religious institutions. This new form of religiosity has been characterized by a 'heightened self-consciousness' of textual knowledge (Eickelman and Piscatori 1996: 39), with the aim of applying it to the self in order to cultivate a pious disposition. Emphasis is placed on organizing one's everyday life in accordance with Islamic standards of virtuous conduct. Many of these practitioners stress the importance of engaging with an authentic, universal Islam and critique the 'backwards' cultural attitudes and practices of older generations (Roy 2004; Schmidt 2002; Jacobson 1998).

The traditions of reform present in the UK are largely a product of older patterns of immigration. South Asian reform movements such as the *Deobandi, Barelvi and Ahl-e-Hadith* – what Bowen (2016: 26–30) has described as the North Indian 'Islamic triangle' – have been highly influential, as have been political groups such as *Jamaat-e-Islami*.[9] The latter has been particularly significant in Tower Hamlets in East London, which has a large and longstanding presence of Bangladeshi Muslims.[10] More recently, Salafi groups have gained prominence thanks to the influx of money from the Gulf countries that has been channelled into the funding of mosques and places of learning, and the provision of free educational material in London and beyond (Al-Rasheed 2005). In Chapter 4, I describe the more recent growth of Somali mosques in London, many of which have been built through local Somali community fundraising initiatives to address social, moral and educational challenges faced by both Somali children and the older generations. First-generation Somalis, who bring along their young or teenage children, are most active in these mosques, and their involvement in these and other Islamic institutions reflects their participation in processes of Islamic reform rarely accounted for in the literature on Islam in Europe, which often privileges the experiences of younger generations.[11]

These Somali mosques are less popular among second-generation Somalis, who in contrast prefer to 'hop around' the diverse, multi-ethnic mosques across the city. As I discuss in Chapter 6, these young people have little appreciation of the reform movements they encounter in London; rather, they distinguish between the different forms of knowledge based on a Sufi-Salafi continuum (Jensen 2006). Like other Somalis, most follow the *Sha'fi madhhab* (school of jurisprudence), but the religious practices of the young women featured in this book cannot be subsumed under a particular tradition or movement. Many experiment with a range of different forms of knowledge, and their commitment to any teacher, group or institute of learning is often not sustained over long periods of time. Throughout the book I present the perspectives not only of committed or practising Muslims, but also of those who claim to 'live Islam' in many other ways. Some state clearly that they are not practising, and are often criticized by more committed friends or relatives for being 'bad Muslims' or for not adopting orthodox modes of Islamic dress and behaviour. Others do practise their faith, but their positions vis-à-vis British society vary. Some are politically engaged, while others are not, and some seek to practise a British Islam, or to demonstrate Islam's compatibility with being British, while others stress the universality of their faith and care little about adapting it to British ways of life.

The Islamic revival in Europe has largely been studied through the lens of migration, integration and adaptation. This is understandable given that the majority of Muslims in Europe are the children or grandchildren of migrants who arrived post-Second World War. However, the majority of Muslims in the UK are British citizens, and certainly most of the Somali women featured in this book hold a British passport or a passport from a European Union country. This book thus questions the extent to which migration, integration and adaptation are useful concepts for analysing the lives of Muslims in Britain. I suggest these frameworks problematically cast Muslims as foreign, and therefore as not fully British, and present Islam as a problem of integration or assimilation and not as a constituent part of the social fabric of Britain. In so doing, I critically engage with two major themes found in the literature on Islam in Europe.

The first seeks to account for the recent rise of religiosity and the prominence of Muslim identities among young people in Europe with reference to their relative experiences of deprivation and discrimination. For example, some scholars have claimed that the stigmatization of Muslims in post-9/11 Europe, and the discrimination, unemployment and socio-economic deprivation faced by many, have encouraged Muslim youth to seek meaning and a sense of belonging through the *umma* (community of believers). It is argued that Islam provides them with a sense of community, support, self-esteem and ways of coping with these challenges of living in a place where they feel they do not belong (Peek 2005; Kibria 2008; Jacobson 1997, 1998). By seeking to explain the resurgence of Islam, I argue, these studies present it as an anomaly, or as a phenomenon that needs to be accounted for, rather than an ordinary dimension of young people's lives. These studies presuppose that with migration and increasing engagement with Western society, migrants will eventually secularize, or privatize their faith, reflecting a modernization and secularization narrative. The resurgence of Muslim public religiosity contradicts this narrative and so demands an explanation. Furthermore, religion is reduced to being a means to an end, and to serving as a source of support, meaning and identity for people in difficult times.

Rather than asking why young people engage with reformist Islam in contemporary Britain, this book asks why this has come to be viewed as a 'problem'. It also explores how and to what effect Somali women engage with teachings, texts and scholars, stigmatizing debates around Islam and a range of other forms of knowledge. Many Muslims do experience social and economic exclusion and stigmatization, and for some this might trigger a more active engagement with their faith. Religion might indeed provide a source of identity and belonging for young Muslims. However, for many of the young women to whom I spoke, religion does not primarily serve a purpose, nor is it seen as a way of dealing with the problems of exclusion. As we shall see, engagements with scriptures, debates and ethical practices are not necessarily, or only, about identity,[12] but involve processes of ethical self-fashioning (Mahmood 2005; Hirschkind 2006; Fernando 2014: 14) and, as I discuss below, forms of aspiration.

The second body of work can be broadly subsumed under the notion of 'European Islam', and has investigated the ways in which Islamic religiosity, practice and organizational life have changed within the European context. As I elaborate further in Chapter 6, scholars have explored the ways in which Islam has adapted to become more 'critical', 'individualized' and hence more 'European' (Cesari 2003; Mandaville 2001, 2003). It is claimed that encounters with secular Western societies have fragmented traditional forms of authority, and Islam has become more privatized and individualized as a consequence (Roy 2004). While this literature has raised important questions about changes to modes of Islamic religiosity over time and space, I suggest that it has also problematically assumed that change occurs primarily in the relatively recent encounter with a modern Europe. It fails to consider a longer history of exchange between Muslim societies and Europe and, in particular, ignores the colonial encounter and the ways in which some traditions of reform originate from this period, and in some cases, in anti-imperial struggles.

As Amir-Moazami and Salvatore (2003) have also shown, this approach juxtaposes tradition against modernity, assuming that with the fragmentation of religious knowledge Muslim traditions are eroded and effectively become 'modern'. This juxtaposition neglects the 'potential of transformation and reform that originates within Muslim traditions' themselves (ibid.: 53). Drawing on MacIntyre's (1981 (2007)) notion of a 'living tradition' and Asad's (1986) elaboration of this concept into the 'Islamic discursive tradition', Amir-Moazami and Salvatore (2003) point to the importance of considering internal processes of transformation that have unfolded over time, as well as changes that occur in the engagement with other competing traditions. If fragmentation does occur, they argue, it is because traditions have undergone internal interventions that are not necessarily a consequence of the encounter with the modern era (ibid.: 55).

This book engages with the question of change and transformation of the Islamic tradition but, like other recent scholarship it also explores processes of reform and change that occur internally within the tradition as part of processes of reform, and prior to migration to Europe, as well as externally in interactions with a European context (Jacobsen 2010; Fernando 2014; Jouili 2015). In a similar way to this existing body of work, it focuses on how Muslims draw on and rework concepts from the Islamic tradition in a secular or liberal European public sphere. It considers both continuities and changes, and the importance of norms and forms of orthodoxy in shaping people's engagements with Islam. In Chapters 6 and 7, I demonstrate how changes unfold as young Somali women engage with the Islamic tradition but in relation to contemporary forms of problematization around the meaning of Islam, ethnicity, culture and nationality. Somali women are not simply changing Islam to 'fit' British contexts, but are employing tools and concepts internal to the Islamic tradition – such as the tensions between interiority and exteriority, choice and constraint – to engage with problematized questions of belonging. Through this process, they are reworking and transforming the tradition from within, even while challenging mainstream notions of religion, difference and citizenship in Britain.

In moving beyond a paradigm that prioritizes migration, integration and identity formation, this book explores the ways in which Somali women aspire for new ways of being in the context of securitized Britain. In so doing, I engage with two bodies of work that have emerged in parallel with each other within the anthropological study of Islam. First, I draw on the work on piety (Mahmood 2005; Hirschkind 2006), which has explored how Muslims engage with the Islamic discursive tradition to fashion themselves as pious subjects through a set of practices and bodily techniques of self-discipline. This work has usefully challenged the secular-liberal notion of agency that assumes an innate desire for freedom, by considering Muslims' desire to fashion themselves into good pious subjects by submitting to norms and forms of power. However, departing from this work, I focus less on discourses of pious self-cultivation and more on how Islamic teachings and texts, alongside a range of other forms of knowledge, are engaged in the process of imagining relations with self and others. I thereby move beyond binaries of Islam versus secular-liberalism, which have framed much of this piety scholarship. I draw on a second body of work that has challenged the homogenous, coherent and linear nature of accounts of pious self-cultivation (Osella and Soares 2010; Schielke 2010a,b, 2015; Marsden 2010; Simon 2009). This scholarship has focused on the everyday lives and complex experiences of Muslims to investigate how pious projects are negotiated and contested in relation to other values, ideas, norms and practices and within particular sociopolitical contexts.[13] Experiences of piety, these studies have shown, are often fragmented, incoherent and ambiguous.

Building on these insights, the following ethnography shows how Somali women engage with pious projects among several coexisting forms of knowledge – ideals, values, practices and models of selfhood – and within a constraining context that has increasingly come to problematize Islam. Rather than focusing on ethics or morality,[14] however, it demonstrates how some of these forms of knowledge, such as Islamic reformist teachings, are connected with ethical projects, whereas others – a desire for fashionable clothing, a professional job or a romantic relationship – are not, but are equally important in understanding these women's complex subjectivities. Different forms of knowledge, whether textual or experiential, are themselves shaped by contextually specific problematizations, and exist not in opposition but in a hierarchical relationship to one another, with some dominating over others at specific moments in time.

Moreover, through the lens of aspiration, this book offers a more complex account of subjectivity than that provided in the anthropological work on Islam described above. While scholarship on piety has theorized Muslim subjectivity predominantly through abstract concepts and ideas taken from the Islamic discursive tradition, the work on the everyday lives of Muslims has moved beyond an overemphasis on pious self-cultivation and discourse. Yet, it has reduced subjectivity to processes of navigating, negotiating or challenging competing or overlapping teleologies of the subject. The latter has left unexplored the multiple means and modes by which these different teleologies or 'moral registers' (Schielke 2010a) are engaged in the making of subjectivities. In a recent critique, Fadil and Fernando (2015: 80) note how work on the 'everyday' has posited the self as 'external to and independent of structures of power (i.e. religion)', reproducing historical binaries of structure versus agency. The authors argue that the complexity, contradiction and ambiguity of 'real' and 'everyday' actions of individual agents are juxtaposed to, and prioritized over, the coherence of religious norms and institutions, thus reproducing a notion of the humanist subject.

In what follows, I argue that subjectivities are more than the occupants of particular subject positions within social, economic and religious structures, but are constituted in relation to the self and other through forms of identification and dis-identification which are discursive, embodied, affective and imagined (Moore 2011: 76). Rather than separating 'grand schemes' or 'moral registers' from the self, and emphasizing resistance or creativity vis-à-vis norms, this book explores the means and modes by which Somali women differently attach themselves to religious norms and ideals, as well as to newly encountered projects, imaginaries or practices, which do not necessarily exist in contradiction to each other.[15] Through this process, it highlights how, through these attachments, Somali women reconfigure their relations to themselves and to multiple others, aspiring for new ways of being and thus intervening, as I elaborate below, within a set of contextually specific problematizations. They articulate new possibilities that exceed, and therefore cannot be reduced to, distinctive discursive traditions – whether Islamic or secular-liberal – nor to particular sets of rules, norms, value systems, moral registers or 'grand schemes'.

Aspiration

This book explores how Somali women who currently reside in London make sense of what it means to be Somali, Muslim and British in post-9/11 Britain, as they go about their everyday lives, working, studying, marrying, raising children, and dealing with personal crises and ambitions. Problematized questions around culture, religion and national identity are made sense of, and reworked, through these events in their lives. For example, at particular moments of change – brought about by political, economic or social factors – the women who feature in this book also imagine and reflect on themselves, on their futures, and on their relations to others and to the world around them in relation to experiences in their life-course. They are shaped by an existing terrain of problematizations, but also contribute their own understandings, and their own solutions. Through their imaginations of self and self–other relations they alter the conditions in which possible responses can emerge and take form.

Contexts of social change are, therefore, also moments of potentiality because they introduce new ideas, discourses and ways of being. The following ethnography explores how these broader social changes are made sense of by Somali women, as they relate these new forms of knowledge to personal trajectories, which in turn give rise to forms of aspiration. Rather than theorizing aspiration solely as a 'cultural capacity' (Appadurai 2013) embedded in particular norms, values, practices and histories, this ethnography unravels aspiration as a human capacity to orient the self forward in time. This orientation fuels engagements with particular forms of knowledge, as well as individuals' efforts to imagine and seek out new ways of being. It is a capacity that is expanded in moments of social change as individuals are faced with new ideas and ways of being and become 'other' to themselves, forcing them to rethink and reimagine who they are and how they relate to those around them. Aspiration, therefore, is crucial to understanding the ways in which subjectivities are transformed.

My approach to aspiration draws on Moore's (2011) concept of the ethical imagination as a human capacity or mode through which individuals imagine relationships to themselves and to others. Moore builds on both a Lacanian understanding of the subject, which foregrounds fantasy and the imagination (2007: 15), and a Foucauldian approach to ethical practice and the making of the subject.[16] Yet her interest, like mine, is not in ethics per se, but in the processes by which subjectivity is formed and transformed by engaging the ethical imagination. While for Foucault (2000: 117) ethical practice is informed by thought and reflection – an ability to stand back from acting and reacting – the ethical imagination also includes embodied dispositions, affect and, crucially, fantasy and the imagination (Moore 2011).[17] Therefore, as Moore (ibid.: 76) elaborates, the relation between the self and other is historically specific, social, embodied and affective, as well as imagined and based on forms of knowing and unknowing.

Furthermore, for Moore the self is part of a 'dynamic relational matrix' (Long and Moore 2013: 4). Relations are interdependent and co-constitutive; they are formative of the subject, but also something upon which the subject can reflect and subsequently transform (ibid.). These fantasized relations to the self and others can have different spatial scales (Moore 2011: 78) but also, I would add, different temporalities. Whereas some relations may be premised on 'detailed empirical knowledge of shared intimacies and spaces ... others are mediated by more distant institutions, structures and imaginaries' (ibid.). Therefore, fantasized relations to kin, pious or non-pious friends, or non-Muslims may be mediated by everyday experiences with these individuals, as well as by global discourses on piety, imaginaries of Muslims in Europe, public discourses on culture, or narratives of financial success. Self–other relations extend across time and space: they may refer both to intimate relations in the home or neighbourhood and to distant individuals or entities, such as God, past selves or future husbands. As Moore's work (2011: 16) demonstrates, in contexts of social change the ethical imagination is brought into play by new ideas, ways of being and people's own theories of change. The experience of engaging with these new forms of knowledge, through reasoned, affective, embodied and imagined processes, involves shifting the entire 'relational matrix' so that these multiple relations are all reconfigured.[18]

New forms of knowledge, whether these are in the form of texts, ideas, discourses or affective or embodied experiences, engage the ethical imagination, enabling new forms of being to emerge. They thus expand the capacity to aspire, and open up horizons of possibility. As I show throughout the book, and as illustrated in the play with which I opened this chapter, many young Somali women in Britain do experience the struggles and limitations of being black, Muslim and female, and they frequently encounter barriers in achieving their aspirations. At the same time, my ethnography reveals a capacity to redirect struggles into potential opportunities, and to recast difficulties as possibilities for striving and transforming themselves anew. The focus, therefore, is not on assessing or determining whether imagined possibilities are accomplished, but on individuals' own understandings of their trajectories, and their engagements with these struggles and possibilities at various points in their lifetime. Unlike accounts of young black Muslim youth in Europe who are often depicted as victims of alienation and discrimination, young Somalis in this book emerge as key agents of change, articulating and transforming what it means to be Muslim, black, female, educated and British. As Cole and Durham (2008: 5) argue, 'youth and children help negotiate new futures', and in what follows youthfulness emerges as a capacity to redirect the self towards a future horizon. In sum, striving unfolds through the reimagining of relations to the self and the other. This capacity for aspiration is experienced as an openness, or a form of becoming – a tendency rather than a movement or project with identifiable trajectories (Khan 2012). I place analytical emphasis on the processes of setting new horizons rather than the realization of particular projects or endpoints. Unlike Khan's analysis of Muslims striving in Pakistan, whereby the ultimate aim is left obscured and unanswered, the efforts to strive among the Somali women described in this book are often directed at managing multiple coexisting endpoints – being pious, modern, educated, good Somali women. Furthermore, aspirations cannot be reduced to what are often categorized as 'religious' pursuits, nor are they embedded solely within socio-economic or political projects. Processes of engaging with revivalist projects constitute one of several different and interconnected aspirational endeavours, such as striving to be modern or professional, a good mother or a feminist activist. Some of these projects are projected forward in the near future, whereas others might be extended into the distant future of the hereafter. These endpoints constitute imagined ideals which shift throughout one's lifetime. What my ethnography highlights is a potentiality to aspire, as individuals imagine new ways of being through novel experiences and engagements with knowledge.

An emphasis on aspiration, I argue, shifts attention towards a more 'positive anthropology' (Fischer 2014; Appadurai 2013) in a context that is increasingly dominated by the language of struggle, threat and disruption. By positioning pious projects as one of many forms of aspiration in contemporary Britain, this book joins recent efforts in downplaying the exceptional nature of revivalist Islam and of pious Muslims at a time when the rise of Islamic religiosity has been viewed as anachronistic, and Muslims have been cast in opposition to European values (Coleman 2013; Schielke 2015).

Furthermore, while retaining an awareness of structural and historical factors shaping experience (Ortner 2016), this analysis seeks to account for actions and motivations not only by looking to the past, and understanding the present as historically determined, but also by understanding the present through the potentiality that is offered by a yet undetermined future. Changes in subjectivity involve processes of thinking, imagining, reasoning and feeling that cannot be reduced to subject positions or models of selfhood. Aspirational projects are always more than reactive responses, or coping tools in contexts of discrimination and alienation. They are imaginative possibilities that emerge in particular situations, and in response to given circumstances, but are never fully determined by them, as they creatively challenge these circumstances offering new possibilities for the future. Attention to Somali women's ethical imaginations, I argue, sheds light on how forms of knowledge are personalized and given meaning, and how processes of change unfold through shifting attachments to texts, ideas and discourses as well as to multiple others. It provides a more complex account of the formation of subjectivity and its relation to forms of power. It also shifts our perspective away from the dominant debates around Islam and the politics of difference to new ways of being that do not necessarily emphasize similar categories of difference.

Outline of the book

This book takes a subjective and generational perspective on processes of change to explore how women who have experienced similar historical trajectories make sense of these changing engagements with ideas, discourses, symbols and texts at various points in time through relations with multiple others. It is organized as follows.

The next chapter reflects on the politicized nature of working with, and writing about, Somali women in securitized Britain, and describes my experience of conducting research in London. Chapter 3 turns to examine the memories of modernity of Somali women raised in the capital Mogadishu throughout the 1960s to 1980s – whom I refer to as the 'first generation'. Specifically, the chapter explores the ways in which notions of *Soomaalinimo* (Somaliness), shaped in relation to ideas of modernity and traditional culture, were made sense of and employed in the shaping of female subjectivities. It is based on competing memories of everyday life during this period, narrated by Somali women who moved to the UK during the civil war in the late 1980s and early 1990s. It sheds light on how these women differently remember and recount the post-independence periods of nationalist fervour, socialist modernity and the subsequent conflict, in light of their experiences of moving abroad and becoming increasingly pious. I argue that unpacking these memories of Somalia's modern past is crucial to understanding new and heightened forms of religiosity in the diaspora. Religious transformations need to be situated in a broader historical perspective that is often missing from accounts of revivalist Islam in Europe.

With the onset of civil war and migration abroad, many of these ideas and pursuits were abandoned, and Chapter 4 details these women's struggles with settling into life in London, their new engagements with reformist Islam and their efforts to raise their children. The recent growth of Somali mosques is accounted for through parents' investments in their children's education and futures, and their hope of raising them as good, educated Somali Muslims in some of the more deprived neighbourhoods in the city.

Chapter 5 turns to the 'younger generations', many of whom were either born in, or moved to, the UK or Europe as small children. It introduces a number of women who are not necessarily committed Muslims but who engage with notions of *Soomaalinimo* and Somali culture in contrasting ways. These young women are actively involved in updating, renewing and transcending what it means to be Somali, and shaping themselves around these new ideas and concepts. The subsequent two chapters focus on a group of young women who have begun to pursue pious projects at particular junctures in their lives, while negotiating these with other ideals and pursuits. Chapter 6 explores their efforts to seek Islamic forms of knowledge among various reformist movements and groups in London. The focus is on how these women understand their experiences of Islam in contrast to those of the older generations. For many of the younger women, practising involves seeking knowledge not in Somali mosques but in diverse, multi-ethnic mosques. This chapter argues that movement across different spaces of learning – what they call 'mosque hopping' – is key to their engagements with knowledge, and to the ways in which they differentiate themselves from their mothers and older kin. The chapter further contributes to discussions around authority within Islam by bringing to the fore the importance of friendship groups, and the reasoned and affective experiences of engaging with particular sources of Islamic knowledge.

Chapter 7 positions young practising women within debates around Islam in Britain. It explores how young women are shaped by – but also respond to – representations of pious Muslims in the media, popular culture and public debate in the UK. It also sheds light on how they transform debates around multiculturalism, integration, Islam and national identity. Specifically, it examines the ways in which these young women engage with the 'problem' of what constitutes the Muslim subject, with a series of interrelated problems around the visibility of Islamic practices, and with the tension between the universal and the particular. The process involves a reformulation of the relationship between exterior practices and interior dimensions of the self and, as discussed in the preceding chapter, a process of reconfiguring what it means to be Somali. By separating themselves from mothers, older kin and non-practising friends, and reworking public discourses on Islam, these women are also transforming the Islamic pedagogical tradition from within by prioritizing the importance of interiority.

The final chapter focuses on marriage to explore how individuals engage with conflicting and overlapping values, discourses and ideals, and manage their relations with multiple others. Bringing together more or less pious women, this chapter is about women's discussions around marriage and ideal husbands, and the forms of imagination and aspiration that it entails. The chapter comes to two interrelated conclusions. First, it shows how individuals fashion themselves not only in relation to a single discursive tradition, but often by negotiating between several in a range of diverse ways. Second, it demonstrates how many young Somali women, whether they are concerned with pious pursuits or not, are engaged in similar processes of rethinking their relations with the self and the other, and articulating novel ways of being. In so doing, the chapter seeks to unsettle the dichotomies between religious and non-religious, or between pious and liberal or integrated Muslims that often dominate public discourses on Islam.

The book concludes by gazing back at contemporary policies and public debates about Islam in Britain. Through a critical analysis of Prevent and the Counter-Terrorism and Security Act 2015, it reflects on the ways in which this legislation shapes and reforms religious subjectivities in particular ways. It subsequently returns to discuss the ethical and political tensions and contradictions of conducting research with, and writing about, Somali women from the point of view of a knowledge-producing institution that has become complicit in Prevent. By drawing on my ethnography, the book proposes a number of alternative visions for a utopian future beyond Prevent and securitized Britain.

Notes

1   Since 2001 the UK government has passed eight terrorism-related acts.

2   Contest is the UK government's post-9/11 counter-terrorism strategy, which includes Prevent, Pursue (stopping terrorist attacks), Protect (strengthening protection against terrorist attacks) and Prepare (mitigating the impact of any successful attack) (Home Office 2011).

3   In the late 1990s and early 2000s, the UK witnessed the proliferation of a series of reports accommodating of religious diversity (Home Office 2001). Practical and financial provisions for Muslims, including the provision of *halal* meals in schools, uniforms that accommodate the donning of the *hijab*, or the right for parents to withdraw children from some aspects of sex education, were introduced and implemented at the local level. In 1998 government funding was extended to the first Muslim schools, the *Islamia* Primary School in London and *Al Furqan* in Birmingham.

4   Criticism of multiculturalism existed before this, but it was not mainstream. For example, see Alibhai-Brown (2001) and Okin (1999).

5   These reports include the *Strength in Diversity* consultation (Home Office 2004b), and the Community Cohesion Panel Final Report (Home Office 2004a). See also David Blunkett's white paper, *Secure Borders, Safe Haven* (Home Office 2002).

6   The report was written by the Community Cohesion Review Team and chaired by Professor Ted Cantle, founder of the Institute for Community Cohesion, which was set up in 2005 (see http://www.cohesioninstitute.org.uk/home).

7   For recent work on multiculturalism in Britain, see Grillo (2007), McGhee (2008), Kundnani (2007, 2012a), Phillips (2007). For discussions on multiculturalism within political theory, see Kymlicka (2007), Modood (2005) and Taylor (1994).

8   According to the 2011 Census, Muslims constitute the second largest religious group in the country (4.8 per cent of the population in

England and Wales), and almost half of Muslims in Britain were born in the UK. The boroughs of Tower Hamlets and Newham in London have the highest proportion of Muslims in the country.

9 In South Asia many of these traditions of reform are seen in opposition to more textual forms of Islam (Maqsood, forthcoming). In contrast to the older generations, young Muslims in the UK are less interested in particular traditions of reform than in engaging in textual forms of Islam that are not necessarily linked with a particular tradition.

10 See Glynn (2002) for a discussion of Islamic reformist movements in East London, and Bowen (2016: 37–42) for a discussion of the East London Mosque.

11 Pedersen's (2014) work on first-generation Iraqi women in Copenhagen is a notable exception.

12 As Lambek (2014: 20) notes, this reduction of religion to identity politics is the result of the secularization and objectification of religion.

13 Schielke (2010a: 29–30) refers to these sets of values, norms and practices which constitute different moral or normative frameworks as 'teleologies of the subject' or 'moral registers'. Deeb and Harb's (2013) concept of 'moral rubric' adapts Schielke's (2010a) 'moral registers' in order to capture the potentially more malleable nature of moral ideals, discourses, norms and practices, and to place more emphasis on values.

14 The anthropology of ethics and morality has flourished in recent years as evidenced in the work of Laidlaw (2014), Lambek (2010), Faubion (2001) and Keane (2015).

15 In so doing, it avoids positing an opposition between religious norms and everyday actions, or piety and other 'non-religious' frameworks, that is found in the literature on the everyday lives of Muslims (Fadil and Fernando 2015: 76). It also avoids an opposition between piety and secular-liberal ethics reproduced in some of the literature on ethics (Mahmood 2005; Agrama 2012).

16 For recent anthropological theorizing on subjectivity, see Ortner (2005), Biehl et al. (2007) and Luhrmann (2006).

17 Foucault (1985: 26–8) identifies four dimensions to ethics. First, the *ethical substance* refers to a part of the self or mode of behaviour upon which the individual works. Second, the *mode of subjectification* refers to the way in which an individual establishes her relationship to the rule. Because the subject is formed within the limits of a historically specific set of practices, this dimension

recognizes the ways in which power summons a subject to constitute herself in relation to her moral codes. Third, the *forms of elaboration of ethical work* or the *techniques of the self* refer to the means by which a subject works on the ethical substance and changes herself in order to become ethical. Finally, the *telos* (plural: *teleologies*) of the ethical subject denotes the type of moral being to which one aspires.

18 According to Foucault (2000), 'forms of knowledge' refer to acts, practices and thoughts which come to be authoritative at particular moments in time and under specific configurations of power. These forms of knowledge provide the grounds for an ethics of the self – the relationship of the self to itself. They thus define particular *telos* of the subject, or using Schielke's (2010a) term, distinctive 'moral registers'.

CHAPTER TWO

An ethnography with Somali women in London

A new Somali studies

As I was writing this manuscript in Spring 2015, Safia Aidid – a Harvard PhD student – began an online exchange using the hashtag #*Cadaan*Studies (Whiteness Studies). This was prompted by the launch of the *Somaliland Journal of African Studies,* which had failed to include a single Somali scholar or student on its editorial board. Aidid wrote a critical letter to the editors, sparking what has since evolved into a global debate about the process of knowledge production about Somalis. The conversation has so far given rise to a blog (http://themaandeeq.com, discussed in Chapter 5), panel discussions at academic conferences and arts festivals, and a workshop at Harvard University. While these debates are not new within anthropology, those involved in *Cadaan* Studies claim that Somali studies is yet to be decolonized. They argue that scholars and researchers continue to deploy colonial epistemologies that essentialize Somalis and reify them as appropriate subjects of study. *Cadaan* Studies is not only about reclaiming Somali studies for Somali people – thus allowing Somalis to produce knowledge about themselves – but also about unsettling colonial ways of knowing, concepts and assumptions that continue to dominate knowledge production about Somalis.[1] The 'Whiteness

Studies' label is therefore intended as a mode of gazing back and interrogating the producers of knowledge about Somalis. Aidid and others involved in *Cadaan* Studies have begun to challenge the conceptual 'whiteness' of knowledge and to imagine a 'new' Somali studies (Aidid 2015).

Drawing on these debates, this book aims to unsettle the dominant modes of researching and writing about Somalis in the diaspora, and to untangle the ways in which these are tied to the governance and politics of difference in Britain. Rather than seeking to resolve a 'problem' pertaining to Somalis, it questions why Somalis have come to be seen as a problem and as particular subjects of study. Throughout the book, I do not define *Soomaalinimo* (Somaliness) but rather interrogate the ways in which categories of difference and identity, such as Somaliness, have been produced historically and shaped through forms of governance. I question why we have taken for granted certain modes of describing difference and, in doing so, have reduced and reified people's lives. Rather than approaching the study of Somalis in Britain through the lens of migration, integration and belonging, I suggest that we seriously ask how and why Somaliness and Islam have become problematized under the current security agenda. I explore how these issues and questions are shaping lives, but also how they are being reworked, disrupted and transformed.

Furthermore, my ethnographic approach is intended to be a process of 'speaking with' rather than speaking 'to' or 'for' Somalis (Spivak 1988). While recognizing the power dynamics inherent in my relations with different groups of Somali women, I present here a contextualized account of our conversations and engagements. I place these conversations alongside those of theorists, scholars, politicians and public commentators in order to treat my interlocutors themselves as theorists. That said, I also question if it is possible for a white European woman, drawing on concepts derived from Euro-American critical scholarship and writing from within a British university, to present a truly decolonized account of Somali lives in the diaspora. I return to these questions in the final chapter of this book, where I reflect on the politics of knowledge production about Somalis in securitized Britain. In what follows I reflect on my experiences of researching and writing this book.

Ethnographic fieldwork in London

My research focused mainly on female members in twenty-one Somali households in London. The decision to focus on women was both a deliberate choice and dictated by the difficulties of gaining access to the everyday lives of Somali men. Some men – mainly the fathers, husbands and brothers of my interlocutors – do feature in my research, and I did conduct twenty interviews, and many more informal conversations, with elderly and younger Somali men. However, husbands and older brothers were often absent from the houses I visited, either because they were working or socializing outside the home or because they lived elsewhere. Moreover, thirteen of the twenty-one homes I visited regularly throughout my research were female-headed either because the couple had divorced or the husband had permanently or temporarily moved back to Somali-speaking territories or, in some cases, because the husband had passed away. As is typical of many other Somali households in London, most of the ones I frequented were relatively large by British standards, with an average of five children per home. My ethnography thus provides a gendered perspective on changes and transformations; it places the mother–daughter relationship at the centre of the analysis and uses it as a lens through which to view historical changes within Somali society and in Britain.

Throughout the process, I have sought to the best of my ability, to omit sensitive material that is inappropriate to share more widely, to protect my interlocutors' anonymity and, in some cases, have sent copies of chapters to those who expressed a desire to read them. Consequently, I have had to change people's names, biographical details, identities and locations. Somalis in London, particularly those belonging to the same clan or living in the same area, are well known to each other, and I have been rigorous in my attempts to ensure that the individuals mentioned or featured are not recognizable, unless they explicitly stated otherwise.

Most of my fieldwork took place between September 2009 and January 2011, and it was followed up at various points between 2011 and 2013 and between 2014 and 2015. It was based mostly in east and northeast London, areas that host some of the city's most long-standing communities of Somalis. While there are relatively large numbers of Somalis in other cities in Britain – such as Leicester, Bristol, Sheffield, Liverpool and Cardiff – and across other European cities – such as Amsterdam, Stockholm, Oslo, Copenhagen and Helsinki – London lies at the centre of Somali diasporic life. In settling in London, Somalis tend to move close to family or clan members, thereby producing a pattern of clan-based settlement across the city (see Chapter 4). Many Somalis live in majority Muslim areas of the city, which are also renowned for their histories of religious migration. The borough of Tower Hamlets, for example, hosts the largest Muslim population in the country (mostly Bangladeshi-born residents), with Newham and Camden following closely behind. Somali-born residents constitute at least an estimated 1.2 per cent of the population of Tower Hamlets (Census 2011), representing the largest single migrant population from Africa in the borough.

At the start of my fieldwork in 2009 I contacted several Somali organizations in Kilburn, Camden and Tower Hamlets. I explained that I was conducting research on generational and religious change. The directors of these organizations allowed me to volunteer with them, introducing me as a student-researcher, and I began teaching English at supplementary classes for Somali teenagers, teaching ESOL (English as a second language) lessons for adults and volunteering at youth clubs in Camden, Tower Hamlets and Newham. I took part in as many of these organizations' activities as I could, including *buraanbur* classes,[2] meetings and celebrations. I also supported a Somali woman in her campaign to become a local councillor and became involved in a local campaign against FGM. For a year I conducted interviews while also writing and editing articles for *Somali Eye*, an English magazine based in Tower Hamlets that catered for a diaspora readership. During and after fieldwork, I volunteered on a weekly basis with Kayd Somali Arts and Culture, an organization that coordinates regular artistic and cultural events – including the annual Somali Week Festival in Bethnal Green and the Hargeysa International Book Fair – in London and in the Horn of Africa. I have since become a trustee of Kayd and continue to be involved in its activities. Thanks to the dedicated and passionate efforts of Zainab Dahir, an expert educator and writer, I continue to take Somali lessons in the hope that I may one day become proficient in the language.

Between April and September 2014, I conducted research in London and Hargeysa, Somaliland, for a project created under the auspices of the Oxford Diaspora Programme on Diaspora Engagement in War-Torn Societies. The research focused on a campaign that emerged in reaction to the decision made by Barclays Bank in May 2011 to shut down the accounts of remittance companies, including that of *Dahabshiil*, the largest Somali money transfer company. I interviewed young Somali activists and directors of Somali youth organizations in London, as well as many other stakeholders involved in the campaign or affected by the account closures. The project enabled me to travel to Hargeysa in Somaliland, where I interacted with many young people who had moved from the diaspora to the city to live and work, or who were volunteering abroad or visiting their families during their summer holidays.

The initial months of fieldwork in London were by far the most challenging. Urban lifestyles rarely allow people to dedicate long periods of time to a researcher. In my case, this was compounded by the fact that I planned to conduct much of my research in domestic settings, in the hope of being able to follow the trajectories of individual women across London. First-generation women in particular were initially, and understandably, sceptical and reluctant to participate. They worried that this was yet another one of the many policy-based research projects targeted at Somali women, which they felt rarely translated into visible improvements in their lives. Furthermore, many women lead busy lives, their time taken up with work, childcare and domestic responsibilities. This undoubtedly played a part in their initial reluctance to participate and their questioning of the extent to which my research would bring them any direct benefits.

To begin with, I was commuting across large distances in London to meet with people. After several months, however, I found a house in Hackney, which gave me easy access to the boroughs of Tower Hamlets, Newham and Camden, where the majority of my research took place. After having moved to Hackney, I noticed almost immediately that I was developing a greater rapport with both the students and the organizers of the Somali-run organizations at which I was volunteering. Nevertheless, it was often difficult to ask questions in these settings, so I began to organize interviews with older Somali women outside these spaces. I conducted both life-history interviews and narrative interviews on their experiences of everyday life in the UK and 'back home' throughout the Somali post-independence period. In total I conducted interviews with thirty first-generation Somali women who had migrated to the UK in the last twenty to twenty-five years from both urban and rural areas across Somali-speaking territories. Some of the women were happy for me to interview them several times, which enabled me to ask follow-up questions or explore themes in greater depth. The interviews always took place in the women's homes and, unless the women were comfortable with it, I rarely recorded the sessions.

Conversations during interviews were often informal and, although I had prepared a list of topics, I usually allowed the conversation to flow naturally, occasionally bringing it back to my list of themes. I began asking about their life histories, which generally required minimal prompting. The women were more than happy to speak at length about their lives, recounting minute details of their pasts and reflecting nostalgically about their youth and the beauty of Somalia, while also expressing deep sadness about the current situation there. I was often shown photographs and pamphlets or was introduced to poetry recitations or music from the 1970s and 1980s. My interview topics also touched on themes regarding their everyday lives in London, their religious education and, particularly, some of the personal, religious and familial changes they had experienced since coming to the UK. In addition, by collecting biographical information on extended family and marriage patterns, I was able to produce kinship diagrams for twenty-one of the families I regularly engaged with during my research.

Several months into my fieldwork, some of the women I met at the community centres in Camden and Tower Hamlets asked me if I would teach them and their children English in their homes. We agreed that I would volunteer my services, and I began spending my afternoons in their homes, teaching, eating, conversing and watching TV in the evenings with the children. At that stage I was visiting six households on a weekly basis, and, through these contacts, I was introduced to other women who were happy to be interviewed or visited on an informal basis. Although I had a very basic understanding of the Somali language, we often spoke in English, or in Somali with a daughter or friend helping to translate. Despite some language difficulties, I managed to develop close friendships with four first-generation Somali women who had lived in Mogadishu until the 1990s. Their stories feature most prominently in Chapters 3 and 4 of this book. I began by teaching them English and accompanying them to *Qur'an* lessons, but we soon developed a more personal relationship and I often went with them to weddings, friends' houses and other social occasions. I spent many afternoons sitting in their living rooms, chatting over a plate of rice and meat or a cup of very sweet and beautifully spiced Somali tea. They also introduced me to their extended network of kin and friends in the local area.

One of the most significant events in my fieldwork was the day I met a young woman in her mid-twenties, who I will call Layla M, at a Somali arts event. It was Layla who introduced me to many other young practising Somali Muslim women in their mid-twenties and thirties. At that point I had mostly interacted with older women, teenagers and some young non-practising women who worked at the community centres where I was volunteering on a weekly basis. It was through Layla and her friends that I began to learn more about young women's understandings and experiences of practising Islam. From the start, she not only showed a willingness to answer my questions patiently, but she also demonstrated an interest in my life. Soon, accompanied by Layla, I began going to Islamic lectures, classes and informal Islamic circles (*halaqa*), as well as weddings, parties and dinner outings. I spent much of my time in the family homes of these young women, as the majority of them were unmarried at the time of my fieldwork and lived with their families. I also accompanied them on a range of activities across and beyond London, including to the Sufi Soul Festival in Sötenich, Germany, a fundraising hike in Scotland, a trip to the Ihsan mosque in Norwich, and several weekends away outside London. At various points during my fieldwork, I also met and interacted with different groups of young women, many of whom were not necessarily actively practising their faith. Some worked at the organizations or projects mentioned above, while others were introduced to me through friends. Their experiences feature most prominently in Chapters 5 and 8. With this younger generation I spoke in English, although they used Somali to talk with their mothers and, occasionally, with their friends and siblings.

The nature of ethnographic fieldwork means that the relationship between a researcher and her interlocutors is never fixed or clearly defined as the researcher shifts between roles. In my case, I moved between being a friend, volunteer, teacher and so on, as people positioned me differently in relation to themselves. For many of the older first-generation women, I was initially very much an outsider; they saw me as a white, young, non-Muslim and unmarried woman with little understanding of the Somali language. The fact that I was Italian, however, facilitated some of my interactions. Several of the women who had been raised in Mogadishu spoke Italian and had Italian TV channels in their homes in London. To my surprise, they enjoyed commenting on the similarities between Italian and Somali cultures and contrasting them with British culture and society, which they considered individualistic, cold and distant. My interlocutors would often comment on the inhospitable attitude of their English neighbours, who rarely greeted them in passing and showed no interest in welcoming them to the neighbourhood. Furthermore, their interactions with non-Somalis were few and far between, particularly if they were not in employment. The fact that I was not British meant that the older women felt free to express quite openly the racism and social barriers they had encountered in British society.

In contrast to my experiences with the older Somali women, many of the spaces that I visited with younger Somalis were incredibly diverse and included Muslims and non-Muslims from a range of backgrounds. The mosques and Islamic institutes and spaces of learning were similarly diverse, welcoming Muslims from different ethnic and socio-economic backgrounds, including many white British converts. As a non-Muslim, I was still positioned by the women as an outsider, even though I was of a similar age and level of education as many of them. Sometimes, my outsider status proved incredibly valuable to my research; some women felt they could open up to me and discuss issues that they felt unable to mention to other Somalis or Muslims. However, it also meant that, whenever I attended Islamic classes and events, I was constantly questioned about my beliefs, my motivations for being there, and whether I would ever convert. Although I tried to be as honest as possible about my beliefs, the young Muslim women I befriended often wanted to know exactly which passages of the *Qur'an* I disagreed with or had difficulty accepting. These questions would then turn into discussions about the different interpretations of the text and the nuances of the opinions of scholars and Muslim feminists.

These exchanges prompted me to reconsider many of my assumptions about religion, Islam and my Catholic upbringing.

The work of feminist scholars on religion and the post-secular (Bracke 2008; Braidotti 2008) influenced my thinking throughout the fieldwork process, particularly as I reflected on my own secular or liberal assumptions and on my interlocutors' quests to practise Islam. By participating in debates about Islamic texts with these young and informed women, I learnt about the ways in which they engaged with textual knowledge and the importance they attributed to reading, analysing, interpreting and debating these texts. However, many of these young women often stressed that there was a limit to their scrutiny of the texts and to their critical engagement with particular verses. Ultimately, for them, one simply had to rely on faith. In their view, they could explain the texts to me, but whether I accepted them or not was ultimately in God's hands. Although they continued to engage in discussions with me, my friends accepted that they only had a limited role to play in my ultimate acceptance or rejection of faith and, after a few months, they stopped questioning me and accepted my participation in classes, daily prayers and fasting.

My experience of conducting research on issues of faith, however, was unsettling. I noticed that I gradually began to speak and act differently, interspersing my English with Arabic phrases, changing my tone and altering my clothing. But more surprisingly, I began to think of myself differently, particularly in the presence of more pious friends. Practising Islam involves, above all, a shift in self-understanding and the establishment of a relationship with God. I often found myself thinking in these terms and reflecting on fate and the presence of God, and reminding myself about the inevitability of death in ways that would have been alien to me prior to fieldwork.

Throughout my research, friends and acquaintances constantly questioned me about my interest in studying Somalis. Somali friends often reminded me of the complex politics of representation into which I was immersing myself by writing about Somali women. For example, from the very first day I met Saynab, a young Somali woman, she questioned my reasons for writing about Somalis and my entitlement to do so. 'Why are you interested in Somalis? What have you got to say that we can't say ourselves?' she would often ask me in a blunt, outspoken way. Her attitude was understandable given the ways in which some white European writers have represented Somalis and Muslims in the mainstream media. On another occasion, an acquaintance expressed her annoyance at white liberals who, she argued, represented themselves as Somali 'experts'. She felt, for example, that the anthropologist Ioan M. Lewis' work on Somalis had dominated Somalis' own understandings of their clan system and Somali society for decades. 'We'd prefer if you didn't dominate representations, so that we don't have to see ourselves through your words,' another woman commented, clearly directing her words at me. It is with her words in mind that I would like this book to be read: it is not a general study of the experiences of Somalis in London, but rather a historically situated account of my experiences of engaging with a small group of Somali women in a particular place and time. It does not seek to provide a coherent narrative of these women's lives, nor a linear historical analysis, but rather explores specific recursive and fragmentary processes of change. It seeks to challenge simplified depictions of Somali Muslim women, and critique the ways in which Islam has come to be problematized in Europe today.

Notes

1   Interestingly, *Cadaan* Studies has coincided with the emergence of Black Lives Matter, which was set up in response to police racism and brutality, and has since evolved into a movement for dignity and justice for all black lives.

2   *Buraanbur* is a form of women's poetry, often accompanied by drumming and dancing.

CHAPTER THREE

Memories of modern Mogadishu

As we became independent,
Our right bore fruit
That you bind us so strongly,
[That] you keep us shut up
[in our homes –]
Is that just?
Is that lawful?
Is it allowed [by our religion]
For you [to do this]?
You make an offense,
And you crossed the boundary.
Give us [at least] part [of our rights].

[Extract from Shabeel Naagood (1968), by Hasan Sheekh Mumin,
Translated by John. W. Johnson (1974: 137)]

'Wait, I'll have a look for them!' Safiya exclaimed as she bounced off the couch and rushed towards her bedroom. I had asked to see photographs of her life in Mogadishu in the 1970s and 1980s, and she returned to her living room a few minutes later carrying two shoeboxes. She kept these tucked under her bed alongside

suitcases filled with clothes and shoes, and some of her most
valuable possessions: her British passport, jewellery, and large
amounts of cash she had saved up for her *hagbad* (money-saving
scheme). The photos were thrown into the box in no particular
order. Some were upside down, others stuck together. Safiya hadn't
pulled them out for a while. Her three daughters had rummaged
through them a few times before, but they hadn't since shown an
interest and, like in most Somali homes, photographs were not
on display in picture frames or on the walls. She was delighted to
have an opportunity to sift through them again, dwell on pleasant
memories of her youth and reminisce with nostalgia of a time of
novelty and aspiration.

Safiya was born in 1960 – the year Somalis gained independence
from colonial rule – in Hoodan, a middle-class district of Mogadishu.
Her father, who had been educated in Egypt, was a government-
employed Arabic and *Qur'an* teacher and worked at the Ministry
of Justice and Islamic Affairs until his death in 1980. Her mother,
who had migrated from the countryside as a young woman, worked
mostly in the home, but was unwell for most of Safiya's lifetime,
so her own mother (Safiya's grandmother) had taken charge of
the house and cared for the children. Safiya's parents were both
divorcees – her father had divorced several times – and, as Safiya
explained, theirs was truly a 'love marriage'. They had met in her
father's local grocery store, which her mother, who at that point had
divorced her first husband, frequented regularly with her children.
When Safiya's mother fell ill, Safiya's father visited his future wife in
hospital and shortly after that he proposed to her.

At the age of five, Safiya completed *Qur'an* school (*dugsi*) and
started her schooling, initially in Italian and subsequently in Somali,
following the introduction of the written script in 1972. Her father
strongly encouraged her to acquire an education. He had wanted
her to go to university and, as she recounted, 'investigate Somalia'
and 'study Islamic religion'. 'At the time I didn't understand why it
was important ... but now I know why,' she explained, referring to
her father's insistence that she study religion. 'He also taught me to
be independent. Without him I wouldn't be who I am, I thank him
everyday.'

Following secondary school she spent two years participating
in the literacy campaigns initiated by the Supreme Revolutionary
Council (SRC) under Maxamed Siyaad Barre, whose regime seized

power following a coup in 1969. She subsequently enrolled at Lafoole College of Education, close to Afgooye, a town approximately 25 km west of Mogadishu. In 1984, following the completion of her degree, Safiya began teaching at a secondary school, and that same year she married her first husband. She taught history and geography at secondary school level, 'not Islamic history ... we weren't *allowed* back then', she explained disapprovingly. But Safiya hoped for more: she was planning to apply for a master's degree in the United States, and had hired a Kenyan tutor to provide private English classes in her home. With a foreign degree she would hopefully be eligible for a good government job, enabling her to play a critical role in the newly independent nation-state.

The photographs she showed me that day displayed relatives and friends sitting, standing and posing. There were rarely any places, landscapes or objects, and most were taken in studios, or in people's homes on special celebrations such as *Eid*. Most of the shots taken in studios were set against a backdrop often featuring a rich tapestry of exotic flowers and plants, in tune with the embellished and bright-coloured clothing worn by the women in the images. Some photographs evoked painful memories: a friend with whom she had lost touch during the war and feared dead; a cousin who had gradually turned blind. But the majority displayed a life of leisure and carelessness. An aunt dressed in tight, high-waisted 1980s jeans, a white shirt and Afro-style haircut on her way to a party, and a friend in a glowing Somali *dirac* (loose and long Somali dress) and a hearwrap posing before an *aroos* (wedding celebration). As we sat on her couch looking through them, Safiya's ten-year-old daughter curled up next to us to take a peek. She giggled at the photo of the aunt who, she remarked, now looked so different in her long black *jilbab* (an Islamic style of dress that covers the head, and drapes over the chest). In one photo with a friend Safiya was dressed in a *guntiino* (wrap-around dress), an outfit she also wore when participating in national parades or celebrations at school and university, and her friend wore a Western-style top revealing her bare shoulders. In another she posed with male friends and cousins. 'Look at this, we're holding each other! That's not allowed now!' she pointed out. Her photographs captured the amalgamation of modern, urban lifestyles with national celebrations of traditional culture. Safiya explained how she used to spend most of her free time attending the cinema and *concerti* (theatre and dance productions), promenading on the beach or dining in restaurants with friends and cousins. 'We all wanted to be modern back then!' she explained, referring to her choice of leisure activities, clothing and employment aspirations.

At the same time, these memories contrasted with her present experiences of frustration and bitterness. Safiya often expressed a sense of loss and dissatisfaction for what she had been unable to achieve since fleeing Mogadishu and resettling first in Rome and then in London. The civil war had shattered her hopes and aspirations, and she had struggled to rebuild her life in the UK. When I first met her she was starting to learn more about Islam, thanks to a neighbour who had given her books and taken her to classes at the local Somali mosque. As she witnessed Somali women in Britain replace their jeans and short skirts with dark-coloured *hijab* and *jilbab*, she contemplated whether she ought to do the same and take more of an interest in her faith.

She was also working towards obtaining her driving licence. She spent much of her time worrying about her daughters, arguing with her separated husband and pondering her situation. Driving around London gave her a sense of independence and allowed her to take some time out for herself. As she had a provisional licence, she was only legally allowed to drive with someone with a full licence beside her, and that's where I came in. We spent many afternoons driving around London in her overheated car; I often teased her for trying to recreate a tropical Somali climate in the small confines of her vehicle. We both became very attached to each other, but at times my presence bothered her and she would act indifferently towards me. I was working towards a PhD, and she reminded me constantly that she would have been doing the same had the war not shattered her ambitions. 'I've worked for my children all my life, and I'm sick of cooking, being in the house. I want to do something for myself,' she often complained. Every few months she embarked on a new project and sought to involve me in her new life plan. After getting her licence, she was planning to enrol again for English classes and work towards a degree, or perhaps learn Arabic, or find a job. She wanted to feel active and engaged, but felt this was a struggle in a country that neither recognized her qualifications and skills nor valued her talents.

Between nostalgia and critique

This chapter is about the ways in which the past is remembered, forgotten and reinterpreted to inform and make sense of the present, and how these acts are 'anchored in present context … [and say] a lot more about contemporary social configurations than about the past itself' (Davis 1979: 31 cited in Angé and Berliner 2014: 5). I focus on how Somali women of Safiya's generation, raised between the 1960s and early 1980s in Mogadishu, and now living in the UK, remember, interpret, narrate and share their memories of that period of their lives. Many came from the urban middle classes, and some were the first generation of women to complete their schooling and in some cases attend university. Given their socio-economic standing, they were also among the earliest cohorts to leave the country as civil war spread across the region.

Safiya's reminiscing over her photographs revealed – what Özyürek (2006) has described as a 'nostalgia for the modern' – a longing for the nationalist, modernist project of the postcolonial period and the initial phases of Siyaad Barre's rule. In political discourse, this modern project was juxtaposed against notions of traditional culture (*dhaqan iyo hiddo*) as 'backwards', but it also sought to reappropriate *dhaqan* as a symbol of *Soomaalinimo* (Somaliness), an authentic Somali culture and a national identity rooted in the past. Safiya's *guntiino* worn for national celebrations, for example, celebrated a nationalist ideology constructed around an authentic Somali *dhaqan*, symbolized by a reified notion of Somali nomad society. Modernity was experienced as a rupture with the past – a reimagining of the self in the present through a process of self-fashioning (Foucault 2000: 312), and a projecting of the self forward in time by reworking elements of the past. This modern project was characterized by a tension between a nostalgic engagement with an imagined authentic traditional Somali past, and a critical distance from this past as 'backwards', non-modern and in need of development.

Safiya's descriptions of the 1970s and 1980s also display a similar bifurcation between a nostalgic longing for a modernist past, as we saw above, and a critical engagement with the widespread 'immorality' of this period. As mentioned, like many women of her generation, she has personally experienced and witnessed heightened forms of religiosity since moving abroad to the UK. In her search for a moral order that she deems was lacking in the latter years of Barre's rule, she has not sought not to revive *dhaqan* (traditional culture) but to engage in a renewed *diin* (religion). She points to the absence of an Islamic consciousness throughout the late 1980s by commenting on the intimacy between men and women in the photographs, the Western clothing worn by the women and her inability to teach Islamic history. These practices are contrasted with the present context in the Somali regions and the UK where these forms of intimacy or friendly relations between men and women are increasingly frowned upon, and where most Somali women don more modest clothing such as the *hijab* (headscarf) or *jilbab*. Looking back at her past, she remembers her father's advice to pursue the study of Islam, which provides her with a justification for her present pursuits. While Safiya's comment on her inability to teach about Islam presents a critique of Barre's anti-Islam agenda, and hence of the immorality of that period, her comment 'that's not allowed now!' referring to a photo of male and female friends and relatives embracing each other, also reveals her derision of stricter forms of religiosity that have emerged in recent years in the diaspora. In fact, Safiya had only recently begun to learn about and engage with Islamic knowledge, but remained critical of 'excessive' or stricter forms of religiosity.

The remainder of this chapter explores this tension between nostalgia for, and critique of, the past by looking at how Somali women have made sense of and reinterpreted notions of modernity, *dhaqan* and *diin* since moving abroad and in light of new and heightened forms of religiosity among Somalis. Throughout, I intersperse an account of the Somali social and political context post independence with women's narratives of the past. The chapter is structured as follows. It begins with a summary of the independence struggle, which culminated in 1960 and was informed by a nationalist and modernist discourse of *Soomaalinimo*, rooted in colonial notions of Somali ethnicity and culture. The discussion subsequently turns to the socialist project of the 1970s and early 1980s. Through the narratives of Safiya's contemporaries, it elaborates on their nostalgic recollections of the post-independence period. The fourth section provides an account of the rise of religious opposition to the Barre regime following the 1975 Family Law, the growth of reformist movements in the region and their critiques of the modernist project. The chapter concludes with a discussion of how Somali women have also begun to appropriate Islamic idioms to critique the modernist period for its lack of morality.

Kapteijns' (with Omar 1999; 2009; 2010) historical insights, and particularly her analysis of Somali popular songs and public discourses on modernity, tradition and moral womanhood between 1960 and 1990, are particularly relevant to this discussion. Building on Kapteijns' work, this chapter also explores changing attitudes towards notions of modernity, traditional culture and religion not only through texts but also from the life histories of individual women, most of whom shared an urban middle-class lifestyle prior to the war. The civil war and migration abroad created a sudden temporal and spatial rupture, separating a period of modernity and nationalist fervour in Somalia from the present condition of conflict and displacement abroad. While Islamic ethics and forms of identification have partly replaced modernist aspirations, what is revealed through the narratives of these women is a coexistence of nostalgia and critique towards the past. I argue that this process of oscillating between nostalgia and critique is crucial to the understanding of this generation of women's present pious aspirations. While this group of women represent a unique middle-class group, their narratives bring to the fore a gendered perspective on everyday urban experiences, which is often missing in mainstream historical accounts of this post-independence period.[1]

In order to make sense of how and why Somali women in Britain have begun to consciously and reflectively engage with Islamic texts and practices, we need to explore how these changes are made sense of in light of their past experiences, and their understandings of modernity and traditional culture. These women's narratives also reveal the ways in which memories of the past are discursive but also affective and embodied (Gidley 2013) – rooted in individuals' attachments to particular objects, practices, places and people. As we saw with Safiya, objects like photographs form a crucial part of the process of sharing experiences with friends of the same generation, but also of transmitting experiences to the following generation. Furthermore, remembering and forgetting through objects, stories and practices also involves reimagining relations with self and other, which extend back in the past as well as into the future.

The following section takes us back to the independence struggle which emerged in the 1940s and culminated in 1960, the year of Somali independence from colonial rule, and the same year of Safiya's birth.

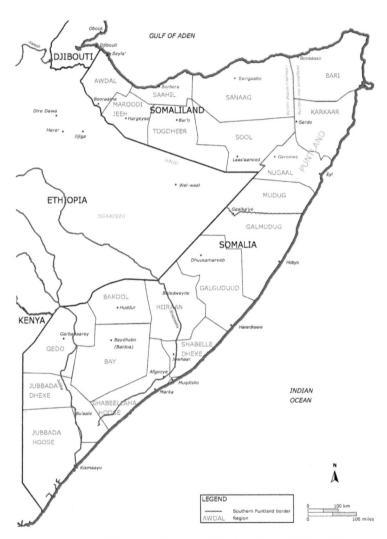

FIGURE 1 *Somali Horn of Africa. Published in Michael Walls (2014: 318).* A Somali Nation-State: History, Culture and Somaliland's Political Transition. *Pisa, Italy: Ponte Invisibile.*

Soomaalinimo and the spirit of modernity

The Somali regions came under colonial rule relatively late compared to the rest of the continent. In 1887, almost three years after the Berlin Conference where the rules for the partitioning of Africa were laid out, the Somali-speaking territories were divided up between four colonial powers. The UK seized the Protectorate of British Somaliland (since 1991 the self-proclaimed Somaliland) and the Northern Frontier District (since 1963 the North-Eastern Province of Kenya), Italy, La Somalia Italiana (present-day northeastern, central and southern Somalia), France, La Côte Française des Somalis (Djibouti since 1977), and Abyssinia (Ethiopia), the Ogaden and Haud areas (Lewis 2002: 40–62) (see Figure 1). This partitioning of the Somali regions was transformed during and after the Second World War, as the British Military Administration took over the Italian colonies in 1941, until 1947 when the Four Power Commission of Investigation met in Mogadishu to decide on the fate of Italy's colonies.

In May 1943 the Somali Youth Club (SYC) – the first Somali political organization – was formed in Mogadishu. Coinciding with the Four Powers Commission, in 1947 the SYC organized as a political party, the Somali Youth League (SYL) (Touval 1963: 86–93). Initially the only party with a pan-Somali ideology, in its memorandum to the Commission the SYL called for a Greater Somalia and for independent rule under the banner of *Soomaalinimo*. According to the nationalists, this pan-Somali identity distanced itself from sectarian and clan-based identities to advocate a shared culture, language and religion:

> We wish our country to be amalgamated with the other Somalilands and to form one political, administrative and economic unit with them. We Somalis are one in every way. We are the same racially and geographically, we have the same culture, we have the same language and the same religion. There is no future for us except as part of a Greater Somalia. (Touval 1963: 95)

A year later a protest by the SYL against Somalia's return to Italy under UN trusteeship was violently suppressed by Italian forces, leading to riots across the city. Yet despite this fatal incident, in 1949

Somalia was declared as a UN trusteeship under Italian administration until 1960 – the year set for independence.

In the years leading to independence, the SYL grew in popularity, particularly among young supporters who had migrated to emerging cities or coastal towns within the protectorate in pursuit of education and employment. It was among this class of young aspiring middle classes that the nationalist identity of *Soomaalinimo* (pan-Somaliness) flourished. Largely articulated by intellectuals and artists, this discourse was supported and disseminated by state institutions such as the radio stations of Hargeysa and Mogadishu. A 'desire to be modern' was a central component of this nationalist project, and included a desire for liberal democracy, a progressive agenda of individual rights and freedoms, formal education based on European models, and economic, scientific and technological progress (Kapteijns 2009: 104). In mobilizing for a nationalist future, however, a uniquely Somali national identity was crafted by drawing on 'tradition', as both cultural authenticity and traditional religious morality. The notion of *Soomaalinimo*, which took shape particularly through popular songs, upheld a 'modern yet moral' and culturally authentic, Somali identity (ibid.: 105–6).

While the discourse of *Soomaalinimo* was part of an anti-colonial identity, it also involved appropriating and reworking ideas of Somali ethnicity, culture and identity that had been shaped throughout the colonial period. Prior to the arrival of the British and Italian administrations, the idea of a 'Somali' collective identity or ethnic marker was not commonly employed as a self-identifier; sub-clan names were instead used to refer to particular groups.[2] Through official discourse and political practices, the colonial administrations classified natives into racial categories, upholding and effectively forging the notion of 'pure' Somalis, and also the perception of Somalis as distinct and superior to black Africans (Besteman 1995: 51–2).[3] As in other colonial settings, policies of divide and rule entrenched and essentialized differences between ethnic groups and tribes (Moore and Vaughan 1994).[4] Through an insistence on delineating authentic Somali 'traditions' and 'customs', British administrators effectively selected, codified and 'fundamentally changed what had always been highly contextualized and customized applications of Somali constitutional principles' (Kapteijns and Farah 2001: 720).

For example, through processes such as 'collective punishment ordinances', the colonial administration effectively 'stabilized' groups which had previously had more flexibility in deciding their own composition and procedures (ibid.: 720–1). Governance of Italian Somalia under De Martino's rule was similar to the indirect rule of district officers in British Africa, further entrenching the power of clans and of customary law; warrant chiefs were created as the official points of contact between government and colonial subjects with little understanding of how the role of *cadis* and chiefs varied regionally and across clans (Hess 1966: 107–8). With few amendments, this governance structure was then appropriated and implemented during the UN trusteeship and the independent Somali Republic.

As Kapteijns (2004: 8) has noted, this articulation of tradition overemphasized men at the expense of women, prioritized politics over other dimensions of Somali society, and presented clanship as the primary principle of sociopolitical organization and an emblem of authentic Somali society. 'Clan' came to serve as a 'governmental technology of power' on which colonial rule should be based (ibid.: 6–8). This rendition of Somali traditions was inextricably tied to the production of knowledge about Somalis, which reinforced an articulation of Somalis as separate, unified and internally homogenous (ibid.). I M Lewis' (1961) ethnographic monograph, for example, published under the auspices of the British colonial government, overemphasized patrilineal kinship and clan as defining features of Somali society, simplifying local realities and presenting a timeless and monolithic conception of a traditional society (Kapteijns 2004).

This idea of cultural authenticity persisted throughout the post-independence period, and was appropriated and celebrated as a national signifier of *Soomaalinimo*, calling for the unification of all five colonial Somali divisions, and an explicit denouncement of clan identity. The myth of a homogenous Somali society was based around nineteenth-century notions of the nation-state as consisting of a group of individuals sharing a similar race, ethnicity, language and religion (Ahmed 1995: 142). Clan and sub-clan identities were seen as the main obstacle to the creation of a modern Somalia united around commonalities of language, culture, religion and territory, and under a young, educated, urban leadership (Kapteijns 2009). Nationalists articulated an idea of a

Somali national heritage and identity by picking and choosing, for the sake of progress and nation building, what was to be kept from what was to be discarded of this heritage. In so doing, they fashioned a new discourse of what it meant to be 'Somali' couched in concepts of cultural authenticity and national identity (ibid.).

This rhetoric of unity, however, was fraught with tensions. First, it was an elitist and urban-based discourse, one that was based on a nostalgic longing for an imagined rural past as the authentic source of culture and identity. Second, colonial boundaries, which had entrenched and marked clan divisions, were difficult to undo. Although in reality the discourse denounced clannism, the importance of clan persisted, and became a struggle for control of the state. As we shall see, the centralization of the state in Mogadishu, and the marginalization of the northern clans under Barre's rule, further shattered the idea of unity and revealed the illusionary nature of pan-Somaliness. Finally, the notion of *Soomaalinimo* was male centred, and presented the struggle for unity as one dominated and led by men. Although women had been involved in the fighting (Jama 1991), they were initially excluded from membership of the SYL, and their struggles remained less visible.[5]

From independence to Scientific Socialism

In July 1960 Somalia and Somaliland merged to form the new Somali Republic, with Mogadishu as its capital. Urbanization continued to escalate as the population of Mogadishu went from less than half a million to more than two million between 1969 and 1990 (Lewis 2002: 265), and other major urban areas, including, for example, Kismaayo, Marka, Baidoa/Baydhabo, Gaalkacyo, Boosaaso, Hargeysa and Berbera, grew rapidly in size. Elected in 1960, the SYL remained in power until the military coup of 1969. It was not long after independence that many Somalis became disillusioned with the new government as the country was plunged into economic stagnation. Aid dependency increased, as did rural proletarianization and corruption; nepotism became rampant and the gap between the lower and upper classes widened (Lewis 2002: Chapter 10). In 1969 the government, under Prime

Minister Egal, came under accusations of clientelism and neo-patrimonialism along clan lines, and President Shermaarke was shot dead in a military coup. Members of the Somali military and police forces announced the rise of a new revolutionary order, and the establishment of the Somali Democratic Republic. In January 1971, the Supreme Revolutionary Council (SRC) under General Siyaad Barre issued its policy programme.

The new SRC oversaw a period of nationalism and reform, which acquired an ideological edge with the adoption of Scientific Socialism in 1970 (Lewis 2008: 39). This led to a period of nationalization of the economy; foreign banks, factories, plantations and other businesses were seized in an attempt to reduce dependency on foreign imports. As the regime developed, the state became increasingly centralized, and university, healthcare and industry were clustered only in Mogadishu – a process that was to antagonize the rest of the country. Among the SRC's mandate were the aims of guaranteeing the right to work, fighting poverty and disease, promoting social justice, eradicating illiteracy, establishing orthography for the Somali language, and eliminating corruption and the tribal system (Samatar 1988: 84–5).

The SRC introduced an official Somali alphabet based on Latin orthography, and issued an intensive and extensive literacy programme. In 1971, all schools were nationalized and old school materials were replaced with Somali textbooks, as Somali became the official administrative and national language (ibid.: 100–3). Following the success of an urban literacy campaign, a rural campaign – in which Safiya and many of her contemporaries participated – was launched which sent 30,000 urban students and teachers into the countryside to teach reading and writing to the nomadic population (ibid.: 102). By 1978, although most schools were in urban areas, student enrolment was on the rise in both primary and secondary schools, and the student university enrolment tripled (ibid.: 102–3). Adult literacy increased from 7 per cent to 10 per cent in 1969, and to 60 per cent in the 1970s. Despite the SRC's commitment to boost employment, many of the jobs created were within state structures, and very little was done to help the agricultural sectors (ibid.).

In February and March 1971 a general 'Campaign against Tribalism' designed to 'exorcize corruption and to resuscitate pan-Somalism and national unity', was launched (Samatar 1988: 107). Drawing on previous nationalist struggles and promoting a pan-Somali identity (*Soomaalinimo*), the aim was to appeal to a united Somalia across clans and lineages by diminishing the roles of clan-based institutions and practices. Somalis were encouraged to call each other 'comrade' (*jaalle*) instead of 'kinsmen', and weddings and burials were no longer designated as clan-based affairs. Instead, marriages were symbolically stripped of kinship and religious significance, taking place in state-owned orientation centres, and burials were to be conducted in local neighbourhoods, although the extent to which these took place is debatable. Emphasis was placed on local settlement as a unit of allegiance (Lewis 2008: 40), official lineage titles were renamed peacemakers (*nabad-doon*), the *diya* (blood money) institution was outlawed and clan alliances were banned (Samatar 1988: 108; Lewis 2002: 209).

The SRC was also committed to furthering women's rights, under the banner of gender equality, and many urban women, including Safiya, benefitted from policies that encouraged women to access education and to enter the workforce (see Figure 3 for a propaganda image celebrating women's involvement in scientific research). Whether Barre's Scientific Socialism led to more gender equality and improved material conditions for Somali women remains contested. As Hamdi Mohamed (2003: 121) has described, the campaign against tribalism weakened traditional family and kinship structures, disrupting gender and age hierarchies. Furthermore, the introduction of free and universal education increased Somali women's enrolment at all levels of education, and improved the public acceptance of women's education, at least among the urban middle classes (ibid.: 124–5). Women also benefitted from policies aimed at equalizing access to paid employment. Despite these advances, however, female enrolment in schools remained lower than that of men, and women remained underrepresented in some sectors, particularly in government jobs (ibid.: 125–6). While many women participated in new grassroots political activities, particularly through the government-funded and -regulated Somali Women's Democratic Organization (SWDO), they remained underrepresented in the upper echelons of party leadership (ibid.: 130). Throughout the 1980s, with a growing economic and political crisis, many of these policies were abandoned or left unimplemented. Barre's emphasis on gender equality emerged as a means of enhancing his global reputation, and an instrument to mobilize support and long-term legitimacy – issues I will return to in the final section of this chapter.

Modernity through the eyes of Somali women

Muraayo's modern middle-class aspirations

Muraayo was a close childhood friend of Safiya, and having lost sight of each other during the war, they met again many years later in London. They now lived only a short drive away, and I often accompanied Safiya to pay her friend a visit in her home in Camden, North London. Our conversations drifted in and out of English, Italian and Somali, depending on the topic. Like Safiya, Muraayo had been a part of the new urban aspiring middle classes. Her parents were the first generation of urban dwellers: her father owned a butcher shop and occasionally worked as a farmer outside the city in his home town and place of birth. Her mother had initially worked in her family shop, selling imported goods from Italy – spaghetti and macaroni as Muraayo specified – but when her husband's business picked up, she stopped working altogether. 'My mother was the queen of the house. She was beautiful and used to sit outside all day. My father looked after her, provided everything she wanted. We were a happy family,' Muraayo recounted.

Muraayo was one of twelve brothers and sisters, and they lived with two adopted cousins, and their maternal and paternal grandmothers, in a large, gated house in the central Boondheere district of Mogadishu. They rented out the spare rooms to couples or larger families. Muraayo attended primary school close to home, and secondary school in the nearby Shingaani district, one of the two oldest quarters of the city. 'We wore uniforms everyday ... white and blue but no headscarves,' she explained, referencing Barre's secular policies at the time. Both she and Safiya vividly remember singing the freedom songs of the Somali Republic after school, and participating in national parades. Muraayo subsequently enrolled at the National University in Mogadishu and completed her five-year agronomy degree in Italian. She now melancholically reminisces about those university days:

Everything was free and the government gave us food, free accommodation. It was beautiful, very green ... we had entertainment, a hall, sometimes the university invited pupils to sing songs, *concerto*, films screening. We were not far from Afgooye town, we could go there to buy something.

She met and 'fell in love' with her future husband while at university, and they married shortly after and moved to Jordan for a couple of years before returning to Mogadishu. They had since divorced and she usually spoke little about him; however, these memories of their first years together always brought a smile to her face.

Following her degree, Muraayo was employed by USAID and worked as a laboratory assistant on the large Juba river dam project. In one of our conversations, she spoke about her busy days running around Mogadishu between domestic chores, entertainment, work and study. Her descriptions also captured her taste for Western foods and goods:

> The thing I miss the most is waking up, going to the market to buy fresh vegetables and fruit, coming home, cooking nice fresh natural sauces, sleeping, going out again, going to the cinema. ... Here in the morning I feel I've done nothing. There were modern big shops, selling everything, clothes, furniture. I really liked Western food, pasta, rice, tomato sauce.

Frequently during my visits with Safiya, the two women would reminisce about the 'good old days' of their youth in Mogadishu, alternating between these and the latest episode of violence in the capital. Muraayo showed me photographs similar to those Safiya stored in the shoeboxes under her bed; alongside these photographic memories Muraayo had also treasured her university degree and training certificates, as signs of her status in Somalia before the war. Some of her photographs were also taken on holidays in Afgooye or in the countryside around Mogadishu, and Muraayo meticulously described the idyllic natural beauty of the place, her feelings of respite from chaotic urban life, and the healthy diet and lifestyle she enjoyed. 'Sometimes in the rainy seasons we went to nomadic areas. ... We drank a lot of camel milk, enjoyed the countryside.' The quality of the food they ate in Mogadishu was also incomparable to the fruit and vegetables found in UK supermarkets, I was often told: 'Here [the UK] the food is bad. It's very cold. We lack vitamin D and miss the sun ... We cover up so our skin never gets any sun.'

On one occasion Muraayo described her long evenings of entertainment in the city:

> When the sun went down, we had a bath and then dressed in *dirac* (Somali dress) or *gonno* (skirt). Boys and girls they went together, but nowadays ... eeeeh! That doesn't happen! Sometimes we went to someone's house, cinema, *concerto*, theatre. Sometimes we had festivals outside, and the government decorated the streets. For example, in Boondheere, and Anseloti, these two places, they did *nikko* [a dance associated with Bantu Somalis] on the streets in the evenings ... so we went there, we watched, we learnt from them. Also near Medina, we had Jazeera beach, and I remember my brother organized for us all to go to that beach, and we would buy food, and sometimes cook on the beach ... we rented a car, and we went with other friends from school, friends from the area, boys and girls, together! But now?

Muraayo qualified her account by explaining that there were certain places that were out of bounds. Dance clubs such as Rooba had Western music, were frequented by 'whites', and sold alcohol. 'Only bad Somali girls went there,' Safiya added. Despite these restrictions, both women felt relatively free to move around the city. Safiya frequently mentioned how, unlike the UK, there was little need for families to worry about their children's whereabouts: 'It was safe because even a stranger would tell you off. So control came from the wider community. People had morality, they knew how to behave ... Somalia was an ideal, perfect, easy life. That's all gone now.'

Muraayo elaborated on the moral boundaries and norms of acceptability that children were taught from an early age:

> It was not necessary to be escorted by a brother or relative. We had boyfriends, but we didn't sleep with them, we only talked. Sometimes you split, sometimes you marry. Parents, if they knew, they'd push for marriage, but if you split, it was ok. Sometimes when a girl became pregnant she didn't know what to do, she was embarrassed, ashamed, and was rejected by her family.

She continued: 'My mother never said, "You are boy or girl," she raised me for who I was.' She did encourage Muraayo to attend *dugsi* and learn the *Qur'an*, and to avoid clothes that were too revealing, but as Muraayo explained: 'It was part of her religion, her culture, her environment.'

Muraayo's and Safiya's depictions of urban life capture a nostalgia for an urban youth culture characterized by leisure, entertainment, freedom of movement and travel, but equally also an embodied sense of morality. Throughout our conversations, Safiya suggested that it was 'all gone now' and Muraayo also hinted that this was a long-lost reality. Her comment 'but nowadays ... eeeeh!', like Safiya's 'that's not allowed now!' in reference to a photo of her cousins embracing each other, is directed at Somalis' excessive preoccupation with gender separation since moving abroad and engaging actively with Islamic reformist traditions.

The women's descriptions of urban life are also reflected in novelist Nuruddin Farah's (2007: 35) account of the Tamarind market:

> This was always abuzz with activities, its narrow alleys filled with shoppers. You could see entire families pouring into its alleys and plazas soon after siesta time, some shopping for clothes, others wishing to acquire what they could find in the way of gold or silver necklaces, many made to order. Stories abounded in which you were told that some of the shoppers came from as far as the Arabian Gulf to strike bargains, well aware that they would pay a lot more for the same items in their home countries in the Emirates or Saudi Arabia. In those days, no bride would get married without a collection of custom-made gold and silver items bought from one of the artisans there.

For Farah, Mogadishu represented a microcosm of the city's cosmopolitanism. Many of the women I met throughout my fieldwork had lived in Mogadishu prior to migrating abroad; even several of those born and raised in the countryside or in other major cities such as Hargeysa or Gaalkacyo had moved to Mogadishu to pursue their studies, or to follow their own or their husband's job. A narrative of modernization was closely intertwined with urbanization and liberalization, whereby the urban stood as a paradigmatic site of the modern (Simmel 1971b).

Throughout the 1970s and 1980s Mogadishu was not only seen as the embodiment of modernity, but was also symbolically, economically and politically situated at the centre of the nation (see Figure 2). In a poem entitled *Mogadishu what happened?* (*Muqdishu maxaa dhacay?*) by London-based Cumar Cabdinuur Nuux 'Nabaddoon', written in October 2003 and translated by Kapteijns (2010: 37) – which I reproduce in part below – the poet talks to the city, reflecting on the 'good life' of the modern era. He romanticizes the city's natural beauty, depicting it as a place of prosperity, leisure and freedom, but also as the centre of administration, secular and religious learning and the central 'nerve' of the entire nation (Kapteijns 2010: 36–7):

> Your beautiful seascape matching the colour of the sky,
> the fish, the ships travelling on and under the water,
> places to swim, tourist sites to visit,
> a central harbour, stable administration, security
> you were graced with everything beautiful ...
>
> The centre of education, organised administration, and general
>   supervision
> institutes, Qur'anic and other schools, mosques to pray in,
> Mukarama road, so beautiful to the eye –
> what is the cause that now country hicks graze their camels
>   there?
>
> Mogadishu, you are the capital of our country
> If, as such you deserve respect,
> if you are the place from where all other towns are
>   administered,
> if you are the heart, head and nerve centre,
> what caused you to be defiled? What happened, Mogadishu?
>
>> [Nabaddoon (2003), translated by Kapteijns (2010: 37)].[6]

Kapteijns (2010: 39) links this spirit of cosmopolitan modernity evoked in the poem with a notion of urbane civility (*ilbaxnimo*), as a set of meanings related to 'the sophistication of people living in urban communities made up of different kinds of people ... aspiring to modern education and to an ideal of gender relations', in contrast to the manners of country people. Muraayo similarly captures this notion of *ilbaxnimo* and sophistication in her descriptions of urban life. Many of the *concerti* and theatre performances she mentions would have taken place at the National Theatre, which was not only a piece of modernist architecture, but also the centre of new forms of modern songs and music styles of the time. It was the home of the famous *Waaberi* band, whose members included the now London-based vocalist Maryan Mursal, singer Magool, as well as Hadrawi – known globally as the 'Somali Shakespeare'. Cinemas were a popular pastime, and many of the women I interviewed spoke about attending cinemas that had retained their colonial names – Cinema Missione, Benadir, Centrale, Supercinema – where the latest American or Indian films were screened, dubbed in Italian. Several remembered James Bond films, Clint Eastwood's Westerns, and the Federico Fellini and Totò productions.

In a recent essay, Italian-Somali novelist Cristina Ali Farah (2014) describes her own memories of the city alongside extracts from a guidebook on Mogadishu published by the government at the time. She remembers watching Bollywood love stories, dangling her legs in the swimming pool at the Hotel Jubba, watching her cousin play tennis, and sitting on the beach looking at what the waves had washed up that day. She also describes the establishment that was also frequently at the centre of my own interlocutors' narrations of Mogadishu: the Azan 'patisserie-restaurant-roofgarden-takeaway-cheesemakers-bakery', which was the only place that produced fresh pasta to order (Farah 2014: 33). It was one of many places that sold Italian goods. Up until the 1990s Italian fashions, furniture and cuisine had been symbols of modern urban civility and sophistication. On my trips home to Italy, many of the women I met in London who had grown up in this period asked me to bring back all sorts of Italian products – a leather bag, jewellery and food. I was surprised by these nostalgic attachments half a century after the end of colonial rule, but I came to appreciate the ways in which they enabled my friends to connect to this particular period of their youth, and to the smells and tastes of everyday life in the modern city.

Similar nostalgia for the modern past was evoked when I visited the *Mogadishu Lost Moderns* photographic exhibition in the Mosaic Rooms gallery in Kensington, West London. Part of the *Disappearing Cities of the Arab World* cultural

FIGURE 2 *Modern Mogadishu c. 1970. Published in Ismail Mohamed Ali (1972: 13)* Beautiful Somalia. *Somalia: Ministry of Information and National Guidance.*

programme, *Lost Moderns* captures fragments of the old Arab town, remnants of fascist architecture, and architectural forms relating to Mogadishu's postcolonial era. Somali architect Rashid Ali and English visual artist Andrew Cross seek out architectural forms and designs that capture the modern glory of Mogadishu and its subsequent destruction. As Ali (2014: 15) explains: 'Modernism … was to have an enduring influence on post independence architecture and the built form, since this was largely seen as a way for the country to assert its identity through architectural forms.' However, in the photographs taken in 2013 after over two decades of conflict, dust and rubble abound, staircases and walls

FIGURE 3 *Showcasing Women's Involvement in Research c. 1970.*
Published in Ismail Mohamed Ali (1972: 54) Beautiful Somalia. *Somalia:*
Ministry of Information and National Guidance.

are crumbling, and goats graze on the weeds that sprawl around
the now largely abandoned buildings. Yet some new developments
appear to be sprouting up again; scaffolding can be seen in the
background, and the National Theatre, originally built in 1969
and destroyed during the war, has recently been rebuilt. While the
buildings mark the destruction and abandonment of the city, they
also remind viewers of the past and suggest that some elements of it
have endured despite the war. The photographs of public buildings,
houses, facades and cityscapes offer a glimpse of hope, suggesting
that the 'modern' has perhaps never been completely 'lost'.

Tradition, culture and morality

As mentioned, an aspiration for the modern in post-independence Somalia was also accompanied by an ambivalent attitude towards traditional culture. On the one hand, the nationalist modernist discourse of *Soomaalinimo*, articulated in popular culture and propagated by the nationalist movement and the postcolonial state, sought to distance itself from some elements of the past deemed 'backwards' and in contradiction to modern, feminist and emancipatory politics. On the other hand, the notion of *Soomaalinimo* gained legitimacy by drawing on tradition, which included notions of an authentic culture and traditional religious morality.

The older women to whom I spoke in London often discussed traditional culture in reference to nomadic lifestyles and clothing such as the *guntiino*, which was also often presented as a 'practical' form of dress that suited the rural lifestyles of nomad women. Urban middle-class women, such as Safiya, might occasionally adopt the *guntiino* and *garbasaar* (shawl) as a way of celebrating Somali traditions. In a similar way, both Safiya's and Muraayo's descriptions of summer holidays in the countryside capture the ways in which nomadic culture was also often associated with natural beauty, a healthy lifestyle and an authentic Somali culture that was not accessible in the city. Trips to the rural interior provided them with a temporary break from the frenzy of urban life, as well as a 'return' to what was conceived as the original, 'natural' and authentic roots of Somali culture.

Traditional culture was also often evoked as a source of morality in the face of a frivolous and immoral modernity, drawn on to assess, and guard against, the corruptions of modern life. The following poem, entitled *In the old days (Beri hore waxaa jiray)*, was sung by two famous vocalists of the late 1960s. It is an exchange between a man who invites women to remain true to their customs and culture, and a woman who ultimately turns away from tradition, which she sees as an obstacle to her own development:

He [Maxammed Jaamac Jaaf]:
In the old days it was custom
that a girl perfumed her hair
and braided it.

She wrapped around her waist
a wide cloth belt with fringes and an ornamental cord
and wore a white dress.
But something has changed.
Something weird with long horns
they wear as hats on their heads
and run all over the market
[Refrain] You, women, have destroyed our culture
You have overstepped the religious law
and destroyed our religion.
Girls, won't you behave?

She [Mariam Mursal]:
What was custom in the old days
and a hundred years ago
and what has been left behind
don't make us go back on that well-worn road
for we have turned away from it with effort.
Now we expect to run and compete
for the sun and the moon
and to lead people.
[Refrain] First get some education and learn how to read and
     write.
Don't try to turn back, you country hick, people who have
     woken up.

[Extract from Kapteijns with Omar (1999: 139)]

The song reveals an ongoing tension between modernity and
tradition and culture, and the ways in which this plays out along
gendered lines. For the male singer, the embracing of modernity
represents a disregard for tradition and a loss of morality, whereas
for the female singer modernity signals education, development and
a break with the past. Interestingly, morality is associated with a
notion of tradition and culture that also includes, and is inseparable
from, religion.

Many of the first-generation women with whom I spoke in
London also drew on this discourse to describe the past. Raaxo, a
woman in her fifties who lived in Kilburn, North London, explained
how 'traditionally' an unmarried woman in nomadic society

braided her hair until she was married, after which she also started wearing a *garbasaar*. Covering after marriage was viewed not only as 'tradition' but also as moral behaviour, and Raaxo pointed out how these practices were largely abandoned in urban areas. Nonetheless, inherited understandings of traditional behaviour, norms and values set moral boundaries. Muraayo's mother allowed her daughters relative freedom to move around the city, but she reminded them of dressing modestly. Modern clothing and urban lifestyles were often seen as frivolous, Western and immoral. As Muraayo remembers, her mother's notion of modesty stemmed from embodied understandings of morality grounded in particular notions of tradition – as Muraayo put it – from 'her religion, her culture, her environment'. Modest clothing was not therefore necessarily incompatible with modern urban lifestyles, but both tradition and modernity could be combined; Muraayo could participate freely in urban life, but she was expected to dress and act modestly in line with traditional norms and customs.

As Kapteijns (2009) has noted, similar tensions between modernity and tradition are observable in popular love songs in post-independence urban Somali society. Drawing on Abu-Lughod's (2000) notion of the 'modern subject', which is premised on ideas of individual desire and emotion, Kapteijns (2009: 109) shows how romantic love, often expressed publicly through love songs, became an important ideal for urban Somali youth of the nationalist period. In some of the love songs, romantic love, based on mutual consent and the solemn commitment of both partners, is portrayed as a central value within marriage. This is juxtaposed with a monolithic idea of marriage in traditional pastoral society, whereby one needs approval from male elders, and where 'the husband-provider [is] in charge of an obedient wife' (Kapteijns with Omar 1999: 132). Nonetheless, this breaking away from an imagined tradition is depicted as incomplete. The concept of tradition, rooted in pastoral traditional culture and customary law, is used as a tool for legitimizing the marriage (ibid.: 149). Companionable marriage, therefore, is discursively depicted as interlinked and inseparable from tradition. The latter is positioned as the seat of morality and is opposed to an immoral modernity; women are hence made to stand as the bearers of morality and symbols of cultural authenticity.

Most of the first-generation women I spoke to drew on a discourse of love and companionship when they discussed their own marriages. They contrasted their own relations with their husbands with those of rural or traditional Somalis, and those of their parents. Seven out of eleven female Somali interviewees with whom I discussed the topic, and who were raised in Mogadishu throughout the 1960s–80s, told me they had married out of 'love'. They often enjoyed reminiscing and recounting their romances. Ubax, for example, had met her husband at a bus stop in Mogadishu, and although she had initially refused his advances, they eventually courted each other for two years before he asked to marry her. Similarly, Safiya described her husband's love and adoration: 'When we got married my husband loved me so much!' Ardo, another woman in her sixties who married a work colleague, explained how she had had several boyfriends, and her 'parents would know, but not always. If they knew they would usually push for marriage.'

As we saw above, it was acceptable for females to frequent gender-mixed environments and to have male friends, but clear boundaries were set based on embodied ideas of traditional practices and customs. Certain areas of the city were out of bounds, and sexual intercourse for women prior to marriage was deemed immoral. There were clear limits to modernity, and even though one could embrace a modern lifestyle there was always a risk that would be viewed as immoral if completely divorced from tradition. Love marriages were accepted as long as moral boundaries were maintained before the marriage, and elders were involved to some extent in the marriage negotiations.

Beyond the Mogadishu middle classes

While I have dealt at length with the lives of the urban middle-class women in Mogadishu, it is important to note that these experiences were unique when compared to women from working classes or minority backgrounds, or those living or originating from elsewhere in the Somali territories. Many of the women mentioned above inhabited the central middle-class districts of the city, but Mogadishu was also characterized by its urban slums situated in the peripheries of the city, which housed many of the more recent rural migrants. Sahra, for example, like many other *Banaadiri*[7] women in Mogadishu, had not enjoyed the same freedom as Safiya and Muraayo. She didn't go to school but instead helped out at home:

> I didn't go out most of the time, I wasn't allowed. I stayed at home. I woke up early in the morning, cooked *canjeero* [Somali pancakes], cleaned dishes, then lunch time, went to the butcher with my dad, then came home, cooked food, then cleaned. After lunch we used to sleep until 4pm and then we made tea in the evenings. Most of the time we didn't cook in the evenings, maybe we made *canjeero*. We didn't go out, sometimes for a wedding or something. Saturday and Sunday I used to go with mum to the mosque to listen to talks.

Sahra's parents, originally from Hargeysa, had moved to Mogadishu in search of employment. Her father was a religious scholar (*sheikh*) and an *imam* in a *madrasa* (school) in the Medina district west of Mogadishu, and her mother made and sold *halwa* and other sweets from the house. Her brothers were allowed out more than the girls, and tended to do the shopping for the family. Sahra told me she barely saw her father, who was often busy visiting sick people, teaching *Qur'an* to their neighbours or conducting wedding celebrations. She married at the age of thirteen, much earlier than Safiya and Muraayo. When we spoke of her marriage, she did not employ discourses of love and companionship but rather explained that it had been 'organized' by her kin. Nor was Sahra able to avail herself of the educational and employment opportunities in Mogadishu, and she rarely used the idioms of modernity, development and freedom to talk about her youth.

Life in the rural areas of the country was also strikingly different. Xalwo, for example, was born in 1961 and raised in what is now the Sanaag region of contemporary Somaliland. She was one of eight siblings and never went to school but, like Sahra, she helped out in the house. She married a paternal cousin: 'We knew each other all our lives,' she explained, 'We would meet secretly to chat behind trees, say things, that we loved each other. We couldn't meet in public places, for coffee or tea.' Like Sahra Xalwo married young, at the age of fifteen. 'I started wearing *hijab* and *abaya* (a loose and ankle-length black robe or dress) after marriage … like it says in our culture,' she explained, referring to the traditional norms and customs mentioned above. She was less likely to have access to the modern clothing or urban lifestyles which characterized Muraayo and Safiya's lives. Her memories of the past tended to focus on the beauty of Somali rural landscapes, the quality of the air, the food and the heat – all things she missed in her small flat in East London.

Furthermore, Safiya and Muraayo often amalgamated their nostalgia for the modern with a nationalist rhetoric of *Soomaalinimo*, and a patriotic longing for a united Somalia. However, this attitude is not shared with many Somali women who originate from, for example, northern or north-east clan families, or those who identify with the independent Somaliland nation-state, or with the Ogaden or the Kenyan north-eastern province. While this longing for the period of modernity might be shared with others who lived in Mogadishu at the time, the rhetoric of a united pan-Somali nationalist project has become separated from the modernist rhetoric, and is more commonly employed by those from southern-based clan families. As a Somali woman in London summarized for me: '*Soomaalinimo* means a blue flag [Somalia flag] in Mogadishu. In Somaliland it means culture, tradition and language. For the Ogadeni it means language, and it's a way of understanding their relation with other Somali regions.' The meaning of *Soomaalinimo* has not only developed over time, but it is understood differently based on past experiences of the post-independence context, and present political orientations.[8]

This unique fusion of nostalgia for a modern past and for a nationalist project was most evident when I attended a welcome event for the newly elected president of Somalia, Shariif Sheekh Axmed, with Safiya, Muraayo and some of their Mogadishu friends in March 2010 at Troxy Hall in East London. The president had been invited by members of his clan, who comprised most of those present and had financed and organized the gathering. For weeks we spoke about the event, discussed our attire, and encouraged friends and relatives to attend. Like Muraayo, many of the other women at the event were dressed in *dirac* and *garbasaar* with their hair uncovered, and some had made their dresses out of a Somalia flag, indicating their political allegiance to a united Somalia. At an event that stressed the importance of the nation, religious markers were downplayed. 'It's not appropriate to wear *jilbab or niqab* (face veil). … Not at this type of event,' Safiya commented when I asked her about it. We shivered for over an hour in the queue waiting to make our way past the stringent security measures, as Safiya and Muraayo joined in the singing of Somalia *ha noolaato* – United Somalia – to keep each other warm.

The hall was packed with thousands of people, and we pushed our way through the crowds to find seats together on the upper balcony. Somalia flags were on display everywhere, accentuating the dazzling Art Deco interior. Hosted by journalist Rageh Omar, the event started off with a prayer followed by speeches, poetry recitals, and musical performances by famous Somali vocalists Farxiya Fiska and Faadumo Qasim Hilowle. When the president finally appeared on stage, he made promises to restore peace and security and to rebuild Somalia, criticized those who were distorting religion to bring about terror and destruction, and appealed to the diaspora for their continued support. Safiya and Muraayo sat for the entire event mesmerized, transfixed, their eyes glittering with excitement as they joined in the singing of the national anthem and cries of 'Somalia *ha noolaato*', while waving their miniature flags in the air. I was surprised at the deference and respect they showed when talking about the president; their show of patriotism transported me back in time. At one point they reminded each other of similar national celebrations and summer youth camps in which they had participated in the 1960s and 1970s, and they spoke once again about their youth and the freedom and beauty of life before the war. For one night they imagined the possibility of returning to a peaceful Somalia that once was. 'I would love to return some day, have a position that matters, do something for my country ... mostly educated Somalis suffer here,' Safiya explained, charting out yet another one of her life plans.

Modernity versus religion: Consequences of the 1975 family law

The law and its opponents

Throughout the Barre regime, religion was viewed as co-constitutive of traditional culture, but it occupied an ambiguous position vis-à-vis modernity and Barre's socialist ideology. In the early years of his regime, Barre sought, at least in rhetoric, to link fundamental values of Islam to socialist policies. In a speech in 1972 he declared: 'Ours is the religion of the common man. It stands for equality and justice. Consequently, socialism as applied to our particular condition cannot identify religion as the obstacle to the progress of the working class and therefore cannot negate it' (cited in Samatar 1988: 108).

Shortly after, however, with concerns about growing opposition from religious leaders, he introduced sanctions on religious expression, and in 1975 passed a new family law, arguing that previous arrangements, supported by religion, had resulted in the abuse and exploitation of women. The year 1975 was to mark a crucial turning point in the country. It signalled a reconfiguration in the Somali collective imaginary of the notions of modernity, Islam and traditional culture, which would have longstanding effects. The struggle for gender equality became merely a backdrop on which these wider struggles played out.

On 11 January 1975 the new family law was passed giving men and women equal rights in divorce and inheritance, and the *diya* practice (blood money) and other aspects of customary law (*xeer*), which were considered a traditional source of gender inequality, were outlawed (Samatar 1988). In a speech at a stadium in Mogadishu and broadcast across the country, Barre announced: 'As of today, Somali men and women are equal' (Baadiyow 2010: 147).

Five days later, on 16 January, Islamic scholars condemned the law from the pulpit of the Cabdulqadir Mosque, which was then the 'epicentre for the emerging Islamic movement' in downtown Mogadishu (ibid.: 138). Opposition arose from reformist activists, members of the Sufi orders, and the traditional Somali *culima* (*waddad*, scholars). Seen as an assault on Islamic values, the law was viewed as a further attempt to secularize Somali society by attacking the sacred domain of the family (Samatar 1988: 109; Baadiyow 2010: 139). *Sheikh* Cabdulasis from the Al-Azhar Mission in Somalia delivered the Friday sermon the following day condemning the law. Following other speeches by traditional scholars, demonstrations against the family law broke out on the streets. Hundreds of scholars and activists were imprisoned, and on 18 and 19 January the National Security Court sentenced to death ten scholars, and jailed six for 30 years and seventeen for 20 years (Baadiyow 2010: 138). On 23 January ten scholars were executed at the Police Academy in Mogadishu.

Baadiyow (2010) explores the multiple factors behind the passing of the law and the state violence against Islamic scholars. The colonial administration, for example, had upset the balance between traditional authorities and Islamic scholars within Somali society by absorbing traditional leaders into its institutions and marginalizing the role of Islamic scholars. While colonial rulers had imposed their own legal systems on Somalia, the existing family law, based on a combination of *Sha'fi* jurisprudence and customary law (*xeer*), had been more or less respected, despite British attempts to codify the law. The postcolonial state had centralized power by reducing the scope of traditional institutions, but the existing family law had remained unchanged, with Article 50 stating that the 'doctrine of Islam shall be the main source of laws of the state' (ibid.: 143–4). The family law of 1975, which significantly changed a law that had until that point remained relatively untouched, was therefore seen as the final blow to the authority of traditional religious scholars.

At the same time, throughout the 1970s there had been a growing presence of activists and scholars influenced by revivalist ideas, many of whom were also opposed to the regime. Scholars had fled during this time to study in Sudan, Egypt, Saudi Arabia and the Gulf countries. Educated in Arab universities they brought back ideas of the Muslim Brotherhood, Salafism and Takfir ideologies (Baadiyow 2010: 152–4). *Sheikh* Maxamed Macallin was one of these scholars who had gained prominence, particularly among young activists during this period, thanks to his religious commentaries. Having completed his postgraduate studies at the Al-Azhar University in Cairo, he returned to Somalia in 1967 and was employed in the Ministry for Justice and Islamic Affairs. He spoke frequently at the Cabdulqadir Mosque, which came to attract many Islamic activists concerned with the regime and its socialist ideology (ibid.: 138). The emergence of renaissance organizations such as *Al-Nahda* and *Al-Ahli* in Mogadishu and *Al-Wahda* in Hargeysa can be dated to this period; many of those involved in these organizations preached ideas drawn from the Muslim Brotherhood. The works of Hassan Al-Banna, Sayyid Qutb and Al-Mawdudi from the Brotherhood, as well as literature drawn from the *Jamaat al-Islamiyah* in Pakistan, had become widely read and available within Islamist circles (ibid.: 152). By the mid-1970s a large part of the opposition to the regime had taken an Islamic edge. As Sadia Ahmed (1999: 70) explains this rebel movement was generally welcomed by people who disagreed with socialist principles or were against the increasingly oppressive practices of the regime. These Islamic revivalist movements, although perceived by some as foreign funded, were supported by others who saw them as promoting 'Somali' religious values and culture.

Saudi influences were not only political, but they also began to pervade society at large throughout the 1980s. Migration to the Gulf states of young, educated men increased in this period, influenced by the oil price boom of the early 1970s. Many left Somalia to work in the oil industry, but also to pursue religious education, do business or flee the political situation (Kleist 2004: 5). As Declich (2000: 296–7) describes, these migrants brought back money, new fashions and consumer items; Saudi Arabian clothes such as the *hijab* started to compete with Western-style clothing, and offered an alternative 'sign of modernity and fashion'. Furthermore, Somalia's geopolitical situation shifted towards the late 1970s. It joined the League of Arab States in 1974, and the loss of support from the Soviet Union after the Ogaden War in 1977 meant that it became increasingly reliant on the (mostly financial) support from Saudi Arabia and other Gulf and Middle Eastern countries. This Saudi influence – also referred to as 'petro-Islam' (Mernissi 1996 cited in Abdi 2007: 202) – led to a further 'Arabization of Somalia', which came to be felt in Mogadishu at the end of the 1980s and early 1990s. The Mosque of Islamic Solidarity was built by the Saudi Fahd bin Abdul Aziz Al Saud Foundation in front of the Parliament building in Mogadishu, and free and compulsory schooling in the Arabic language was implemented in the mid-1980s. Sufism, which had been the original form of Islamization in many Somali areas, started to come under attack by reformist groups (Abdi 2007). Some of its practices, such as the *nabi-ammaan*, had already been a source of criticism by literate modern urbanites who labelled them 'traditional', and as pertaining to the 'uneducated peasantry' (ibid.: 313).[9] In the 1980s these criticisms were voiced through revivalist idioms, as activists condemned these Sufi practices as inauthentically Islamic. Urban intellectuals, including many women, were influenced by these ideas and turned to practice the form of spirituality advocated by the followers of the Muslim Brotherhood (ibid.: 316).

Baadiyow (2010: 150) proposes three main reasons to account for why Barre introduced the 1975 family law at that moment in time, and subsequently launched a campaign against the scholars who opposed it. First, Baadiyow suggests that these policies served as a way of entrenching socialist ideology by curbing traditional practices that curtailed gender equality. Second, Barre may have been driven by geopolitics, and the need for foreign assistance. The new law served as a way of competing with Marxist Ethiopia for Soviet support by flagging up Somalia's socialist credentials.[10] Finally, as suggested above, it may also have been an attempt to further curb the influence of traditional scholars and to quash the emerging Islamic movement, both of whom were becoming strong opponents of the regime.

Barre's stance towards Islam, however, remained unclear. In a speech he delivered during the 1970 *Eid-al-Adha* celebrations, he proclaimed that 'the Somali Democratic Republic will spare no efforts to follow the path to prosperity. ... This path is clearly laid out by Islam, and the active work of the religious leaders in the field of education and morals, will be a source of inspiration and assistance' (Barre 1971: 61). He suggested that Muslim leaders were indeed the 'teachers of nations and people', and that religious ideas and actions ought to be directed towards the progress of the nation (Declich 2000: 296).

Religion, modernity and traditional culture reconsidered

The 1975 family law was eventually amended in 1980 to comply with the general principles of Islamic law, but it was to have wider implications for Somali society. Scholars have shown, for example, how contemporary Islamist movements in the Somali regions can be tied to this period of opposition to the Barre regime (Baadiyow 2010). More importantly for the purposes of this chapter, however, the law also marked the beginning of the demise of the nationalist project and discourses of modernity that had dominated the previous decades. Gradually, over the following decades, Islamic morality came to take precedence over the notions of *Soomaalinimo*, and of modernity, and particularly over the collective discourse of gender equality, which had been a crucial symbol of this turn towards the modern (Kapteijns 2009: 119). Gender equality came to be associated with the modern, and hence, was positioned as antithetical to Somali morality of which Islam was a crucial part. In addition, new frictions began to emerge across clan and religious lines, challenging the notion of pan-Somali unity and fragmenting the notion of *Soomaalinimo*. Although traditional Somali culture and morality had until this point been seen as inseparable from Islamic morality, as I noted above, this also began to shift. Following the continued rise and popularity of revivalist movements, religion came to be singled out from traditional culture within public discourses. This period marked the origins of a reformist discourse, which became hegemonic in the late 1980s and advocated an 'authentic' religion in opposition to cultural norms and habits. I will return to this discourse in the following chapters, but in the remainder of this chapter I will focus on how these reconfigurations of the modern, religious and traditional culture are manifest in the memories of urban middle-class women in London and how they shape their present engagements with their faith.

Caasha-Kin Duale was one of the few female lawyers in Somalia during the 1970s and 1980s, and the only female defence council in capital punishment cases. She was born in Beledweyne, Central Somalia, but when she was five years old, she moved to Mogadishu with her family where her father worked for the government. Caasha married a patrilineal first cousin who worked as a medical doctor in the capital, and together they had five children. Having completed her law degree in 1979 at the National University, she first worked as a legal adviser for a government insurance company, and later began practising as a criminal lawyer. As the only female senior partner in her law firm, she struggled to gain the respect and trust afforded to male lawyers of her stature. On one occasion she described how one of her male clients, who in 1988 she had defended and who eventually was spared the death sentence, turned to her after the case and thanked her by saying: 'I should congratulate myself because I put my life in the hands of a woman.' She now recounted this with a smile on her face, but at the time she had been deeply hurt by this remark.

During one of our meetings Caasha provided me with her own analysis of the causes and effects of the war at the end of the 1980s. 'In my lifetime when I was growing up and working in Mogadishu, people had core values,' she began, in reference to the 1960s and 1970s, 'I could not go to my neighbour and beat her up and take her stuff right? But that's exactly what happened.' She elaborated with a detailed account of a moral shift that occurred in the 1980s:

The problem is the government are in charge of maintaining the moral order and core values. But when morality changes there is nothing that can stand between the rights and wrongs of people. Before, those who grabbed public property were pointed at, people who took bribes were pointed at. After 1979 those who achieved high positions but were not corrupted were pointed out as weak … . Rebel clan members who would die in combat with the government would have their corpses not buried or their limbs attached to a bar on the side of the road as a deterrent to other rebel groups. It started in the Central Somalia and it became the norm. There was no respect for the dead. In the old Somali war ethics the elderly, women, children and religious people got immunity. After 1979 all this changed – indiscriminate killing became normal and rape of women belonging to rebel clans became a used weapon. What happened is that in the 1990s there was no morality, no war ethics, all boundaries of decency and human respect were crossed, those people who grew up in the 80s will never know of that morality that existed before that.

Her discussion then turned to a description of the 1975 family law, and the religious opposition to the regime that ensued. Caasha had been an advocate for the Barre regime's progressive agenda, and had campaigned in support of the new legislation. The family law had to be changed, she reasoned at the time, as it stood as an impediment to women's acquisition of equal status in Somali society. However, she later elaborated that she had been wrong and misguided in supporting these legislative changes:

> I was in favour of that law. But I didn't know my rights as a Muslim woman. … Now I do, because I went back to study it and discovered that I have more rights than what any man-made legislation could grant me. I know why Islamic laws [on inheritance] make sense. … People like me, who didn't know the religion, supported the law. Barre never put equality in practice. There were no high positions, no ministries given to women, and women needed to challenge stereotypes in every aspect of life. In the *Qur'an* I have learnt it says to cover for modesty but not to submit to men. Polygamy is allowed with the clear reservation that men must be able to provide equally for all his wives, if not, one wife is good for him. But the problem is with men's interpretations of the *Qur'an*.

In the first part of our conversation, Caasha tied an absence of morality to the incompetence of the state, its perpetuation of corruption, and its inability to maintain the moral order and many of the 'core values' – traditional Somali values – that sustained Somali society prior to the 1970s. Safiya made a similar comment during one of our conversations, suggesting that the streets of Mogadishu in the early 1980s were no longer as safe as they had been; crime was rampant, and one could no longer rely on the 'wider community' to maintain moral order. In Caasha's account the Barre regime is presented as violating traditional Somali culture, and disrupting the stability and continuity of Somali society. In the second part of our discussion, Caasha suggested that the absence of religious knowledge in modern socialist Somalia, and in her own life, was also a contributing factor to moral breakdown in Somali society. According to this narrative, religious values are viewed as separate from traditional cultural values, and the absence of a conscious and intellectual understanding of Islamic law, norms and values is presented as the leading cause of the moral breakdown. Women's lack of knowledge of Islam, which Caasha linked to the absence of religious instruction during this modern period, meant that men have interpreted the *Qur'an* to further their own ends. Gender equality, according to Caasha, can only be achieved through Islam. A proper, conscious understanding of religion by and for women, Caasha suggested, will enable them to implement equality not only in rhetoric but also in practice – something Barre failed to do.

Religion forgotten

According to Caasha, her religious awareness has come about by engaging with texts in an intellectual and reasoned way. Fahiimo, a Somali woman raised in Mogadishu throughout the 1970s and 1980s, with whom I also discussed the 1975 family law, similarly suggested that Barre's secular socialist policies had produced a generation of Somali women with a limited understanding of Islam. Unlike her own parents who had never learnt to read the *Qur'an*, Fahiimo had attended *dugsi* (Islamic school) from an early age where she had learnt to pray, and to read and recite the *Qur'an*. However, outside these classes, she explained, religion was marginalized. As mentioned above, Safiya and Muraayo also commented on how religion was 'not allowed' or not actively embraced in public life throughout the 1970s. Looking somewhat critically at her own religious learning, Fahiimo remarked in relation to her *Qur'an* lessons: 'There was no explanation, you just learnt by heart ... with no application to our lives.'

Her own parents, had lived for most of their lives as pastoralists. Despite their illiteracy, and the fact they had not studied the *Qur'an*, they had a different kind of knowledge of Islam – a 'practical' or embodied sense of religion – that was inseparable from Somali traditions, norms and ways of being. As she described to me:

> My mum knew religion ... she was not learning from the *Qitab* (the Book), she was just talking, memorizing, and she would say what to do and not to do ... like covering her hair, *salat* (prayer), Ramadan, cooking for the poor in Ramadan. ... She knew you had to do the right things to go to *Jannah* (paradise) ... like not hurt someone, not say bad things, respect people. ... She was always telling us what to do ... . Religion is really the basis of Somali culture, that's why we are good people.

On another occasion, Fahiimo discussed with Safiya and her other friend Ubax what had happened with their own generation. Safiya explained:

> Our ancestors knew religion and we knew the *Qur'an*, but in 1960 everything changed and we wanted to be modern. We had to wear trousers to school. Religious scholars were killed by the government, we all started to have education. ... But religion says that a boy and girl must not meet until he asks her family and they agree. They must meet with the family before they are married. But in our generation boys and girls were running away, getting married and then coming back to families. ... That's what happened. ... That had become our culture. We had forgotten religion.

According to Safiya and Fahiimo, religion had been a visible and crucial part of their ancestors' lifeworlds: as Safiya put it, previous generations 'knew religion'. In contrast, her own generation had learnt to read and recite the *Qur'an* and knew *about* the fundamentals of the faith, but had failed to put these into practice: they had 'forgotten religion'.[11] It was not necessarily the lack of an engagement with the texts, but an obsession with the modern that had led Somalis to ignore what they already knew, and hence to abandon the practical sense of religion their parents and ancestors had. Modernity had stood in the way of a true realization of their faith.

Similarly, Fahiimo explained on one occasion that she had learnt about basic religious precepts, but that the government and society at large had discouraged public manifestations of Islam. She blamed the government and its socialist policies, rather than modernity for the lack of morality:

> Our government didn't allow religion, it didn't allow the *hijab* in school. Barre used to send religious people to jail, so most of the people didn't know their religion. ... Even the children used to throw stones at people wearing *hijab* in Somalia. ... Their parents told them religious people were bad and dangerous. But gradually the parents started to realize themselves and change.

Religious knowledge was previously understood in practical terms, linked to action rather than to a set of facts, or an ability to read the texts. Her friend Ubax continued the explanation: 'And then suddenly some religious scholars started to go around and tell people voluntarily in the streets, sending messages about religion. Barre only had power in Mogadishu, the rest of the country was free.' Ubax was referencing the sudden shift that occurred following the 1975 family law with the growth of revivalist movements and loss of authority of the Barre regime outside Mogadishu. While religious people had previously been mocked or silenced, they were suddenly welcomed and listened to; they had turned from dangerous individuals to freedom fighters struggling against the immorality and corruption of the regime.

Both Fahiimo and Ubax accused Barre, and his repression of religion, for their own ignorance of Islam. Similarly, other women noted how it was not modernity per se that had erased religion from everyday life, but rather Barre's anti-religion policies, his corrupt practices and his manipulation of clannism that had contributed to the breakdown of Somali society. For others, what had been forgotten was a lived experience of religiosity, not knowledge of texts and scriptures. Some first-generation women looked back nostalgically at Sufism as the authentic Somali religion that had first been suppressed as 'backwards' by the Barre regime, and later as 'unIslamic' by reformist movements in the country. Deqa, for example, was born and raised in Mogadishu but moved to Italy aged seventeen, where she completed her degree and later moved to the UK for further study. She did not consider herself particularly religious, and often criticized Somalis for adopting 'Arabic' customs and clothing and for assuming illiberal attitudes towards non-Muslims. She considered herself a Muslim, but had not embraced the reformist understanding of Islam. She explained: 'Back in the day Somalia was more Sufi, we were Muslims but we were not drawing on Saudi traditions ... we all shared this religion.' Deqa looked back at what she claimed was a more authentic and moderate form of Islam which existed in the past, and with which she continued to identify. This particular form of religiosity, she claimed, constituted the essence of *Soomaalinimo,* and the true way of being both Muslim and Somali.

As we have seen, the ways in which Somali women raised throughout the 1960s to the 1980s in Mogadishu remember the past shed light on their current aspirations and forms of identification. These processes illuminate their experiences of war and the current political context of the region. These practices of sharing memories have created new forms of sociality, bringing together Somali women in London through the emotional, embodied and affective exchanges of memories. At the same time, these practices have reinforced boundaries between women who do not share similar interpretations of the past. Safiya and Muraayo have found each other again after decades apart, and their experiences of nostalgia for a modern, nationalist era have brought them together with others who share a similar orientation towards the past and present. Their critical attitudes towards the immorality of the past and their engagement with reformist teachings have also connected them with women like Fahiimo. However, these new forms of sociality have also reinforced frictions, and distanced these women from those who might not similarly partake in their nationalist understanding of *Soomaalinimo,* or perhaps those who are less interested in engaging with Islamic reformist teachings.

According to Özyürek (2006), Kemalists in Turkey search for modernity in the past because it can't be found in the present or the future. In contrast, for many first-generation Somali women, modernity existed in the past, but it was incomplete or immoral. For these women modernity can be redeemed in the future by embracing Islamic ideals. Such ideals offer Somali women a possibility of critiquing the past, but also of looking forward to an experience of modernity, albeit one that is 'moral' and ethically grounded. Somali women look backwards at a nationalist modernity of their youth, and forwards at the possibility of a moral modernity of life in exile. As Boyer (2012: 25) points out: 'Nostalgia always carries with it a politics of the future.'

Barre's collapse, and Safiya's flight

By the early 1980s following an intense period of drought, dwindling aid, a shrinking economy, a growing ecological crisis, and a costly counter-insurgency, Somali society was on the verge of collapse. As the urban populations grew, energy production was unable to keep up. The Ogaden War of 1977 had caused an influx of thousands of Somali and Oromo refugees into Somalia. The 1974 friendship treaty with the Soviet Union, which had brought money, weapons, and administrative and organizational support to Somalia, was revoked. This all further impoverished the country and weakened the regime (Lewis 2002: Chapter 10). In 1980, following the Soviet Union's backing of Ethiopia, Somalia signed a deal with the United States, exchanging the use of their airbases for military support (Samatar 1988: 141).

Furthermore, throughout the 1970s and 1980s, much of the socialist rhetoric had not been translated into reality (Samatar 1988), and Barre began to exploit clan divisions to his advantage. The government became increasingly reliant on quashing political dissent through fear and violence. Nuruddin Farah's trilogy of novels *Variations on the Theme of an African Dictatorship* vividly capture the everyday realities of censorship, imprisonment and violence under an increasingly authoritarian military regime. Resistance to the regime was intensifying in the north, as the Barre regime exacerbated the political, economic and social differences between the north and south. Barre sought to crush opposition through imprisonments, executions, confiscations of businesses, and other forms of coercive or violent means (Adan 1994). Two major opposition groups formed: the Somali Salvation Democratic Front (SSDF), which was largely dominated by the *Majeerteen* clan based in Ethiopia, and the Somali National Movement (SNM), led by the *Isaaq* clan and initially launched in London. As the SNM took hold of the city of Hargeysa in 1988, Barre ordered a series of aerial strikes that flattened the cities of Hargeysa and Burco, killing thousands and forcing many to claim asylum abroad. In 1991 the United Somali Congress (USC), which aimed to unite all opposition groups and take hold of the government, ousted Barre from Mogadishu, who sought exile in Nigeria until his death. The other groups refused to accept the USC's authority, leading to inter-group and inter-clan fighting, the spread of conflict across the country, and the eventual collapse of the state (see Kapteijns 2013: Chapter 2; Laitin & Samatar 1987: Chapters 5–7). That same year the Republic of Somaliland, the former British Protectorate, building on the struggles of the *Isaaq*-led SNM, declared independence, putting an end to a nationalist pan-Somali struggle.

At this point in time, Safiya was busy pursuing her English lessons in order to apply for a master's programme in the United States. She was also pregnant with her second daughter. When conflict reached the capital she spent most of her days in the house, too scared to set foot outside. The day she went into labour, she was unable to reach a hospital and no midwife was on call to assist. 'My daughter was born in my kitchen … without a doctor, without a midwife, without any help. I had to call the neighbours. … I gave birth standing.' After a painful delivery, and convinced she had lost the baby, Safiya shut herself in her bedroom, exhausted and demoralized. 'We had already prepared for the burial when Idil [her eldest daughter] went to have a look and she saw the baby moving in the cot and realized she was still alive!' A few days later Safiya and her children got into a truck which drove them all the way to the southern Somali border, and into Kenya. Thanks to her husband's connections with the Italian embassy, she was able to gain a visa and board a flight for Italy with her children a few months later. She left behind her dreams for her future, but carried with her two daughters who were to grow up far away from her beloved homeland.

Notes

1 There is a body of work that focuses on women's involvement in the independence struggle (Jama 1991; Aidid 2010; Hassan et al. 1995), and women's experiences of war, state collapse and exile (Mohamed 2003; Gardner and El- Bushra 2004), but no substantial account exists of the everyday urban experiences in post-independence Somalia (with the exception of Mohamed 2003).

2 The Somali clan structure and the ways in which it has been shaped historically through colonial and postcolonial forms of governance have been dealt with at length (Lewis 1961; Mansur 1995; Kapteijns 2004).

3 Nonetheless, Italian efforts to create a Somali identity in order to cultivate anti-Ethiopian sentiments during the Ethiopian war failed as hostilities between Somali sub-clans emerged (Hess 1966: 181).

4 In 1941 this form of British colonial rule was also exported to former Italian Somaliland which came under the British Military Administration.

5 A group of women went on to found the Somali Women's Association in 1960 as a women's section of the SYL, and the more radical group, the Somali Women's movement in 1967. Women were also actively involved in the nationalist movement and with political parties post-independence (Aidid 2010).

6 I have left out the final stanzas of the poem, in which 'Nabaddoon' describes the decay and destruction of the beautiful idyllic city he captures in the initial stanzas. See Kapteijns (2010) for further details.

7 The *Banaadiri* are mercantile communities of Arab origin who typically live in the coastal cities of southern Somalia.

8 Furthermore, while some associated and conflated modernity with socialism, emphasizing values of equality, unity and progress, others clearly distinguished between the two.

9 The *nabi-ammaan* are Sufi celebrations where women eulogize female personalities such as Eve and Fatima. Since the 1980s they have become less common among women in the Somali regions (Declich 2000). See also Kapteijns (1995) for a discussion of the marginal role of *sittaat* (songs sung by Somali women for the distinguished women of early Islam) in contemporary Djibouti.

10 The Soviet support was subsequently lost prior to the 1977 Ogaden War. Throughout this period Somalia had become a site of competition for infrastructure investment between the Soviet bloc and Western capitalist states.

11 As I discuss in the following chapters, most women did not know the Arabic language nor were there any Somali translations of the Qur'an available at the time. Most of the teaching was based around recitation and memorization of the sacred texts.

CHAPTER FOUR

Tuition centres and Somali mosques: Raising good daughters in London

As a genuine mother she suffers agonies
Her family torn by the godless, split by social services,
Unable to sleep, goaded by worries,
Expecting no guidance, no partner by her side,
She feels so shattered and gripped by thoughts
And bad memories, she grieves until dawn
And raises her arms, prays for Allah's goodwill.

[Extract from Gocasho *(Recollection) by Caasha Lul Mohamud Yusuf (2012)*
Translated from the Somali by Said Jama Hussein and Clare Pollard for the
Poetry Translation Centre.]

Once a week for over a year, I sat on the London underground heading north, getting off at Kentish Town station and walking for ten minutes to Bilan's flat. Located in a large council estate, the small three-bedroom house provided just enough space for her and her five children. Nonetheless, Bilan took great care in furnishing and keeping it clean and tidy. Her living room was adorned with a soft brown leather couch facing a small TV screen, a wooden glass cabinet containing books and an assortment of objects from trips to Egypt and the Somali regions, and a dining table that the children used for their homework. They had a single computer in the corner by the window, which was fought over by the children most afternoons. Bilan had approached me towards the start of my fieldwork, when I was teaching at a supplementary school run by a Somali community organization. She asked me to help her two teenage daughters – Mulki and Nawaal – with their homework, and I agreed to visit their home once a week and to offer my support free of charge. Bilan almost always prepared food for my arrival. Macaroni and cheese or lasagna were favourites with the girls, but most often it was a Somali rice dish, which they regularly refused, opting instead for cereal or a snack, or begging Bilan (usually in vain) to go out to the local chicken and chip shop.

After an hour of work, we often sat on the couch with tea and biscuits to watch *EastEnders* or, depending on the time, other shows such as *X Factor* or *Crimewatch*. Late evenings were spent watching TV series, romantic comedies and chick flicks. Bilan sat and watched TV with us, interrupting occasionally for a clarification; her English was not fluent and she occasionally missed some of the nuances in the plot. If nothing of interest was on TV, Mulki or Nawaal would switch on the computer to sift through their Facebook updates or search for their favourite YouTube videos. Kesha, Puff Daddy, Kings of Leon and Beyoncé accompanied our evenings, as Mulki and Nawaal sang along and danced in front of the screen. The occasional roar of 'baby' made Bilan jump and demand they switch off whatever 'filth' they were consuming. Her daughters diligently obeyed, only to switch it back on a few minutes later when Bilan had left the room to attend to a household chore or to answer the constant stream of phone calls from friends and relatives. Their older brother was more severe with his monitoring of their Facebook usage and criticism of their skinny jeans and tight revealing tops, and they rarely allowed themselves such liberties in his presence.

Bilan was often exhausted in the evenings, when she would slump on the couch next to us. She worked three different part-time jobs during the day, but also looked after her children single-handedly. Originally from the north-eastern areas of the Somali regions (present-day Puntland), she had grown up in the central Waaberi district of Mogadishu with her paternal grandparents and uncle. After completing her primary school education, she worked in a family grocery store until she married aged eighteen and moved in with her husband and his mother. Their marriage was short-lived, and she divorced and remarried just before the civil war, when she escaped to Kenya with her second husband. They resettled in London two years later, in the early 1990s, and moved into a flat in the borough of Camden close to her paternal family. Shortly after the birth of her fifth child, she separated from her second husband, who moved to live on his own in North London. Her family members lent her money when she was short, and she was also involved in a local *hagbad* (money-saving scheme). After their separation, her husband helped very little with expenses and the small amount of money she made, she explained, was spent on her children's education. Her sons and daughters attended extra tuition classes twice a week, as well as *Qur'an* classes on Saturday and Sunday in a Somali mosque which was a short bus journey from their flat. She also gave her children small amounts of weekly pocket money which enabled the girls to buy the latest Primark top or a new brand of lipstick.

One afternoon, several months after I had started teaching in their home, I was sitting in the kitchen eating Bilan's tomato sauce spaghetti with her and her eldest daughter. By that point I had grown accustomed to Bilan's complaints about some of her children's performance at school, or her sudden angry outbursts at their neglect of their household duties. This time, however, it was different. She turned to me and sighed: 'I can't buy anything for myself. I wanted a new tablecloth as the old one is ruined but I have spent all my money paying for tuition. I have nothing left.' Before she could continue, however, she was drowned out by her daughter who, failing to pick up on her mother's distress, turned to me to describe the latest summer fashions – boots, leggings, dress – and her plans to transform her wardrobe. Bilan tried to interrupt, but Mulki's stream of consciousness was unstoppable:

I want to go to Cambridge, own a mansion in Canada … with a massive living room, not like the Somali one, ours is too cramped, too cluttered. My mansion would be simple but massive, a flat screen TV covering the entire wall. … My mum would have a wing of the house to herself. … Everyone would have their own room, and a cupboard each. And I'd only have one child, so there would be few people in the house.

Both mother and daughter vented their mutual frustrations and aspirations, each struggling to be heard over the other. Bilan's sacrifices to educate and provide for her children were drowned out by her daughter's desires for conspicuous consumption, wealth and status, and an escape from her present circumstances. I sat there in silence, taken aback, wishing that mother and daughter would stop talking to me at the same time and turn to listen to each other instead.

This chapter is about the first generation of Somali women to arrive in the UK following the civil war, and their efforts and struggles to live, work and raise their children abroad. It starts with a description of the migration and settlement patterns of Somalis in London, in order to provide a backdrop to the financial, practical and emotional experiences of Somali families in the UK. It subsequently describes the ways in which Somali women have replaced a desire for the 'modern' with pious pursuits by drawing on a reformist discourse which advocates a separation between Islam and 'traditional culture'. By fashioning themselves into 'good Muslims', they have also begun to rearticulate their understandings of *Soomaalinimo*, and of 'Western' British society and culture.

I suggest that these changes have been manifested in Somali women's temporal reorientations: in a distancing from the past and from their immediate circumstances in the UK, and a projection towards a moral, peaceful and more prosperous future for generations to come. Efforts to transform themselves into 'good Muslims' are therefore inseparable from concerns about raising 'good daughters' in Britain. During my fieldwork I often heard older women explain the importance of being 'good role models' to their daughters by dressing and behaving appropriately and, importantly, practising their faith regularly. They had to transform themselves into 'good Muslims' in order to become 'good Somalis' and to shape the generations to come.

In the final sections of this chapter, I describe how mothers' efforts to raise educated, upwardly mobile, good Somali Muslim children in Britain have led to the proliferation of institutions such as Somali tuition centres and mosques across London. As the title of the chapter suggests, these institutions have become symbols of Somali women's investments in their children's future. The incident in the kitchen that afternoon with Bilan and Mulki, however, reveals how mothers' intentions are at times at odds with those of their teenage daughters, who seem more concerned with American popular culture and separating themselves from their Somali upbringing.

From Somalia to Britain

Somali settlement in the UK originated long before the onset of the civil war, with the earliest Somali migration dating back to the nineteenth century. During the period of British colonial rule in the former Protectorate of Somaliland, migrants worked as sailors and traders with the British merchant navy and established communities around major UK ports, such as London, Liverpool, Bristol and Cardiff (Kleist 2004: 4). The Somali community in the borough of Tower Hamlets in London originated in this period and consisted of males, mainly from the British Protectorate, who were automatically entitled to British citizenship. While some settled permanently, many continued to maintain economic and social ties with the Somali regions. With the expansion of the steel industry in the UK during the 1960s, Somalis who were already in the country began to settle in the midlands and in the north in order to take advantage of growing industrialization. During this period some also migrated for study, women and children began to join the men, and the communities were further expanded (Harris 2004: 22–3).

It was not until the outbreak of civil war in the late 1980s and early 1990s that a large number of Somali refugees moved to the UK. Most of these early arrivals applied for asylum and were granted refugee status and later became citizens. The UK had few asylum claims until the late 1980s, but in the early 1990s applications increased following the spread of conflicts across the globe (Van Hear 1998). The UK Parliament passed a number of immigration and asylum laws during this period which, along with visa requirements, made legal migration increasingly difficult (Lindley 2010: 117). Migration costs increased as a consequence, and some were forced to lie about the purpose of their visit and use false documents in order to enter the country and seek asylum (ibid.). While some women were fortunate to come directly, many others spent time in refugee camps (Horst 2006) or in transit in Ethiopia or Kenya prior to their relocation, while others still arrived through a smuggling process. Over the last two decades most applicants have been granted Humanitarian Protection or Discretionary Leave to Remain, although this has been declining over the last few years (Open Society 2014: 28–30).

Those who moved throughout the 1988–91 period were largely from the north-western areas and had escaped following Barre's bombings of Hargeysa and Burco in present-day Somaliland. Those from southern areas arrived following the state's collapse in 1990. Because of the high costs of migration, many of the refugees tended to be from urban areas, and many of my interviewees, including the women I introduced in the previous chapter, had been part of the educated urban middle classes. Fahiimo, for example, had spent several years in a camp in Mombasa where she married her second cousin and gave birth to her first daughter. With financial and practical support from her extended family in the UK, she arrived by plane in 1993. Her parents remained in the camp but subsequently relocated to Gaalkacyo, present-day Puntland, their original place of origin, while one of her sisters went to Norway and another to Canada. Her experience captures the ways in which Somalis have become scattered transnationally across the globe. Many remain connected through phone communication, Skype or regular visits.

Those from rural or disadvantaged backgrounds arrived much later, in the early 2000s, thanks to support from their extended families. For example, Faadumo, who was from a minority clan and therefore less well connected, explained how she had first driven to the border of Kenya and Somalia:

> I sold my jewellery and I had a small amount of money, and I took my kids. My mum and my dad went to Ethiopia and I decided to come to Europe. I knew someone who could help me with visa, I had to pay him and he said he'd take me to America. I went first to Germany, we stayed there, then we went to Holland and the UK. First they didn't give me refugee status, they didn't believe me because I had stayed 2 weeks in Germany. I told them I had only transferred; the man said he would take me to America. Then when we came here I stayed here. ... I arrived here in 2002.

Faadumo's journey highlights the difficulties of reaching the UK legally in the early 2000s but also how, for some, the UK was an unexpected and unplanned destination.

Today, Somalis arriving in the UK are mostly secondary migrants from the wider diaspora who hold refugee status or citizenship in another EU country (Lindley and Van Hear 2007). These migrants are highly qualified professionals and many avail themselves of transnational connections in the UK in order to pursue further study or employment, or to join their families and settle in already established communities (Nielsen 2004). Many also see more potential for creating a 'Somali identity' in the UK because of the larger community and longer history of settlement (Open Society 2014: 41). And some come to avail themselves of the growing Somali entrepreneurial sector that is flourishing in London. The UK is also perceived as having a stronger welfare system and as being more welcoming than other European cities thanks to its multicultural ethos.

Over the last two decades, Somalis have also begun to return to the Somali regions, both temporarily and permanently, as the situation has stabilized in this period. In 1991 Somaliland (the former Protectorate) declared independence, and in 1998 neighbouring Puntland declared itself an autonomous region, attracting numerous returnees who began to set up businesses and search for work with local or international NGOs or in the public sector (Hansen 2006). While some Somalis constitute a 'part-time diaspora' (Hammond 2012) – spending half the year in the Somali regions, pursuing business opportunities and occasionally marrying a second wife – others return to spend their summer holidays with family and friends in the region.

Settling in London

The UK now hosts the largest and most established Somali community in Europe, with official figures estimating that 99,484 people of Somali origin reside in the country and that 65,333 live in London alone (Census 2011).[1] As mentioned, London has historically been an important site of migration, particularly for those from the former Protectorate of Somaliland. The Somali National Movement, the rebel group that fought against the Barre regime throughout the 1980s and that was central to the formation of present-day Somaliland, was also founded in East London. Like the United States, as described by Cawo Abdi (2015), London is imagined by Somalis across the globe as an 'earthly *jannah*' (paradise on earth). It is viewed as a final endpoint in a process of step-migration, although the reality of life in London often proves to be a struggle and far less idyllic than imagined. Over the years London has hosted a range of Somali public figures, from exiled Somali politicians and intellectuals to famous artists and musicians. Many of the Somali diaspora TV channels (such as Universal and Horn Cable), radio stations (Somali Voice, Nomad Radio), websites and newspapers (BBC Somali, *Jamhuuriya, Qaran* news and *Hiraan*) are based in the city, and a large number of diaspora organizations and cultural and artistic events (such as the annual Somali Week Festival) attract Somalis from across the diaspora. London is one of the headquarters of the largest Somali remittance company, *Dahabshiil*, and also a key source of remittance contributions to the Horn of Africa (Lindley 2010: 116).

The group referred to as the 'Somali diaspora' in London is uniquely diverse when compared to other European and US cities in terms of socio-economic and educational background, lineage, regional and political orientations, and time of arrival in the UK. In London there are a high number of educated and skilled Somalis as well as less skilled recent arrivals. Settlement has been largely determined by lineage (Griffiths 2002: 104). As one of my interviewees, a woman in her late fifties, explained to me: 'When I applied for asylum, I told them [the authorities] about the people I knew in London, my family, so then I was put in council housing near to them.' This pattern of clustering near one's family in certain areas of the city has also meant that Somali cafés, restaurants, shops and Internet points have become meeting points for elders from particular clans.[2] Scholars have noted how experiences of war have further accentuated and reified clan divisions in the diaspora (Bjork 2007; Griffiths 2002). As we saw in Chapter 3, divisions between those who identify with a Greater Somalia and those who take on more regional identities (e.g. Somaliland, Puntland) have also become particularly pronounced.

Local community organizations have also developed around lineage structures (Griffiths 2002: 100), giving rise to a large number of small charitable and community organizations spread across the city.[3] This pattern has frustrated government officials, who often bemoan the fragmented nature of the Somali diaspora. As Griffiths et al. (2006: 892) note, local councils in the UK, influenced by a race relations and multicultural paradigm, have been driven by a need to address 'unified and readily identifiable refugee communities'. As Lindley has argued (2010: 122), these complaints belittle the nature of the violence experienced across the Somali regions and the historical (and colonial) roots of these divisions. As we shall see in Chapter 5, this perpetuation of clan has become a target of criticism among younger Somalis, who have sought to differentiate themselves from the older generations by emphasizing unity and anti-tribalism.

Intra-urban and urban–rural divisions have continued to be a marker of status among Somalis in London. Many of the middle classes, for example, could afford to travel abroad throughout the 1990s and often had family connections in the UK. Compared to rural or urban lower-class and minority women who arrived much later, the middle classes were advantaged in terms of accessing housing, acquiring English language proficiency and other qualifications, and finding employment. Notions of urban civility and education, which were crucial markers of status differentiation in 1970s Mogadishu, continue to permeate social relations in Britain. I heard several middle-class women remark disparagingly about 'uneducated Somali women', considered rough in their manners, ignorant about history, tradition and religion, and at times lacking in values and civility. As Muraayo, who I introduced in Chapter 3, remarked: 'Many Somalis came from different educational backgrounds. ... Young brides who came here only to get married. ... These women are happy to get married and sit at home, clean, cook and do nothing. They don't care to study things.' For Muraayo, education was a marker of superior status and class. However, she also pointed out that these differences were overlooked by the larger British public who, much to her disappointment, viewed Somalis simply through their legal status as refugees. 'When we came here we all became refugees. ... We're all the same now,' she remarked.

Life as a refugee woman

Many of the middle-class women I worked with had found their circumstances radically transformed, and their previous aspirations for education and employment significantly curtailed on settling in the UK. 'If the civil war hadn't happened my life would've been better. ... I would be teaching, studying ... have a good job ... but I had to do the housework, look after my children,' Safiya lamented. Many felt that their lives had become increasingly centred on the home and the family, and that they were no longer able to move about freely and carelessly as they had done in Mogadishu. As Muraayo hinted above, being housebound is also seen a sign of lower status.

Describing the difficulties Somali women have had to endure in the UK, Raaxo, a woman in her fifties explained: 'The situation in the UK is a shock for active Somali women. Many Somali women are housebound. What can they do? They feel they don't fit in, they can't work because their qualifications don't count, and they can't speak the language. They don't know a lot of people, and they have big families to look after.'

Repeatedly I heard women express how they felt lonely and alienated in London as they rarely interacted with their non-Somali neighbours and felt British people were generally unfriendly and unwelcoming. 'When I'm not working I'm sitting at home feeling isolated. I feel nowhere. Back home, you could go everywhere eat together, people would visit, neighbours spent time together,' Muraayo reminisced. In Mogadishu, many of these women lived with extended female family members, most of whom supported the women with child-rearing and housekeeping duties. It was common for children to be raised collectively by their grandmothers or other older female relatives, and for more prosperous women to have more time for study and work. Somali families were rarely nuclear, but rather extended households constituted around a patrilineal lineage and clan support system.

Patterns of settlement around clan in London have enabled some women to partly rebuild these networks, but the process has been partial as families have been scattered transnationally. In London many have moved into small flats, which can only accommodate immediate family members. Limited access to networks of support has meant that the women have had to take on more household tasks than they were used to back home. 'Here there are few relatives around, so we have to take children everywhere, or leave them with a friend. And sometimes it becomes a burden,' Safiya explained. Furthermore, it is often women who are responsible for maintaining 'affectionate social relationships' among transnational distant family members, for example, by sending remittances (Lindley 2010: 141).

In addition, men are largely absent from the household due to high rates of separation and divorce. My data from twenty-one Somali households across London reveals the prevalence of households where husbands are rarely present and only intermittently exercise influence. In her research with Somalis in Bristol, Carver (2015) analyses some of the popular stories evoked to explain high rates of divorce. The *qaad*-chewer[4] narrative, for example, features a husband who experiences a loss of status on his arrival in the UK, as he is unable to provide for his family with his limited earnings, and his role of provider is usurped by the state. As a response he takes to chewing *qaad,* further neglecting his familial duties until his wife throws him out. The 'freedom junkie', a counterpart to the first narrative, features a wife who has acquired new freedoms and power in the UK and, realizing that the husband is no longer of any material or practical support, throws him out. Carver notes how these narratives are often presented as explanations for high divorce rates among Somalis in the UK. They reproduce culturally specific criteria while speaking to majority white British values and discourses – such as individualism – and reinforcing a stereotyped national discourse of the 'ideal Muslim family' as a nuclear, stable family with the husband as provider.

In many of my conversations with older women, elements of these two narratives surfaced at different times. Several blamed men for their inability to adapt to changing circumstances. Ikhlaas, who divorced after a couple of years in the UK, explained how her husband 'hadn't got used to a European lifestyle where we share things. You wash dishes, I dry. You take the children out, I cook. Men don't accept the change in culture. ... In Somalia it was ok because we had *eeddo, habaryar* [paternal and maternal aunt] to help with children and the house. ... Here we don't.' Ikhlaas was pointing out how the absence of extended family has had an impact on women's expectations of their husbands in the home, but also how men have been unwilling to accept these changes. Echoing elements of the *qaad*-chewer narrative, Ubax, another first-generation woman, placed the blame on men's marginalization and loss of status in the UK, rather than on their own inability to adapt to changing circumstances and norms:

> Men come here and they get angry, frustrated, they can't control themselves ... because here they don't accept you, you become nothing and you lose your confidence. ... It's women who keep the family going. Back home men had responsibility for their home, their family. ... But when they come here they become reluctant. They start chewing *qaad*. They can't find work, or they can only work as cleaners and drivers. I know a man who was a doctor and now he's a cleaner.

The loss of status due to social, educational and economic barriers has meant that few men are able to fully support their households and thus lose their role as breadwinners. As Ubax's quote implies, men are often criticized for spending most of their time talking politics and chewing *qaad* in Somali cafés and restaurants instead of supporting their families. Women are perceived as having greater adaptability to altered economic and social conditions, and for those who had previously been dependent on men, state benefits have allowed them to secure an income for themselves and their children, leading to a sense of the 'disposability' of men (Griffiths 2002: 111). The 'displacement of male authority in the home' is perceived as having had significant implications for the stability of the conjugal couple (ibid.: 112–13).

The above-mentioned women felt justified in their decisions to separate or divorce by suggesting that the men had neglected their cultural and Islamic duty as 'providers' and had also failed to 'update' and 'modernize' their ideas about gender and to adapt to changing circumstances. Other women, however, were critical of the sense of 'disposability' that had developed in the diaspora, and of the 'freedom junkie' role acquired by women. Safiya explained how 'women get benefits, college, education here and they realize they don't need a man! But it's not good.' She continued: 'They should also respect men and understand.' Several of the men I interviewed reiterated this point, bemoaning the fact that women had acquired new sources of financial support and were making new demands on their husbands. They claimed that women often found that they no longer needed a husband unless he could contribute to the household in significant ways. 'Women have changed here. They are using benefits to support the family and they have different expectations of us,' one male interviewee described.

These narratives around the 'female-headed household' have become so widespread within the Somali community that they have also been appropriated by Somali and non-Somali activists, commentators and policymakers. Most recently, for example, the narrative has been used to support a ban against the import and consumption of *qaad* in the UK. *Qaad* chewing was seen as a cause of the absence of men in Somali homes, and hence of a host of interconnected problems ranging from gang violence among Somali youth to low educational achievements and high rates of unemployment. Resonating with public discourses of moral crises and the dangers of 'female-headed households', these tropes have tended to simplify the situation and assign the notion of 'absent men' too much explanatory power. Furthermore, they neglect the ways in which households are often characterized by an unstable number of residents. In some of the households I visited during my fieldwork it was not always clear who lived in the house at any one time, or whose authority mattered on a given issue. In cases where the husband was absent, there may have been other male relatives, such as a brother, uncle or son, who might take charge of certain decisions regarding the home. In other instances older female relatives might assume authority. In addition, the husband could be absent for part of the year – either visiting family or working abroad – and therefore might not be fully missing from the home.

Given the situation outlined above, Somali women in the UK often struggle to pursue education or to find a stable full-time job. Employment levels are low and those who do work tend to be clustered in low-paid occupations, such as sales, customer services, care work and cleaning (Open Society 2014: 67). Several of the middle-class women who were highly educated and had worked in Mogadishu found themselves unable to find suitable employment: language barriers compounded by the fact that their qualifications were not recognized in the UK meant that they had to either begin their studies again or accept low-paid employment. Several women expressed how they felt stigmatized in the workplace and in the public space for being black, sounding foreign, or donning the *jilbab* or *hijab*. Ubax, for example, spoke fluent English but had interviewed unsuccessfully for several local council jobs. 'They look at me in this thing [*jilbab*] and straight away I know I have little chance,' she explained.

At the start of my fieldwork many women with small children received enough welfare support from the state to enable them to study, train and look after their children. However, I noticed how this changed with the introduction of the coalition government's Welfare Reform Act in 2012. Somali families were disproportionately affected by the significant cuts in benefits brought about by the universal credit scheme as reductions in benefits did not take into consideration household size, which tends to be above average among Somalis (Open Society 2014: 85). Some women who had previously been considered unfit to work because of a disability saw their benefits reduced and were forced to rely on other family members for support. Others abandoned their studies to find work or struggled as they sought to balance childcare and household duties with full-time employment.

Furthermore, older Somali women have been disproportionately affected by poor health – common diagnoses include arthritis, lack of vitamin D, stress and anxiety, diabetes and depression – which impact their ability to work (Tiilikainen 2005; Kamaldeep et al. 2006). Social isolation, discrimination and overcrowded housing have had further adverse effects on health (Cole and Robinson 2003). Fahiimo, for example, developed acute back pain a few years after she moved to London. She blamed the weather, the lack of physical activity, and the damp and poor living standards in her home. Her back pain had made it difficult for her to work and had forced her to remain at home, further isolating herself from friends and family. Her children and their future became a primary concern for her: 'I had planned to study in the UK and to go to university, but when I arrived I clung so tightly to my child. ... I didn't trust anyone, I didn't want to leave her with anyone. I wanted to do medicine in Somalia, but I stopped caring here.' Having lost support from family and unable to trust anyone, Fahiimo felt isolated and turned her attention to her children. This turning inward was partly a reaction to the isolation and marginalization experienced in the UK and to the perceived 'corrupting' effects of 'Western' society. As a result, like many other Somali women, Fahiimo began engaging with Islamic reformist knowledge in the UK with the aim of fashioning herself and her children into 'good Muslims' and hence 'good Somalis'. This was not only an attempt to vindicate the past for its absence of morality, but also an attempt to look forward to the future for herself and her family.

Religious reflections

The refugees celebrate their sadness, reminiscing. They engage a million man-hours of refugee time in introspection and self-analysis: consequently they feel more depressed at the end of the day than when they woke up. To be a refugee is to be suicidal. Is it why a vast number of them become religiously reflective, pondering on the curse which has paid them and their country a visitation? (Farah 2000: 30)

As we saw in Chapter 3, experiences of post-independence Somalia and the civil war have been interpreted through an Islamic lens. An absence or ignorance of religion is seen as the cause of the corruption and immorality of the modern socialist period. Indeed, many feel that their country has been 'cursed' – as Nuruddin Farah suggests – for its immorality and disobedience to God's commands. Learning about Islam in the diaspora has therefore enabled them to make sense of the failures of the Somali nationalist project and, in some cases, the limitations of socialist and modern aspirations. 'If you disobey *Allah*, what do you expect? Punishment,' Bilan stated bluntly in one of our conversations on the topic.

Focusing on religion has also enabled Somali women to distance themselves from past and present troubles that continue to pervade the region. On one occasion I was sitting in Safiya's kitchen with her and a friend when she received a phone call from her brother in Mogadishu about a bomb that had gone off that day in the capital. When she hung up the phone, she had tears in her eyes. We sat for a few minutes in silence until her friend interrupted us, saying: 'I don't like to think about the world. ... I wish I could think about heaven only ... since I've started researching religion I don't think about what's happening in my country. ... I cannot change that. What's happening is beyond our power. So I pray.' For Safiya's friend, religious awareness has enabled her to turn her attention away from violence and disorder and to accept her powerlessness to enact change in the world. She has turned her attention towards an elsewhere and a distant future – to God, prayer and the hereafter – as a source of support and fulfilment.

Somali women have also begun to reflect and analyse their experiences of becoming a refugee in the diaspora through Islamic idioms. Nafisa, another first-generation Somali woman, explained how she felt when she first arrived in the UK: 'When I came to this country I found I was a number in the Home Office. I felt I had lost my identity, tradition, culture, religion.' Her experience was like that of the afore-mentioned Muraayo's, who, in being marked as a refugee, had been stripped of other differentiating markers of status. By being labelled a refugee, Muraayo had come to be seen simply as vulnerable, poor, displaced and uprooted.[5] Nafisa explained that her interest in religious knowledge arose after a period of introspection in which she thought about herself and how she was viewed by the mainstream public in Britain: 'It's a reaction to being uprooted. ... I wasn't feeling in control of my life, I didn't know what would happen to my life. Insecurity makes you choose to either blend with people, or to keep your own identity. And you go back and find out: what is my identity?' She explained to me that when she first moved to the UK she experimented with 'trying to blend in': she remembers going to a pub and dressing up like the locals wearing trousers. But she still felt that she stood out. 'Then I realised how important my image was to others. For example, I started covering my hair, and before in Somalia I never used to. Here I started because I was asserting who I was: a Muslim woman from Somalia. People know you're Somali, Muslim ... and coming here we needed this protection.' In asserting her 'own identity', Nafisa chose to adopt visible symbols of difference, such as the *hijab*. Altering her dress and manners was a way of asserting who she was and hence enabled her to maintain or rebuild a sense of self.

The experience of moving to a radically different setting and experiencing 'strangeness' encouraged many to search for self-coherence as Faadumo, who arrived in the early 2000s, explained:

> I came here when I was 22 and I started to realize that I was strange. I was different, this wasn't my culture, I didn't belong here. So I thought a lot about myself, I started to think that I wasn't even a good Muslim. I had been raised a Muslim, I knew *Qur'an*, I knew *hadith* (reports of statements or actions of the Prophet), but I started thinking that I wasn't good. In Somalia I wore miniskirts, I was always with friends, doing this doing that. But here I realized it was important. Lots of other Muslims were more religious than me. I put on *hijab* straight away. I saw others here as well wearing *hijab*, but I realized it was the best thing for me here. Maybe it was a psychological thing, something unconscious, that made me think: who am I if I'm not even a good Muslim.

Like Nafisa, Faadumo had a similar experience of feeling alienated from her context and of stressing her Muslim identity above the Somali one. Her experience of difference forced her to reflect on her past self and recognize the way in which Islam offered her not only a form of identification but also a moral project of self-formation. Surrounded by other Muslims in her neighbourhood, she was inspired by their experiences and began adopting the *hijab* and practising more frequently. By emphasizing her pious pursuit above her Somaliness, she was also able to connect with other Muslims. Faadumo's remarks also highlight the ways in which the notion of a 'good Muslim' had turned into a dominant idiom among Muslims at the time of her arrival in the UK in the early 2000s. This was particularly the case in the areas of East London where Faadumo settled when she first arrived and where Islamic revivalist teachings were becoming widespread.

The threats of 'British society' or 'Western culture' were recurring concerns for many of these women, often posited in direct opposition to Islamic virtues and Somali traditions and culture. In Chapter 3 I described how modern aspirations in the 1970s and 1980s were similarly viewed as frivolous and immoral, existing in tension with notions of tradition and culture. Thirty years on, the imagined notion of the 'modern' has been replaced by the 'West' – a symbol of an Anglo-American culture and way of being. While mothers appreciate some of the positive elements of the 'West', such as education, prosperity, and welfare support, other aspects are seen as immoral and corrupting. Premarital relations, alcohol, drugs, individualism, disrespect for elders, and conspicuous consumption are posited as some of the corrupting elements of Western society. Western clothing – skinny jeans and tight tops, for example – are seen as symbols of a liberal culture that is pulling young people away from Muslim values and Somali cultural norms and practices.

Learning Islam in Somali mosques

First-generation Somali women have begun to engage with their faith in new ways, emphasizing recitation and memorization of the texts as well as understanding the meaning with the aim of applying it to the self. Many have begun to read Somali translations of the *Qur'an* or access religious books and CDs in Somali. These resources are readily found in Somali shops or Islamic bookshops, which are often located close to some of the major mosques in London. Several of these institutions, such as the East London Mosque or the London Central Mosque in Regent's Park, run *Qur'an*, *tajwid* (recitation and pronunciation of the *Qur'an*) and *tafsir* (exegesis of the *Qur'an*) classes in Somali, and many community groups also organize informal *Qur'an* lessons. The British Somali Community in Camden offered supplementary classes in various disciplines for young people and *Qur'an* lessons for mothers who accompanied their children. The lessons were run by a first-generation Somali woman who lived in the local area and had limited formal training but had taught herself Arabic and Quranic recitation.

Over the last ten to fifteen years, Somali mosques have also sprung up across London offering classes for older men and women as well as children. Examples of these mosques include Al-Huda Mosque in Stepney Green, East London, the Masjid Al-Risaalah and Islington Islamic Centre, and the Assunnah Islamic Centre in Tottenham in North London, and Shepherd's Bush Mosque in West London. The term 'Somali mosque' is used to refer to mosques which are managed by Somalis, and they often run many of their classes in Somali language. Because few older women are fluent in English or Arabic, these places of learning allow Somali women to access and understand Islamic scriptures and provide a familiar environment and a space of socialization with friends and relatives. Most of these institutions are attended by the first generation and their young children. They often offer women-only classes alongside lessons for children on Quranic recitation (*tajwid*), or the study of *hadith*. Most mosques follow the *Shafi'i madhhab* (school of jurisprudence) and many are not associated with a particular reformist movement but include committee members from various Islamic schools of thought. Some, however, have a reputation for following more literal traditions (e.g. Tottenham mosque) or spiritual ones (e.g. Elephant & Castle mosque).

One of the first mosques to open in London was Al-Huda in Stepney Green, East London, opened in 1999 with support from community funding initiatives (see Chapter 6, Figure 5). The women's prayer room at Al-Huda is located in the basement and accessed through a door on the right-hand side of the mosque. A soft, clean carpet decorated with a prayer mat design – a vertical rectangle with an arched top pointing south-easterly towards the *qibla* (the direction of prayer) – lines the floor. The room is clean and relatively bare aside from small *wudu* (ablution) facilities located in the corner and an office with a computer and copies of the *Qur'an* and other holy books. The call to prayer, the Friday sermon and other talks delivered from the men's prayer room on the top floor are often projected through a loudspeaker. The mosque occasionally runs courses and classes in Somali and English for older and young women, depending on interest and demand. English language flyers advertising local courses and lectures, bookshops and Islamic shops are displayed on a small shelf near the stairs; occasionally one finds flyers in Somali advertising a local community event.

Transforming the self

As a consequence of engaging with texts and Islamic reformist teachings in London, many older Somali women living in London today, who twenty years earlier would not have concerned themselves with Islamic clothing, have begun to don the *hijab*, *abaya* and *jilbab*, justifying it as a process of 'religious awareness' (Talle 2008; Berns-McGown 1999). This is not a process unique to the diaspora context, however, as this clothing – which had previously only been worn by Arab and Persian settlers – had become increasingly popular throughout the late 1980s in the Somali territories as a consequence of the influence of Islamic reform movements. Nonetheless, for many women this religious awareness has coincided with the war and with migration abroad. As Safiya explained: 'With time we have changed our dress, our way of talking and interacting with men. ... Now we know the meaning of the *Qur'an* ... thanks to translations, books, people around me talking about it the whole time.' Safiya had only started learning about religion in recent years because of the influence of Fahiimo, whose husband had encouraged her to 'research' Islam several years earlier. Safiya and Fahiimo had begun attending *Qur'an* classes and lectures at the local Somali mosque with the aim of implementing these teachings in order to fashion themselves into pious subjects. Like many of her friends, Safiya retrospectively described her lifestyle in Mogadishu as morally 'wrong' and ignorant of religion. 'Step by step I started studying and I realized I was wrong,' she explained. Whereas a few years previously she might have enjoyed wearing colourful *dirac* at weddings, watching romantic films and listening to music, her increased knowledge of Islam had, she claimed, taught her that these cultural practices should be discouraged.

> When you see food and it doesn't look good you say: that's not good! But you've only seen it then, you haven't tried it. When you

try and taste it, it's actually good. I've tried and tasted religion now, and it's like I'm becoming a Muslim again. [It feels like] I used to belong to another religion and I'm only now becoming Muslim.

Fahiimo herself had been through a similar change. She began to wear *hijab* when she married in Kenya, but only on arriving in the UK did she come to understand the importance of reading and understanding the meaning of the *Qur'an* and knowing and reasoning about Islamic rules, obligations and requirements. Although, as a child during the 1970s, she had regularly attended *dugsi* and been taught to recite the *Qur'an* and *hadith*, to pray and to fulfil religious obligations, she now considered this knowledge insufficient and inadequate. She had never been told the meaning of what she was reciting, nor why it was important. She explained: 'In Somalia ... I knew I was a Muslim, but I didn't understand the meaning and I didn't understand the *Qur'an*. Before I thought that dress was [a matter of] culture, but here I have started understanding and realizing that the *Qur'an* says to veil. I understand the meaning.' Fahiimo added that since coming to the UK and accessing the translation of the *Qur'an* in Somali, listening to CDs and attending lessons and lectures, she had begun to reflect and mould her behaviour according to Islamic obligations grounded in the texts.

For many, these religious transformations have been accompanied by processes of rationalization and self-reflection, as revealed by the following comment by Safiya:

> Before in Somalia we knew [about] religion, but we didn't understand it. ... It was like driving a car without having taken lessons. Before I knew how to drive, but now I have a full understanding of it: I know what I have to do to turn, park, go around roundabouts. ... Now we know what religion says and we're much more conscious about it, so we can explain our behaviour.

Religion, like culture, had previously been a part of everyday practice, like driving a car without lessons, learning to cook or perform daily tasks. Having begun to reflect on religion, Safiya no longer understands it as inherited, but as consciously learnt in formalized ways. Furthermore, religion has not only been objectified but has come to serve as a body of knowledge that informs and enables one to scrutinize behaviour. Like many other first-generation women, Safiya has begun to draw on Islamic reformist discourses which emphasize the purification of culture; religion has been cast as a conscious, collective moral framework used to monitor and assess an increasingly objectified and reified notion of culture.

Fahiimo explained that, since moving to the UK, religion has helped her decipher which parts of culture are *haram* (forbidden) and which ones are compatible with Islam. Not wearing *hijab* and backbiting, she claimed, were aspects of 'Somali culture' that religion had taught them were wrong. Other women frequently mentioned clan divisions, dancing to music and ignoring gender segregation. Sufi practices, such as visiting graves and emotional mourning at death, which had up until the late 1980s been relatively widespread particularly in rural areas of Somalia (Declich 2000), have now come under attack as being cultural and not Islamic. I often heard women criticize those who continued to engage in these Sufi devotional practices, accusing them of committing *shirk* (idolatry). Engaging in pious projects has become a way of purifying and moralizing Somali culture, and of striving to become 'good Somalis' by being 'good Muslims'. Whereas for some this entails recovering 'forgotten' religious practice, which they claim had been part of Somali traditions and ways of being, for others it entails a new process of learning about and reflecting on Islamic texts and teachings, and using these to reform Somali traditions in new ways. The question of where to draw the line between religion and culture and what practices to abandon, however, is often a source of debate and disagreement, as I will show in more detail in the chapters that follow.

Investing in the next generation

Engagements with Islamic knowledge have led Somali women to focus on themselves, as well as on their children, with the aim of fashioning them into 'good Muslims' and hence 'good Somalis'. As we have seen, formalized Islamic education has played an important role in this process. Between the ages of eight and sixteen, Somali children are typically sent to *madrasa* at least once or twice a week.

Some attend informal classes in domestic spaces, for which parents pay a small contribution every week. Increasingly, however, many have begun attending a local Somali mosque along with their mothers. Furthermore, Somali community centres have begun to play an important role in shaping the moral and aspirational outlooks of young Somalis. Caasha-Kin, who I introduced in the previous chapter, co-founded one of the few female-led Somali community organizations in the 1990s, which coordinated a range of projects for Somali women and teenagers, ranging from supplementary English classes, Somali youth clubs and cultural activities to providing health training to mothers. 'Language, culture, religion and identity', Caasha-Kin claimed, were key elements she sought to communicate to young teenagers during the cultural activities. Among many other activities, she campaigned to introduce Somali as a GCSE subject in Camden schools and ran a Somali cultural programme in a local primary school, introducing children to Somali language, games and poems. Her aim was to 'give them an identity', helping them find out about 'who they are'. Unlike some of the women introduced above, who separated religion from culture, Caasha-Kin presented religion as part of Somali culture, as two interlinked forms of knowledge that should be transmitted to the younger generations.

Alongside stressing the importance of religious instruction and cultural knowledge, parents also hope that their children might achieve a higher status and greater wealth within British society. Ensuring they perform well at school and study at a higher education institution has become a primary concern. As a young Somali woman put it: 'My mum has always told me that education is the only thing that can never be taken away from you.' Having lost everything in the war and unable to provide for their children in other ways, they have placed their hope in education as a path to social mobility. In so doing, they have also drawn on their experience from 1970s Mogadishu, when education was equated with empowerment, status, development and progress. As we saw with Bilan, they have invested their savings in extra tuition classes which they hope will secure status and a more stable and prosperous future for their children.

As a consequence, Somalis have become popular customers at private tuition centres, and charities and community centres across the capital have begun offering supplementary classes and homework clubs for Somali children. Examples include the private companies Best Tutors in Edmonton or Prime Tuition in Brixton, where Somali customers abound, the charity Somali Education Centre in Islington, and many other organizations set up and managed by Somalis. These centres are also a place of socialization and, for some Somalis, a source of employment: some Somali women I knew organized the catering in these centres or worked as playground supervisors, while younger Somalis were often employed as tutors and support staff.

Availing themselves of the demand for moral and secular education in a Somali cultural environment, new hybrid institutions have emerged. During my fieldwork a new Somali mosque was established in the borough of Camden in North London, providing supplementary tuition and Islamic schooling for both older and younger generations in a Somali setting. Somali women from the area were largely responsible for raising the £1.5 million for the mosque through personal networks and by advertizing the initiative on Somali satellite TV channels. *Sheikh* Mukhtar, a former mathematics teacher who arrived in the UK as a young teenager, was involved in setting up the mosque. He explained to me: 'These mosques were set up around a local need, to address gang violence ... following Mahir Osman's death ... the problems faced by youth, educational failures. Committees were largely made up of local people.'[6] Like many other Somali mosques, this mosque arose as a way of tackling Somali mothers' preoccupations with their children's educational achievements, but they also assuaged their fears that their children were losing their cultural and religious values to 'Western' society.

When the mosque was first opened, *Sheikh* Mukhtar began running tuition classes for Somali children who were falling behind or experiencing problems in school. A few years later, the mosque was relocated nearby and replaced by a Muslim secondary school, which attracts mostly Somalis and other Muslim children from the area. In early 2015 the school had over 140 students, six Somali and seven non-Somali Muslim teachers, and six Somali teaching assistants, and was planning to teach A-levels (school qualifications typically for sixteen to eighteen year olds) for the first time. 'Within the Somali community the emphasis is on being a good Muslim and Somali, with a good educational attainment. Here we offer all of these things,' *Sheikh* Mukhtar explained. The school also runs supplementary classes for young people in English, mathematics and Arabic, and evening *Qur'an* classes for older women.

Throughout my fieldwork in 2009, I attended some of the classes with Fahiimo and Safiya at what was then the newly established mosque. The lessons for women were in Somali and involved over twenty middle-aged, first-generation Somali women. The mosque had only just opened and still smelt of fresh paint. The women sat in a circle on the ground in a simple room on the top floor, where the furniture consisted simply of a red carpet and white-washed walls. The teacher also taught *tajwid* to older women at one of the local community centres and organized informal lessons in Somali women's homes. The class followed a similar format every week, focusing primarily on reciting and memorizing the *Qur'an*. In turn, the women repeated passages from the *Qur'an*, with the teacher correcting their vocalization and pronunciation. The class, which lasted over two hours, usually concluded with the Somali translation of the pronounced passage of the *Qur'an* or *hadith* and a brief explanation of the meaning of the text followed by a short discussion.

These lessons conveniently coincided with the classes arranged for Somali children, which were also very similar in content and structure. The classes were mixed, with approximately eighty children divided into classes of fifteen to twenty students. The students were taught, in a combination of English and Somali, and among other Somali siblings, cousins and friends, how to read, recite and memorize the *Qur'an*. Throughout the class, the children were instructed on the meaning of the *Qur'an*, the forty *hadith* and the *sira* (life of the Prophet), as well as the fundamentals of their faith and obligatory rules and regulations. Most of these children's classes followed a rule-based approach to learning and were run by and for Somalis, thus equating religious education with ethnicity and culture. As we shall see in the following chapters, both of these elements are disputed by second-generation Somali women who reflect critically on their Islamic upbringing as being excessively 'cultural'.

Raising 'good Somali daughters' in Britain

I began this chapter with Bilan and her two daughters, both born and raised in Camden, London. Like many other first-generation

Somali women, Bilan had hoped to return to Somalia once the violence subsided. As time went on, however, this became an ever-distant possibility. Every news of an attack in the region placed a further dent in her aspiration to return. Life in exile had not been easy for her as she felt estranged from mainstream society and struggled to care for her five children with limited support from her family, the small income from her part-time jobs and dwindling welfare support. Looking forward, like many others, she has turned to Islamic teachings in making sense of the past, reorienting her aspirations, and fashioning herself as an ethical person. She has also encouraged her children, including her young daughters Mulki and Nawaal, to follow suit, pushing them to learn about their faith, but also to perform well at school in the hope that they may become socially and economically mobile. Engaging with pious projects of self-fashioning has enabled her, and the other women discussed above, to seek absolution for the immorality of the past, but also to distance themselves from the current situation in the Somali regions and the struggles endured in the UK. They have turned inwards to focus on themselves and their families, projecting their aspirations onto generations to come and, in some cases, into the distant future of the hereafter.

These new forms of striving, articulated through Islamic reformist discourses, have also transformed dominant notions of Somali moral womanhood, as I explained in the previous chapter. Kapteijns (2009) has described how, until the 1980s, Somali collective understandings oscillated between a desire to be 'modern' and a commitment to 'tradition' (as a particular construction of Somali cultural authenticity and traditional religious morality). This tension also played out in discussions about moral womanhood – ideas of what a 'good' woman ought to be like. However, since the 1980s, this moral public identity based on notions of Somali tradition began to give way to an Islamic morality. While Islam was previously an intrinsic part of *Soomaalinimo*, as I described in the preceding chapter, and 'Somali morality was seen as coterminous with Islamic morality', Somali tradition and culture have become increasingly divorced from Islamic morality (ibid.: 120). Emphasis has centred on the objectification and rationalization of faith, as well as a purification of culture or tradition through claims of accessing a 'true' or 'authentic' Islam. As a consequence, Islam has come to provide these women with a moral basis from which to 'pick and choose' among objects, attitudes and practices that are thought to constitute Somali culture. Somali women who do not make these separations between religion and culture are often criticized by other religiously minded women for being traditional. Increasingly, both Islam and Somali 'culture' are being transmitted not only through everyday practices in the home, but as a set of objectified values, practices and objects, as we saw with Caasha's cultural activities.

Hence, Somali moral womanhood has come to be associated with pious ideals, and with the process of fashioning the self according to Islamic virtues. These women have been actively involved in seeking to cultivate virtues such as modesty (*al-haya'*) and patience (*sabr*) in an effort to transform themselves and their relations with others, and to fashion a new mode of sociality. Faadumo claimed that 'researching religion' had changed her attitude towards others, making her less angry and resentful. 'We no longer shout, swear, scream ... I have become calm. Reading the *Qur'an* has made me less stressed and angry,' she explained. Others emphasized how they had learnt to become more forgiving and generous towards friends and strangers. Bilan, for example, told me on one occasion how she had newly learnt to reflect on her actions and apologize when she thought she had hurt someone. Others have made a more conscious effort to avoid backbiting or gossiping, a vice that is seen by many to be particularly widespread among Somalis. Ubax, another first-generation mother explained: 'People are backbiting the whole time. ... Now I tell them that it's *haram* and I ask them not to tell me these things. I don't want to gossip. I tell them to call me if there's a problem, if not I don't want to talk about these things.' Turning towards religion has enabled these women to reform their behaviour, and reorient it towards God and the implementation of pious virtues. It has also encouraged them to reimagine their relations with Somali friends and relatives in new ways, and to overcome past tensions and present divisions and conflicts.

An emphasis on the cultivation of modesty has most visibly manifested itself through the donning of the *hijab* and *jilbab* among the older generations. As Faadumo explained, wearing the *jilbab* has provided her with a sense of security, but also enabled her to claim a moral high ground and defence against others' judgements: 'I feel secure in my *jilbab*, I feel good, relaxed and comfortable. ... I know no one is looking, judging, and if they are I know I'm doing the right thing, so I feel good about myself.' Young daughters have been encouraged to adopt this clothing from an early age with the hope that they may continue to wear it later in life. The *jilbab* and *hijab* have also become symbols of this renewed engagement with faith, and signs of collective morality and honour. Whereas in post-independence Somalia, morality was represented and embodied by traditional dress, this has now been replaced by Islamic dress. Traditional clothing, such as the *guntiino*, has come to be considered insufficiently modest for everyday interactions and appropriate for women-only events. Modest clothing is seen as a marker of piety, morality, and of a 'good Somali' wife or daughter, and associated with a discourse of honour and shame. A daughter or a wife who does not cover can often be the source of gossip, and can be seen to bring shame (*ceeb*) on her family. Even those who do not regard themselves as religious might cover their head when they attend Somali events, or visit Somali relatives. Traditional culture, therefore, is no longer being seen only in juxtaposition to the modern, as explained in Chapter 3, but rather in opposition to Islamic reformism, which has replaced culture (*dhaqan*) as the seat of morality.

Furthermore, 'Western' society has come to replace the 'modern' as both a place of opportunity and source of progress and development, but also of immorality and a threat to Somali culture and Islamic ways of being. As we saw in the initial vignette of Bilan and her daughters, British and American popular culture enters the home through TV and computer screens, and Somali mothers embrace or tolerate this to varying degrees. They do, however, also hope that their children will not abandon Somali ways and seek to inculcate these in various ways. This doesn't always succeed and, as a last resort, parents may opt to send their children back to the Somali regions to spend time with their relatives and to learn about their culture, norms and values in what is known as *dhaqan celis* (return to culture). Mothers hope that a return to their roots, religion and proper modes of behaviour will also teach them to stay out of trouble in the future.

Although Somali womanhood has come to be equated with notions of a 'good pious Muslim', as the following examples demonstrate, for many women being pious does not necessarily make their daughters sufficiently 'Somali'. Safiya, who often spent hours complaining and worrying about the behaviour and whereabouts of her daughters, put it bluntly: 'My daughters just don't behave like Somalis do.' Her elder daughters were not only uninterested in religion but also enjoyed clubbing, did not don the *hijab* or modest clothing, and had a steady stream of boyfriends. Having been to a *madrasa* as younger children, they had stopped attending as teenagers. Safiya often criticized Idil, her eldest, for her choice of clothing, which in her view was too revealing and immodest. However, it was not only Islam that she wanted her daughters to embrace. Safiya felt that her daughters were not 'proper Somali daughters': although they spoke the language fluently, they did not behave according to traditional or cultural ways as they were undisciplined and had little responsibility and respect for their families. 'My daughters are not good Somali daughters. ... I want them to take responsibility, to help at home, to look after their younger sister, to be disciplined. ... But here in the UK multiculturalism has made it hard for me.' Safiya felt that her daughters were slowly slipping away from her; she realized that they had adapted to Western society and were moving away from Somali customs and norms.

On another occasion she elaborated further: 'I feel different from my children. We don't have the same feelings even though we are mother and daughter. And I don't know if how I raise them, they will raise their children.' This sense that her daughters did not experience the same feelings was perhaps indicative of their loss of an embodied sense of what it meant to be Somali – a habitus, or a set of norms and modes of behaviour into which Safiya felt she had been socialized. Culture, for Safiya, was not necessarily a set of objectified values and practices, but consisted of embodied values and modes of behaviour, which she felt the younger generation brought up in the UK did not necessarily share. Being a good Muslim, from her point of view, would be one step in the right direction, but it would not necessarily make her daughters fully Somali. Fahiimo, whose daughters – unlike Safiya's – prayed regularly, attended Islamic classes and wore *hijab* and *abaya*, agreed with Safiya that her daughters were similarly insufficiently Somali. 'They're not like us, they don't think like us,' Fahiimo claimed, alluding to a similar embodied sense of tradition.

Furthermore, the growth of reformist Islam among Somalis in London has not been embraced equally and unproblematically by all. Whereas both Safiya and Fahiimo saw their pious pursuits as compatible, if not reinforcing of their Somaliness, others have viewed the Islamic resurgence as a threat. Ardo, a woman in her early sixties, who was not particularly pious, was critical of the ways in which the *jilbab* had acquired a form of orthodoxy among Somalis: 'They all copy each other ... they aren't more religious, they are just scared of being judged and they compete on who's covered most! I think they have nothing to do, so they spend their time worrying about *halal* (permitted, lawful), *haram* (forbidden, unlawful) and so on,' she claimed. I also heard others, including Muraayo, criticize Somalis for being 'too extreme'. On one occasion she elaborated: 'Here we are not fighting by gun, but fighting by voice. For example, when I'm wearing like this [a loose *garbasaar* on her head], some people outside ignore me.' Muraayo was suggesting that more religious Somalis were not only judgemental but also unfriendly and cliquey, closed off to others they deemed insufficiently pious. Other first-generation women are critical of what they view as an 'Arabization' of Somali culture. In embracing reformist Islam, these critics claim, Somalis have adopted a new culture and a set of foreign practices, and forms of clothing. These criticisms tend to be voiced by women who appeal to a form of religiosity practised by their parents and grandparents, and who view Islam as an embodied part of the lifeworld and as an intrinsic part of being Somali. Raaxmo, for example, criticized the way in which this new religiosity or 'Arabization' had eroded Somali culture. Music, she explained, had accompanied her throughout her youth: artists such as Mogool, Hibo Nuura and Maryam Mursal and other vocalists were frequently heard on Radio Hargeysa and Radio Mogadishu. This newfound religiosity, influenced by Salafi ideologies, was instead 'destroying Somali culture, music and traditions'. Similar criticisms have been made by Somali intellectuals, such as Bashir Goth (2015), who wrote a famous blog post entitled 'A *jihad* against Somali Music in the Land of Freedom' following the famous vocalist Hibo Nuura's decision to end her singing career after widespread criticism by Somali *culima/'ulema* that music was *haram*.

As I shall explore in subsequent chapters, efforts by parents to fashion good pious Somali daughters are often met with resistance. Bilan, for example, accepted her daughters' preference for Western films, music and entertainment, but tried her best to speak to them in Somali, to encourage them to socialize with their cousins and Somalis in the local area, to take them to a Somali mosque twice a week, and to pray regularly as a way of leading by example. However, she watched with disappointment as her daughters rejected Somali food, refused to reply to her in Somali, or were unwilling to attend Somali community events. 'Erghh it's full of Somalis,' they would often respond; being 'too Somali' was considered 'uncool' or 'backwards' according to the girls. As Mulki suggested in the initial vignette, she hoped to distance herself from her Somali upbringing and kinship obligations, to move out of her mother's 'cramped' flat and to aspire to greater wealth and status.

In the next chapter, I return to the intergenerational tension between Mulki and Bilan with which I opened this chapter to explore how young women born or raised in London insert themselves within these discussions around morality, gender and tradition in light of the growing influence of reformist discourses. In particular, I look at how young people are similarly separating culture and tradition from an 'authentic' Islam, while seeking to reinterpret, update, celebrate and transcend Somali culture and *Soomaalinimo* in new ways.

Notes

1   These figures use 'place of birth' as a proxy for the size of the population. Those who are born in the UK – the so-called 'second generation' – are therefore not recorded. Within London, the borough of Brent has the largest population of Somalia-born residents.

2   For example, Tower Hamlets and Newham are known to be predominantly *Isaaq* (*Habarjeclo*) areas, Brixton and Streatham are thought to be *Hawiye*, Kilburn, Acton and Paddington largely *Daarood*, and Camden and Islington a mixture of southern Somali clans.

3   There are 236 'Somali' charities officially registered with the Charity Commission in the UK (Open Society 2014: 119). The most-established community organizations include Ocean Somali Community Association, Kayd Somali Arts and Culture in Tower Hamlets, the Anti-Tribalism Movement in Hammersmith and Fulham, Somali Cultural Centre and Somali Youth Development Resource Centre and London Somali Youth Forum in Camden.

4   *Qaad (or Khat)* is a stimulant plant chewed across the Horn of Africa and the Middle East. In 2014 the UK classed it as a Class C drug and banned any imports into the country.

5   In the UK Somalis are also viewed through the categories of race, ethnicity and religion as black, African, Muslim minorities. These categories fail to capture the ways in which older-generation Somalis identify themselves. Many feel they are neither black Africans – a label they assign to minority groups such as the Bantu – nor like other Muslim women, such as those from Bangladesh and Bengal, who they view as lacking independence and autonomy.

6   Somali teenager Mahir Osman was killed in Camden in 2006 during a fight between rival gangs.

CHAPTER FIVE

Updating *Soomaalinimo*: Young Somalis and the problematization of culture

She lives in me, the mother of Mogadishu.
Her face is my map of the motherland.
Her head holds the secrets of Xamar (Hamar).
A remarkable woman,
The mother of my mother.

[Extract from 'Mother of Mogadishu', Hamdi Khalif, (2013)]

A play on FGM

Throughout my fieldwork I volunteered on a campaign project entitled Community Against FGM (Female Genital Mutilation). Implemented by a local Somali community organization in Tower Hamlets, East London, and led predominantly by young, second-generation Somalis, the project aimed to raise awareness about female genital cutting or mutilation and was targeted predominantly at first-generation Somalis.[1] At the heart of this campaign was the message that FGM was a cultural practice that had no legitimacy in religious texts. The project recruited a small group of Somali religious scholars, mostly from the east London area to cooperate and reach a consensus on the illegality of FGM in Islamic law, and to raise awareness about the cultural nature of the practice. Despite initial disagreements among the scholars about the extent to which circumcision was *sunna* (based on the Prophet's teachings), those who were able to find a consensus on the issue were invited to participate in a series of workshops in schools, community centres and mosques with Somali women and men across different age groups. It was hoped that the scholars would use their authority in the community to exert their religious opinion and override any cultural understanding of the practice.

The project culminated in a play entitled *The Muted Cry*, which was first performed in October 2011 during the Somali Week Festival (Figure 4) to an audience of mostly Somali women of different ages and only a few non-Somalis and Somali men. Somali Week is an annual event that takes place during Black History Month (October in the UK). Funded in part by Arts Council England, it is held annually at Oxford House in Bethnal Green, East London, and aims to celebrate Somali arts by inviting a range of international Somali poets, writers, comedians, artists and musicians. The festival brings together audiences of different ages to participate in a variety of events – from poetry readings and plays to musical performances, discussion panels and comedy sketches.

The performance of *The Muted Cry* sought to highlight, but also bridge, a generational divide. Written by young director and playwright, Abdirahman Yusuf Artan, the actors were predominantly young Somalis born or raised in the UK. The play features Hodan, a young Somali girl who is taken by her mother from the UK to Hargyesa, Somaliland on holiday, where she undergoes FGM before returning to London, traumatized by the practice. As the play unfolds, familial conflicts and disagreements are revealed: Hodan never appears on stage and her father, worried of tarnishing the reputation of the Somali community and the honour of his family, prefers to brush the incident under the carpet. The mother is informed by her son of the criminality of her act and the possibility of prosecution, but she is unperturbed and concerned only about her daughter's health. Meanwhile Hodan's cousins and brother, all second-generation Somalis, are angered and frustrated by these reactions. They debate the religiosity of the practice, finally appealing to a Somali *sheikh*, who appears on stage holding a *Qur'an*. The stage lights are dimmed and a spotlight highlights his upper body as he informs the audience that FGM is a non-religious, cultural and traditional practice; he says there is no Islamic evidence for the practice, except for a 'weak *hadith*'. The *sheikh* continues:

> Moving on to the way Somalis practice female circumcision, that method is one which is opposed to Islamic ruling and tradition and it has nothing to do with Islam. This method is one which is traced back to ancient cultures and traditions and religion is very much opposed to it. The religion is opposed to everything which harms the person, their body, their mind and psychological well being. Therefore, it is unlawful and forbidden and this harmful way Somalis practice female circumcision should be stopped. Everything that harms a Muslim person is not allowed and forbidden. May *Allah* guide us to the right path. (Artan 2012)

The play concludes with a call for the eradication of the practice, reiterated by the following dialogue among the younger generation:

Ali: Youngsters … are we crazy, or empty of any thought process, have we no shame. … We, the educated, we, who claim to be modern and yet we have been convinced that some cultural and traditional practice … .

Naima: This method of female circumcision brings shame on to the culture and tradition of the Somalis, it is a stigma and black spot against the Islamic religion and it is damaging and traumatic for girls, it is unlawful and totally forbidden in Islam. Everyone else has progressed and is in the twenty-first century apart from us.

(*Enters a crowd of young women and men*)

Mukhtaar: Who is pushing this practice? Are men supporting this, are women propagating this practice. Guys speak up, are you guys supporting the continuation of this practice in our community?

Guys: No … No … No.

Naima: Are the girls happy for our community to become a butcher house for girls?

Girls: No … Nooooooooooo. No!

Naima: Then what devil is pushing this practice in our community and why won't it stop?

Ali: I will tell you why this practice will not stop: it is because of the lack of knowledge and the lack of power and connection of our community which is helping this practice. Look, none of us here support this practice, yet still it is going on … . (Artan 2012)

The performance was followed by a panel discussion with representatives from the anti-FGM organizations Daughters of Eve, *Negaad* – a Somaliland-based NGO – Forward UK and Equality Now. Diverse arguments were raised against the practice: some used the language of rights; some highlighted the health and medical implications; while others gave graphic descriptions of the practice, condemning its brutality. Referring to the play, many of the panellists emphasized the necessity that religious scholars begin a public dialogue and avoid delivering conflicting messages regarding the practice.[2]

The play sends a clear message that FGM is a cultural practice that must be discarded because it contradicts religious practice and belief.[3] It draws on an Islamic reformist discourse that advocates an 'authentic' universal Islam, based on an absolute truth and 'purified' of cultural or traditional norms and practices (Jacobson 1998; Roy 2004). Circumcision is thus cast as a negative and uncivilized cultural, ethnic and traditional practice that religious knowledge should seek to eradicate. As we saw in Chapter 4, the older generations are beginning to appropriate this discourse that separates religion from culture. In the play the younger generation avail themselves of the legitimacy of this narrative in forwarding a religious argument against FGM. At the same time, they criticize the older generations for not fully embracing and implementing this separation, and employ the Islamic reformist discourse to differentiate themselves from the first generation.[4]

The Muted Cry reveals how reformist discourses of 'religion versus culture' reinforce the associations between religion, education, awareness, modernity and future progress, in contrast to cultural traditions and norms. They provide a way for young Somalis to separate themselves from public perceptions of Somalis as 'backwards', constrained by their cultural traditions, and thus not fully integrated into British society. As I discuss below, debates around the demise of multiculturalism in Britain tend to cast certain 'minority practices', such as FGM, as backwards, traditional and illiberal, and hence as incompatible with British ways of life (Phillips 2007). The young people in the play are taking up these ideas and directing them at their parents' generation, blaming their lack of knowledge for perpetuating these 'barbaric' practices. In so doing, the divided character of the Somali community is cast as an impediment to progress, and religious knowledge as a means of 'educating' and thus uniting Somalis and enabling them to collectively select among elements of their culture that do not conflict with religious textual knowledge. Islam is presented as embodying 'modern' values and as the solution to the 'problems' of integration often projected onto minority groups in Britain.

Originally written in Somali, but translated, directed and performed by young Muslims in English, the play marks a clear generational divide. Hodan's mother forces her to undergo FGM and her father ignores the younger generation's plea to reflect on, and confront, the problem and consult a *sheikh*. The woman is represented stereotypically as the carer of familial morality and well-being, as well as emotionally vulnerable and easily persuaded by others, whereas the father is presented as authoritative and the defender of family honour. Both parents are portrayed as adopting a cultural attitude and uncritically performing cultural practices. In the final scene described above, only the younger, educated and modern generation stand at the front and call for the eradication

FIGURE 4 *Somali Week Festival 2016. Courtesy Kate Stanworth.*

of the practice. Ali cries out to the young to reflect and act rather than passively allow the practice to continue in order to avoid the errors of his parents' generation. According to these young people, their parents are unable to effectively 'pick and choose' which cultural practices ought to be discarded (e.g. FGM) and which ones are compatible with Islam and can be retained. The young must scrutinize their actions and values in order to separate themselves from the practice; only reflection on these unconsciously adopted cultural elements, which are associated with the past, will enable progress into the future. The play is, therefore, a critique by second-generation Somalis of their parent's inability to approach culture as object, to fully separate religion from culture and act independently of culture.

Problematizing culture

It is trite to say that culture has been a contentious concept in anthropology. However, just as anthropologists have turned away from it, culture has, in recent years, entered public debate and politics. Through claims to authenticity and uniqueness, culture has come to serve as a form of governmentality, institutionalized in multicultural policies. In turn, it has been appropriated as a way of making claims on state resources as well as being implicated in contests of representation and value (Phillips 2007; Moore 2011: 34–5).

As I argued in Chapter 1, debates around multiculturalism and diversity, which surfaced in the UK throughout the late 1960s and have more recently centred on the demise of multiculturalism, have given rise to a range of problematizations around the meaning and make-up of culture. As a result, a series of interrelated queries around a subject's relation with culture, and what it means to have or belong to a culture, have emerged as areas of knowledge and governance, and as political issues that need to be addressed and tackled.

Baumann (1996) has argued that British hegemonic public discourse equates community, ethnicity and culture, and reifies culture as an imprisoning cocoon and as a determining force. Building on this insight, Phillips (2007) explores how a reified culture is used in multicultural legal and policy frameworks. She contends that minorities have often been represented as bounded communities defined through their cultural characteristics and juxtaposed to a liberal autonomous self. Culture, she maintains, is employed across the political spectrum as a way of demonizing and stereotyping individuals from minority, non-Western groups. Multicultural frameworks have made recourse to culture as a way of referring to race, thereby defining groups in totalizing ways, seeing people as separate and different to the majority culture, and thus predicting the behaviour of minority groups. For example, whole ranges of behaviours deemed unacceptable, such as forced marriages or FGM, have been attributed to cultural characteristics. This deployment of culture has produced a 'radical otherness' and has depicted minorities as incapacitated by culture and as lacking in autonomy. It has produced 'a determinist understanding of culture that represents individuals from minority or non-Western cultural groups as controlled by cultural rules' and as juxtaposed to the liberal, autonomous agent (ibid.: 101). Scholars have shown how these cultural representations, which are readily accepted in popular discourses, have also been highly gendered. Minority men are often depicted as defenders of cultural traditions and perpetrators of violence against passive female victims (Ewing 2008). This notion of culture relies on the stereotyping of minority – and very often, Muslim – gender relations, and serves as a means of suppressing difference.

This culturalization of politics has also been fed by the social sciences and their concern with diversity (Yúdice 2003). The literature on cultural and religious change among Somalis in the diaspora has sought to address and offer a range of responses to the questions that are problematized in public and political discussions. For example, scholars have explored the changing sense of being Somali in the diaspora from the point of view of integration (Hopkins 2010; Valentine and Sporton 2009; Berns-McGown 1999; Valentine et al. 2009), or the changing relationship between Somali ethnicity, culture and Islam (Hopkins 2010; McMichael 2002; Tiilikainen 2003). While I do not dispute the data presented in these studies, and in fact build on them throughout this chapter, my theoretical approach departs from this literature. My work does not assume a particular understanding of Somali culture or of Somaliness. Nor do I seek to address the questions of belonging, identity, integration or assimilation. Rather, the remainder of this chapter returns to young Somali women and the ways in which they navigate around these problematizations and seek to fashion themselves through reworking their understandings of, and relations to, Somali culture. Building on the historical narrative developed in the previous two chapters, I explore how notions of *Soomaalinimo* and Somali *dhaqan* (culture), and their relationship to *diin* (religion), are being disputed and transformed in various ways by a range of the younger Somali women born or raised in the UK.

Problematization, Foucault (2000: 118) argues, not only 'develops the conditions in which possible responses can be given; it defines the elements that will constitute what the different solutions attempt to respond to'. These women's ideas and relations to culture, I suggest, are shaped but never fully determined by a number of discourses and practices: liberal forms of governance around culture in Britain; historically specific ideas of Somali culture; and reformist discourses on culture and authentic religion. As evidenced in the FGM campaign, many young Somalis have come to approach culture as object – as a set of objectified practices and values – and hence to engage with *Soomaalinimo* as a willingly chosen identity. At the same time, the objectification of culture has not emptied the notion of meaning, nor rendered it static or fixed in the past. Somali culture, for many young people, can be shaped and updated, modified and modernized, challenged and transcended. Engagements with culture reveal the ways in which some young Somali women seek to fashion themselves as autonomous, authentic and modern subjects (Taylor 1994) by engaging the ethical imagination and transforming their relations with self and other in specific ways.

The chapter is organized around three different groups of young Somali women who constitute the one-and-half and second generations and are between the ages of twenty and forty. First, I return to the FGM campaign to present Leyla Hussein, a young Somali female activist. I point to the ways in which she articulates critiques of culture as patriarchal and determining, and how she elaborates her own liberal attitude to Somaliness. I subsequently turn to Idil and a group of young Somalis who, in different ways, seek to update and modernize the meanings of Somali culture on the basis of their engagements with UK popular culture. Finally, I conclude with a number of young Somali women who attempt to unpack the bounded nature of Somaliness by challenging the boundaries of culture, or transcending these categories altogether. Unlike the young women who feature in the following chapters, many of those introduced in this chapter are not necessarily active in their faith, although they share these critiques of culture with more pious women. Furthermore, almost all identify as Muslims but make sense of their faith in varying ways, highlighting the analytical difficulties of demarcating the pious from the non-pious and piety from secular or liberal norms. Their perspectives are crucial to understanding the multiplicity of experiences, and the relations between different young Somali women in Britain.

'I have Leyla culture'

I met Leyla Hussein,[5] and several other young Somali women active in various feminist or anti-racism initiatives, through my involvement with the FGM campaign. As a psychoanalyst, feminist and founder of a non-profit organization, Daughters of Eve – which aims to protect the rights of young people from FGM-practising communities – Leyla Hussein is well known across the UK for presenting the 2013 Channel 4 documentary *The Cruel Cut*. Now in her early thirties, she grew up in Saudi Arabia and Italy before returning temporarily to Somalia and subsequently moving to the UK with her mother and siblings. Her parents were among the educated professionals in post-independence Somalia; her father worked as an engineer and her mother as a nurse.

Leyla currently lives with her daughter in a warm colourful flat within walking distance of her mother's flat in East London. On my first visit I remember noticing a purple tablecloth on her coffee table showing the words 'Fight for Women' and the silhouetted figures of the Suffragettes, which exemplified the way in which activism permeates her everyday life. I had known Leyla for several years when I asked her to meet to discuss her involvement in the FGM campaign and other Somali initiatives in London. She launched straight into the topic and explained how Somali culture was not all-encompassing, but constituted only one dimension of her life. 'I have Leyla culture, I don't represent anyone,' she exclaimed. She referred me to one of her Facebook posts with an image of 'Nine versions of Leyla' (Figure 5). The nine 'versions' featured Leyla in a red *hijab*, a Somali *shaash* (scarf) tied in a southern Somali style, a Somali *dirac* (dress), a traditional *guntiino* typically associated with a Somali nomadic tradition but redesigned using West African print, an afro hairstyle, and a long red elegant evening gown, among several other images. 'I wanted people to know I was all these things! The fact is I want to be on a ridge,' she explained, 'I see myself in multiple ways, through multiple perspectives, I love being like that. That's just me, I don't really fit in anywhere, but I like being on a ridge because it means I can see lots of different sides.'

In each of the photos, Leyla was not only emphasizing a collective identity as Somali, Muslim, African or Western, but also, through her poses and props, capturing different elements of herself as modest, shy, loud and fun, intellectual and engaged, and so on. Each photo grasped an element of a multiple and constantly shifting self, and together the images captured her uniqueness or personal authenticity (Taylor 1994). Charles Taylor has described how a new understanding of individual identity emerged at the end of the eighteenth century. Individual identity became attached to an ideal of authenticity that emerged with the decline of hierarchical society and of socially derived processes of identification. Morality became anchored in an individual's feelings – in a 'voice within' – and being in tune with one's feelings became a fundamental part of being an independent and fully human. A new form of inwardness developed, while satisfaction became associated with 'recovering authentic moral contact with ourselves' (ibid.: 30). A century later, with the rise of romanticism, this notion developed into an idea of the self as something that one creates and makes up as 'a work of art' and in opposition to the demands of social life (Appiah 1994). As Foucault (2000: 311) has also remarked, 'to be modern' involves taking 'oneself as object of a complex and difficult elaboration'. In describing herself as 'being on a ridge', Leyla was emphasizing her uniqueness, and her ability to transform and work on herself as a 'work of art'; her authentic self was not socially inscribed but derived from within. However, she was able to identify and externalize these internal authentic characteristics, identities, and elements of the self, and to navigate and appropriate these in various ways. What made her unique was a recognition of her multiple selfhood and a willing appropriation and rejection of various practices and values.

Furthermore, Leyla was emphasizing her autonomous engagement with these collective identifications, her ability to stand back and choose, and to own herself. These different outfits and poses were masks or identities that she could willingly adopt and discard as she saw fit. She could seemingly move in and out of these different roles – none of which fully captured the authentic

Leyla. Her ultimate aim was to acquire multiple perspectives, which she claimed gave a more nuanced understanding of herself and her engagement with the world. While others tried to fix her in a particular category, Leyla claimed she could transcend these labels – she could effectively select and choose what aspects of culture and religion to adopt and when.

Being Somali was also only one dimension of herself. 'I'm African first and then Somali,' Leyla explained to me. Emphasizing her commitment to a pan-African identity and ideology, she positioned her Somaliness in Africa rather than in relation to the Arab peninsula and Islam. Indirectly, by prioritizing her African identity, she was criticizing the older generations for perpetuating an idea of 'pure' Somalis as superior and distinct from black Africans (Besteman 1995). She continued by describing her Somaliness as based on 'the food I eat and cook, the language I speak, the clothes I have, the history, heritage ... the values ... such as caring for people who are vulnerable. That's *Soomaalinimo* to me.' 'But', she added, there were elements of culture that she felt should not be a part of it: 'That stems from my feminist values. Things like FGM, violence against women, slut shaming, patriarchy.' For Leyla, Somali culture should

FIGURE 5 *Nine versions of Leyla. Courtesy Leyla Hussein.*

be purified not by selecting elements that conflict with religious prescriptions, but by eliminating practices that contradict a notion of gender equality. Leyla had been involved in the FGM campaign and she agreed that drawing on Islamic reformist discourses was an effective strategy for discouraging the practice. However, she preferred to evoke a rights-based discourse in critiquing gender inequality and what she described as the 'patriarchal' dimensions of her culture. FGM, according to Leyla, was a cultural practice that ought to be discarded not only because it was counter to Islamic teachings but also because it restricted the rights of women and girls.

For Leyla, Somaliness is treated as interchangeable with Africanness, Muslimness and Britishness, and extrinsic rather than constitutive of the subject; it is composed of a set of values, practices and objects to embrace at will (Brown 2006b: 301). However, these different collective identities are not static or fixed, as is often assumed in debates around culture and the politics of difference. Rather, Leyla was suggesting a purification or revision of culture, one that erased patriarchal elements that were incompatible with liberal values of equality. While most Somalis, typically older kin, embodied patriarchal norms unquestioningly and were hence incapacitated by culture, she was able to step outside of it and rid it of its problematic dimensions.

Reforming culture and religion

Leyla's effort to articulate a unique and authentic 'Leyla's culture', by detachment and liberation from culture and religion, developed in reaction to what she perceived to be social and cultural constraints. As Leyla elaborated:

> I'm constantly being told I'm not Somali enough, I'm not Muslim enough. People accuse me and say: you've left your *dhaqan* (culture) behind. My first reaction is: well, what do you mean, what is *dhaqan*?! They don't really have an answer! They just repeat 'you've lost your *dhaqan* and *diin* behind' like a broken record. I tell them *dhaqan* has nothing to do with hijab. Women used to wear something loose on their heads after marriage. Also, they say I've lost my *diin*, but they just say that. Have they read the *Qur'an*? It says to be modest, but says nothing about

covering from head to toe, it just says 'cover your outer body'. This is just a culture of misogyny, and religion is being used to promote it. The most important thing is not to judge. Sometimes I tell them: well actually, Islam says that you shouldn't judge others, so you've broken one of the most important aspects of the faith. If you pick up the book maybe you'd know that!

Leyla felt she was constantly on the defensive. Somalis who accused her of losing her *dhaqan* had completely misinterpreted the meaning of culture. They were equating religion with culture, interpreting the absence of the *hijab* as a sign that she had abandoned not only her faith but also her cultural roots. Leyla explained otherwise, separating culture from religion. Rather than suggesting a reformed culture based on Western or liberal ideals, however, she turned to a traditional notion of Somali women and gender relations which she associated with her mother's past. This enabled her to develop a critique – also often voiced by Somali liberal thinkers – of the 'Arabization' or 'Islamification' of Somali culture.

As a child she had discovered that her mother featured as a traditional nomadic Somali woman on a stamp in the 1970s, and had recently found this image on social media with a caption that romanticized nomadic lifestyles: 'Somali nomad girls do not require makeups. They have a natural beauty' (Figure 6). Leyla explained that at the time the photograph was taken, government officials had visited her mother's school in Mogadishu and selected her for the image. Unlike all the other children, she had been wearing a white *guntiino* that day, as her school uniform had been stained. Her hair was plaited into two small braids and a traditional headband was tied around her head; the government officials turned her into a nomad girl, into the symbol of Somali culture and of the Somali nation-state. 'This is what Somali *dhaqan* means ... a *guntiino*, no bra, *shaash*, braids, no *hijab*, you could probably see her nipples in the white dress!' The *hijab*, Leyla insisted, had nothing to do with authentic Somali culture, nor did an excessive focus with covering and protecting women's femininity. By referring back to the past, she pointed to what she considered an authentic Somali culture which existed prior to the growth of Islamic revivalist movements in the 1980s. While this nomadic culture had its own 'patriarchal' dimensions, she claimed – in line with her critique of FGM – that these should also be abandoned.

The problem with Somalis, she insisted, was the 'culture of misogyny' and patriarchy that allowed certain practices to continue, such as men dictating what women should wear. Interestingly Leyla fully acknowledged that this performance of culture was staged (her mother was not a nomad but had been born in the city) but that it nonetheless remained an authentic culture, one that was slowly vanishing with the growing influence of reformist movements. Like her mother, who could adopt Somali culture even though she herself was not a nomad girl, Leyla could select among aspects of clothing, or particular values and practices, to present herself as authentically Somali.

Leyla's reference to her mother also points to the importance assigned to mothers as transmitters of cultural knowledge in the diaspora and in a context where men are largely absent from the home. As we saw with Bilan and Mulki in the previous chapter, the relationship between mothers and daughters is fraught with tensions. Young women are critical of their mothers, particularly of their 'cultural' attitudes to Somaliness and Islam. However, despite these criticisms, young women often show deferential respect towards their mothers, idolizing them as authentic sources of Somali knowledge or praising them for the struggles endured in giving birth and raising them in difficult circumstances. Poems are written in praise of one's *hooyo* (mother), and young Somalis often remind each other about the *hadith* that paradise lies under a mother's feet.[6]

Leyla's feminist critique and reappropriation of a past Somali culture, however, did not go unchallenged, as evidenced by the backlash she received following the Channel 4 documentary *The Cruel Cut*. Some accused her of being too Western and 'unSomali'. For example, her explanations and critiques of FGM were viewed as excessively graphic. This language particularly alienated first-generation Somalis, who described it as shameful (*xishood*) and 'too Western'.[7] Others criticized Leyla for perpetuating a political agenda that demonized minority cultures for their 'backwards' practices (Phillips 2007). Continued talk about FGM, these critics claimed, reflected badly on Somalis and only led to more intensified policing, scrutiny and stigmatization. For Leyla these criticisms were unfounded. Ignoring the existence of these 'cruel' practices amounted to a form of racism in adopting different standards of judgement for black minorities than for the white majority. For Leyla, criticisms of being 'unSomali' were targeted at her because she was a woman and therefore had to stand as a symbol of collective morality. A man, she insisted, would not have been criticized in the same way. 'Around the time of the documentary ... I was getting so many bad reactions ... mostly by older Somalis. ... I'm a diaspora woman, divorced, not wearing a *hijab* and with a daughter. I was not what they wanted, I represented all the wrong things,' she argued, suggesting these critiques were personal and targeted her gender and marital status discriminatingly.

In a similar way, Leyla's decision not to don the *hijab* on a regular basis is seen by older Somali kin as an abandonment of both religion and culture, even though Leyla claims it is neither. On the one hand, she sees the *hijab* as an item she can adopt and dispense with as she pleases, as we saw in her discussion of 'Leyla's culture'; religion is treated as an identity and as a collection of values, practices and objects that one can pick and choose accordingly. Donning the *hijab* is also given a symbolic value, representing her Muslim identity to self and others. In the quotation above, Leyla criticizes an over-privileging of external signs of religiosity. Being Muslim, she informs her critics, is first and foremost about adopting the correct values and internal attitudes; it is about being forgiving and non-judgemental towards others. In so doing, she twists her critics' statements by suggesting that it is Somalis' judgemental attitudes towards her that are in fact un-Islamic, not her uncovered hair. In emphasizing the importance of interiority and critiquing Somalis for their overemphasis on external practices, she echoes similar comments made by young pious Somali women, who I introduce in Chapters 6 and 7. Yet contrary to these young women, Leyla adopts Islamic virtues willingly and is less concerned with cultivating these through practices and bodily techniques of self-discipline (Mahmood 2005).

While Leyla identifies as a Muslim, she also recognizes that practising Muslims tend to dismiss this claim as inauthentic. From their point of view, she is often compared to Ayaan Hirsi Ali, the famous Dutch-American author and former politician of Somali origin known for her inflammatory remarks about Islam and for the controversial documentary *Submission* (2004) she directed with Theo Van Gogh. Yet Leyla pointed out in our conversation that she was neither anti-Islam nor a liberal critic of Islam; for her, Islam was itself liberal and compatible with feminism, and she did not view these traditions in opposition with each other. She further felt that the divisions between pious and non-pious women problematically positioned her as a 'bad' Muslim and delegitimized her way of being religious. 'I was recently told by a close friend that I was a *jihadi*, I really represented the real meaning of *jihad*. ... "Leyla you're a *jihadi*, you fight for women's struggles, you dedicate your life to it" that's what she said!' Leyla and her friend interpreted her struggle against patriarchy through an Islamic notion of struggle. In construing herself as an autonomous agent, Leyla was drawing on liberal feminist critiques of culture, romanticized notions of Somali culture drawn from her past, Muslim identity politics and a notion of interiority derived from the Islamic tradition. In so doing, she was casting a new way of being in reaction to stereotyped notions of a good Somali or a good Muslim.

SOMALI NOMAD GIRLS DO NOT REQUIRE MAKEUPS. THEY HAVE A NATURAL BEA

FIGURE 6 *Leyla's mother dressed up as a nomad girl. Courtesy Leyla Hussein.*

Objectifying culture

As both the FGM play and Leyla's experience illustrate, engagements with problematized notions of culture reveal the ways in which young second-generation women are refashioning themselves vis-à-vis their parents' generation and, in so doing, engaging the ethical imagination. In the previous chapter, we saw how being Somali is considered 'uncool' and 'backwards' among young teenagers, whereas here we see how young women seek to reform culture by separating out elements of culture that are viewed as 'backwards', from those that can be appropriated and celebrated in particular ways. In the FGM campaign, Islamic values are employed to select among elements of culture, whereas with Leyla feminist ideals are employed to reject 'illiberal' dimensions of culture.

What is at stake in these critiques is not only a question around the make-up of culture, but also one of how to engage with culture. Young people suggest that culture determines the actions and practices of their parents. Commenting on the culturalization of political and civil conflict, Wendy Brown (2006b) argues that liberalism has imagined and positioned non-liberal people as ruled by culture in opposition to liberal people who *have* culture. This juxtaposition is played out in a series of oppositions between non-liberalized culture and moral autonomy, freedom and equality. The liberal subject is assumed to have an ability to abstract herself from a context. The opposite consists of an 'organicist creature considered to lack rationality and will, [whereby] culture and religion … are saturating and authoritative' (ibid.: 301). For the liberal subject, culture and religion become a 'background' that can be 'entered' and 'exited'; culture is thus rendered extrinsic rather than constitutive of the subject, it becomes 'food, dress, music, lifestyle, and contingent values' (ibid.). Whereas the liberal subject constitutes an 'optional' relationship to culture, the non-liberal subject is determined by cultural rules.

This optional attitude to culture is evident in *The Muted Cry* and in Leyla's engagement with both culture and religion. Young second-generation Somalis present themselves as 'modern', 'choosing' subjects, who are able to approach culture in a liberal way. This attitude is also manifested in the ways in which many second generations ridicule 'traditional' Somalis for their habits and their 'typical Somali' forms of behaviour. A running joke between many second-generation Somalis in London refers to two imaginary figures, Xaliimo and Faraax. These names signify the stereotypical, traditional, Somali woman and man, and are often used by younger women to mock mothers, older kin and new arrivals from the Somali regions. These figures are given old-fashioned names and their behaviour resonates with ideas of tradition and culture. Xaliimo is said to be abrupt, wears mismatching colourful *dirac* and *garbasaar* (Somali dress and shawl), has a traditional conception of gender relations, often makes embarrassingly racist remarks[8] and is overly preoccupied with the clan. Xaliimo is cultural, rather than religious, and therefore ignorant of both British culture and religious knowledge. By mocking traditional behaviour, young Somalis present themselves as different, educated and aware of these unconscious dimensions of culture. Humour is used as a way of separating themselves from older Somalis.

As I have illustrated in the previous section, young Somalis, like some of their mothers, stress the importance of choosing the aspects of Somali culture which are compatible with ideas of the modern or with liberal feminism, and rejecting conflicting practices, objects and values (e.g. FGM, clan ideology). Moore (2011) elaborates on this process of objectification in her discussion of alternative rites of passage (ARP) among the Marakwet in Kenya. As a consequence of pressure from NGOs, ARPs have been implemented as a means of eradicating the practice of FGM by celebrating positive cultural values and practices and discarding others, like the play I described above. ARPs, Moore claims, have emerged as a set of 'identifiable processes and practices' which stress key 'positive' cultural values, while rejecting traditional practices such as FGM. These rites position parents as tied to culture and represent a transfer of power from parents and kin networks to pastors and NGOs. As Moore (2011: 53) points out: 'Choosing the good parts has become emblematic of modern ways of thinking and doing, as people increasingly engage with a process of self-fashioning cast in the idiom of new forms of knowledge.' Embracing the 'good' parts of culture is crucial to young second-generation Somali women's processes of self-making. These engagements are drawn from multicultural policies and discourses in the UK that reify cultural difference and equate it with ethnicity and bounded notions of community (Baumann 1996).

At the same time, young women emphasize and celebrate the 'good' parts of culture by participating in cultural events, eating Somali food, reading, reciting and writing Somali poetry, or in Leyla's case, wearing traditional clothes such as the *guntiino*. Valentine and Sporton (2009: 742) note how, for young teenage Somalis, the importance of 'being Somali' was produced through everyday domestic practices – from the language spoken, clothing worn and faith practised through to the food eaten (see also Hopkins 2010). Canab, a young second-generation woman, had set up the first Somali society at her university, and had been an active participant in a second-generation-led movement campaigning against clan ideology and for political change in Somalia. She also often shared with me her passion for Somali arts and poetry. 'I love that aspect of Somali culture and I love to revive it in my own self,' she explained. She had begun to compose her own poetry in English, drawing on traditional Somali poetry genres. When I discussed this chapter with her over dinner at my house, she added: 'When I speak Somali, I really like it cause I feel it's what makes me Somali, and I'm proud of it. … When I look at myself in the mirror wearing a head wrap, I feel that somehow I'm connecting to my grandmother, I look at myself and think of the connection between us … through this object.' Embracing the 'good parts' of culture was a way for Canab and many other second-generation women to connect with older female Somali kin – who are viewed as transmitters of cultural knowledge – through a willing engagement with what they perceive to be a shared culture. Similarly, poet Hamdi Khalif traces her connection to the Somali regions through her matrilineal connections. As she notes in her poem 'Mother of Mogadishu'– which I have reproduced in part in the epigraph – her grandmother lives 'inside' her. Her connection to Somali places, practices and stories is mediated through her embodied connection with her mother's mother. In another stanza she remarks that 'her eyes are my *faynuus*, guiding light,' suggesting her grandmother provides her not only with a connection to the past but also with support for the future.

Somalis talk about culture as a set of inherited practices, values and objects that they choose to embrace. However, in selecting among identifiable elements of culture, I suggest the content of culture has not remained static nor has it been emptied of meaning. Some, like Leyla, understand being Somali by reference to a romanticized past, purified of its patriarchal elements. As we shall see in the following vignette – which introduces Idil, the young daughter of Safiya who featured in Chapters 3 and 4 – others have actively sought to revive Somali culture in specific ways.

Niiko dancing as culture

It must have been a rather strange sight for Idil, returning home from a long day at university. Her mother Safiya, who is regarded by Idil as relatively computer-phobic, was sitting in the living room with her face glued to the computer screen and her Italian friend/anthropologist slouched on the couch beside her. But in fact, true to self, Safiya was not engaged in any profound computer programming or analysis. Instead, she was undertaking one of the more commonplace and elementary of computer tasks: sifting through a YouTube search for 'Somali songs' and translating the lyrics for me. We had been chatting all afternoon, lazily sipping Somali tea as the topic of conversation drifted to Somali music and dancing. Safiya was reminiscing about the 'good old days' in Mogadishu as she excitedly clicked on the mouse switching from *buraanbur* poems to popular romantic tunes.

Once Idil had made sense of the situation, she tried to slip away to her room, but Safiya, at that moment, had a flash of inspiration; she called Idil back and asked her to demonstrate her *Niiko* dancing to me. Since this is a very sensual dance which involves moving hips and bottom to a drum beat, it is contentious among religiously minded Somalis; *Niiko* is rarely performed at religious weddings or in mixed gatherings. Because Idil was not, unlike her mother, practising Islam, she did not mind performing it in front of both male and female company (something Safiya wilfully turns a blind eye to). In fact, it was one of those aspects of 'Somali culture' that she was proud to celebrate and, acquiescing to her mother's wish, Idil returned from her bedroom with a flowered *dirac* and a scarf tied around her hips to accentuate her bottom. After a quick search on YouTube for the correct drum beat, she turned her back to us, stuck out her bum and swayed to the beat. It was beautiful, controlled and rhythmic, and she showed me the way she had adapted the movements to reggae in order to dance in nightclubs. But while Idil was dancing, Safiya's two Somali neighbours, Fahiimo and Ilhan, dressed in black *jilbab*, walked into the house. Fahiimo sat on the couch, watching and smiling, but Ilhan remained standing, observing with her arms folded and a stern look of disapproval painted across her face. For a while no one took any notice, but after a few minutes Ilhan had had enough and she dashed to one of the shelves, picked up the *Qur'an* and began reciting the opening *sura* (chapter). Once finished, she turned to Safiya and reminded her that music and dancing were cultural practices that were *haram* (forbidden) and incited *Shaydaan* (Satan). I had foreseen the response before the *Qur'an* was even put down because a mood of mischief had crept into the air, particularly between mother and daughter. Safiya jumped up and also began dancing, while Idil swayed more energetically, lifting her long *dirac* to reveal her bare legs.

I introduced Idil, Safiya's daughter, in Chapter 4 and elaborated on Safiya's criticisms that Idil was not a 'proper Somali daughter'. When I first met Idil she was nineteen and in her first year of university. She divided most of her time between her studies, a part-time retail job, and socializing and partying with her friends. She was also actively involved with Nomad Radio, a web-based radio programme featuring Somali shows, music, and other issues relating to the Somali community in London. Idil had arrived in the UK aged nine and settled in Camden with her sister and mother. She initially had difficulties in school, struggled to learn English and got embroiled in various incidents of street violence. One afternoon she came home with her face covered in bruises and it was then that she decided to start focusing on her studies. 'I started to realize and learn that you can be different, you don't have to be a part of those things,' she explained.

Her involvement with Nomad Radio provided her with an opportunity to engage with her Somali heritage, but in a way that she considered fun, entertaining and British. In a discussion about her involvement she stated: 'It's important to keep my culture. I speak, write and read Somali,' and specified, 'but British culture has become more of my culture, it defines my sense of right and wrong. … I'm British but at the same time I don't go to that extreme, drinking, drugs, and sleeping around. That's where my boundaries are.' Idil was carefully crafting her own authentic sense of morality by picking and choosing between sets of values and practices which she associated with each culture. *Niiko* dancing was one of several dimensions of Somali culture that she had actively embraced and enjoyed celebrating and displaying to others. Taught by an older cousin, she had learnt to update and adapt this practice to suit a variety of contexts, ranging from weddings to clubs; *Niiko* was a part of her Somali culture and whether it conflicted or not with religion was not a concern for her at that point in time. Interestingly, *Niiko* is a dance that the majority of first-generation Somalis associate with the minority *Bantu*, who are descended from pre-Somali populations and recent immigrant eastern Swahili groups originally brought to Somalia as slaves (Lewis 2008: 6). For Idil's parents *Niiko* is therefore not necessarily an authentic Somali dance, but one that has been appropriated from minority cultures of African and slave descent.[9] Nonetheless, Idil's appropriation of *Niiko* is a way of reworking and updating an objectified notion of Somali culture. As mentioned above, crucial to her deployment of this notion of culture is the way in which she fashions herself through a creative, willing and autonomous engagement with culture in contrast to her parents. As I show in the following section, Idil and her friends were also involved in updating and modernizing Somali culture by drawing on British popular culture.

The *Niiko* incident above reveals some of the tensions around the make-up of culture and the elements of Somali culture deemed suitably compatible with religion, which I also pointed to in relation to the FGM campaign. On the one hand, a conflict unfolds between Ilhan and Safiya over where to draw the line between religion and culture. Ilhan, a first-generation religiously minded mother, had identified most forms of dancing, including *Niiko*, as a cultural practice in conflict with a religious requirement and awareness of modesty. These treatments and reifications of culture and religion are, I have argued, historically specific. Some first-generation Somali women have only recently come to adopt a discourse that separates religion from culture and identifies certain practices as cultural (whether Somali or Bantu). Similarly, many young practising women, who I introduce in the following chapter, voiced similar critiques about cultural practices such as music and dancing.

Instead, Safiya, who was familiar with *Niiko* from her days growing up in Mogadishu, had only recently begun learning about Islam. For her, performing the dance at home in female-only gatherings did not make her a 'bad' Muslim. In pushing back against her friends, she remained somewhat critical of religious attempts to erode elements of her culture. She was torn between conflicting interpretations and prioritized her loyalty to her daughter and passion for dancing above appeasing her religiously minded friends. Safiya's participation in the dancing demonstrates also the instability of the category of culture and the arbitrary nature of separating religion from culture; it indicates the impossibility of fully reifying culture as object, and the difficulty of transforming embodied practices such as dancing into cultural objects.

Idil's appropriation of *Niiko* is in part a conscious reaction to critical voices among young and older Somalis who seek to purify culture and eradicate these practices. Unlike her mother, who had started engaging with Islam recently, Idil was not particularly concerned with practising Islam. Like Leyla, most of her close friends were Somali, but they were not active in their faith. In conversation, Idil presented to me her typology of young pious women. First, she identified those who had been raised religiously and who confused culture and religion. These women hadn't chosen to practise their faith and Idil claimed they also lacked 'ambition'. 'I want to do stuff, have a career, become a writer. ... I'm not like them,' she explained, echoing some of her own mother's aspirations as a young woman. Second, she identified 'practising' Somalis, or those who had consciously become religious at a particular point in their lives. The latter were deemed more acceptable only if they had actively chosen to practise with 'pure' intentions – with the aim of connecting with God rather than finding a husband. 'Many hijabis start practising only to find a dude to marry,' she stated on one occasion, accusing them of hypocrisy.

Idil also assumed that her disinterest in religion was only temporary and that she might one day start practising Islam:

> I guess I'm just not at that stage ... there are still so many things I want to do before. For example, I don't want practising to get in the way of my future. ... I have so many other things to think about right now. ... I want to go travelling, partying, enjoy myself, I just want to get those out of the way before I start practising.

Religion at that moment in time was perceived as a constraining force, much like some of the 'backwards' traditional practices outlined above. According to Idil, it was not future oriented, but rather acted as an impediment to her current aspirations.

Updating and modernizing culture

Over the last decade, a large number of Somali youth activities, organizations and projects have emerged in London and competed for funding with the more traditional community organizations run by first-generation Somalis. These initiatives provide a space in which Somali youth have explored new ways of presenting and celebrating Somaliness, but also of encouraging young Somalis to be successful. Events such as the annual Somali Week Festival organized by Kayd Somali Arts and Culture (Figure 4), which I mentioned above, or SomFest, an evening of arts and entertainment for Somali youth launched in 2014, are prime examples. Websites, radio channels and magazines dedicated to Somali youth culture also abound.[10]

During my fieldwork I attended Miss Somali, an event organized in 2010 in West London by a group of young Somalis associated with Nomad Radio, including Idil and her friends. Promoted as an event that encouraged 'Beauty with Principles' and one that would build 'socio-economic bridges in the community', Miss Somali was advertized across London and was awaited with excitement by Somali youngsters. Organized in a conference hall and costing £20 per person, the event was marketed as a glamorous, modern and professional affair. The logo, which appeared on the Facebook group and adorned the stage, captured the manner in which the organizers sought to merge traditional Somali culture with modern ideals of education and development as well as contemporary styles. It was described on Facebook as follows:

> The Union Jack (in the shape of Somali speaking territories) is supposed to represent 'integration' into the UK. The leaves symbolize peace, natural beauty, and cultural and traditional backgrounds (roots). The scroll at the bottom stands for intelligence, development and perseverance. We've chosen the colour scheme to signify sophistication, sleek and modern. Silver was purposely considered as it is a precious (hence the crown), classy, elegant and distinguished [sic]. We have had a lot of positive feedback about the logo, many people said it was creative yet simple.

I attended the event with my friend Deqa, a woman in her late thirties who had spent her teens in Mogadishu and subsequently moved to Italy to attend university in Rome. She had recently moved to London in search of employment and worked part-time at a community centre. She arrived beautifully dressed in a *dirac* with a silk *garbasaar* gently wrapped around her shoulders and her hair nicely done up. 'I never wear this!' Deqa laughed, 'but at a Somali event it's ok!' Although the *dirac* originates from the northern Somali territories, it only became fashionable among Somalis in the 1960s (Akou 2011) and among Somalis in the diaspora it has come to symbolize traditional Somali cultural dress. It is typically worn at weddings and other Somali events.[11]

As we made our way up the red-carpeted stairs, with handrails decorated with pink ribbons, I could not help but notice that the event was reminiscent of *The X Factor*: the jury was positioned in the front row, the lights were dimmed and there was an air of forced glam and sophistication. The resemblance might not have been unintentional, as the Saturday night programme is one of the most popular shows among young people in Britain, and those with a Somali heritage are no exception here.

In contrast to Deqa, most of the young women were dressed in formal Western evening wear and the men had donned suits. I felt underdressed in my knee-length black dress and flat brown leather boots. Professional photographers had set up a studio at the entrance to the theatre for anyone interested in having their picture taken, and a few volunteers were selling soft drinks at the bar. This was nothing like the many community events organized by elder Somalis; it purposefully aimed at celebrating Somali culture while portraying it as modern and fashionable.

I could sense Deqa's unease with the spectacle that was unfolding in front of her. Not only did she feel older than the people present, but she also felt more authentically Somali. Throughout, she commented on how these youngsters knew very little about Somali history and culture, which became apparent as the evening progressed. The event consisted of musical and theatrical entertainment, but its centrepiece was a fashion show or beauty pageant, during which the contestants were assessed on their outfits and their answers to various questions posed by the jury. The contestants walked down the catwalk in front of the jury, showing off four different outfits.

Traditional wear constituted one of the four categories and each contestant was asked a question about Somali culture. The only contestant in *hijab*, who had tailored her dress out of a Somali Republic flag, was asked to describe the flag and label the five Somali territories in the Horn. Deqa sighed at the response, relieved these young girls had at least a little knowledge of their country. Another young woman was questioned about her favourite Somali food. The event continued with the women displaying a series of contemporary Western outfits, interspersed with performances by aspiring female Somali poets, a Nigerian comedian and the rapper Que. When Miss Somali was announced, the clapping and excitement of the audience drowned out her voice. She pranced back on stage provocatively holding a Somaliland flag above her head and, as a crown was placed on her head, the crowd erupted in further applause.[12] Deqa looked away, irritated by what she saw as a divisive political statement in a space that, for her, was meant to be celebrating pan-Somali traditional culture.

As we walked away from the event, Deqa commented on her disappointment with the event. 'Most of it had nothing to do with Somalis!' she complained. Having been raised in Mogadishu, Deqa was slightly older than these young people and had vivid memories of life in Somalia. She felt that younger Somalis raised in the UK were ignorant of what was really and authentically Somali. What was made clear by the event, however, was that for young second-generation Somalis, celebrating culture was about embracing and displaying objectified aspects of culture – clothing, food, flags and a set of facts. Furthermore, for young people it was important to rejuvenate and 'modernize' culture, to make it 'glamorous' and to repackage it in specific ways.

This element of modernizing culture was also present in *The Muted Cry* play and in Leyla's efforts to purify culture of its patriarchal elements. It is also manifest in young people's critiques of clan politics. Echoing Siyaad Barre's anti-tribalism policies (discussed in Chapter 3), second-generation Somalis often criticize the older generations and Somalis 'back home' for prioritizing members of their own clan. Drawing on narratives of modernity and progress, this attitude is seen as 'backwards', divisive and dangerous, and viewed by these individuals as the cause of civil war and continued conflict in the region. In *The Muted Cry*, for example, the youngsters critique the Somali community for its divisiveness, and suggest this as a reason for the continued practice of FGM. This criticism of the fragmented nature of Somalis in the UK has long been a concern for the UK government, which, as I noted in Chapter 4, has sought to promote and encourage unity based on ethnic groupings (Griffiths et al. 2006: 892). Young Somali activists have responded to these narratives about the diaspora by stressing their unity and integration in the host society (Liberatore forthcoming). Efforts to 'modernize' culture and to present themselves as educated, modern, ambitious and unified should also be seen as ways of challenging the continued problematization of Somalis in Britain. Critiques of clan have played a crucial part in these processes and have also served as a strategy by which young Somalis can present themselves as distinct from the older generation.[13]

This critical attitude towards the divisive nature of Somali society is particularly true of many of the young people born or raised in the UK who decide to return to the Somali regions temporarily or permanently to volunteer or work in government, UN organizations or the NGO sector. Echoing the perspectives of many of her peers, Cawo, a young woman in her mid-twenties who left Mogadishu aged six and who was planning to return to the region, explained:

> It's our country and we need to do something about it ... so much education can come from the Somali community in London and I want to go back and help my people. I have a responsibility ... I have memories that are vivid of how life was back then. ... I know the country has so any problems, but we're the ones who have to fix it.

Many of these young people employ a discourse of 'difference making' (Hansen 2013: 155); their knowledge and skills acquired abroad are seen as contributing to development back home. They present themselves as more educated than locals, and hence able to 'fix' the problems plaguing the region. I have repeatedly heard young returnees criticize the work mentality of other Somalis in the region, referring to their short working hours, afternoon *qaad*-chewing sessions and their reliance on clan networks. As one young woman who had recently returned home explained: 'It's so hard to do anything back home without referring to your clan. I tried to work in a hospital, but I was told that I should go through my clan ... everything is so nepotistic there.' Critique of clan is therefore intertwined with returnees' self-presentations as modern, disciplined professionals. Influenced by development institutions and discourses and a growing desire to contribute to the recovery and development of post-conflict Somali society, they emphasize their 'professionalism' through notions of development, modernization and democratization, and in opposition to clan-based politics and forms of engagement organized through clan relations (ibid.).

In their efforts to update what it means to be Somali in Britain and present themselves as modern, professional Somalis can also be cast as inauthentic by the older generations, as we saw with Deqa. Many of the older mothers I met throughout my fieldwork lamented that their children had lost any sense of Somali culture despite their involvement in these sorts of events. As explored through the perspectives of Safiya and Fahiimo, being Somali is a way of being, feeling and behaving associated with the past, which their daughters have largely lost to Western culture. More pious Somalis, as I explore in the following chapters, also view some of these efforts at reviving Somali traditions, such as the Miss Somali event or *Niiko* dancing, as 'unIslamic' or as less important than their religious pursuits. As we saw in the *Niiko* incident, Ilhan, Safiya's religious friend, had labelled music and dancing *haram*. The final section of this chapter focuses on young Somali women who are rejecting or struggling with what it means to be Somali and are hence pushing the boundaries of *Soomaalinimo*.

Transcending *Soomaalinimo*

Xafsa had a complicated relationship with her Somali origins and didn't appreciate being asked about it. 'I don't really feel Somali ... I don't like so many aspects of being Somali,' she repeatedly told me whenever the topic arose in conversation. Raised in Sweden by her mother, she decided to move to the UK to live with a maternal aunt as a young teenager. Living in North London she inevitably spent a lot of time around her Somali cousins, but she had few close friendships with Somalis of her age. In her final years of school she enjoyed going out clubbing with non-Somali friends, much to her relatives' disapproval. She moved out of her aunt's flat when she started her degree and began distancing herself from her Somali cousins and acquaintances. This was a difficult period for Xafsa as she began reflecting critically on – and ultimately rejecting – her faith, while also experimenting with her sexuality and eventually identifying as queer to her immediate friends. She initially chose to hide her sexuality and lack of faith from her family, at least until she felt ready to confront them. Furthermore, she struggled to reconcile these aspects with her Somaliness. Being queer and Somali, she thought, were incompatible and, as a consequence she distanced herself further from all things Somali.

But in her mid-twenties she started thinking and wondering about her origins; she decided it was time to visit her parents' birthplace in Puntland. She had never been there before, and had only spent the first few years of her life in Mogadishu, where her parents resided before the war. Explaining her motivations she noted: 'I think it's important to ask those questions: Who am I? Where am I from? Where do I belong, and where am I going?' Her journey was an emotional experience; she met her grandfather, uncles, aunts and cousins for the first time, and brought them suitcases of clothes, mobile phones and other items she had saved up for all year. But the experience of 'going home' was not an easy one and it generated anxiety and discomfort. Like many young people raised in Europe, she felt very different to Somalis of her age who had never left the region; she missed the comforts of life in the UK and struggled to adapt to the climate, food, manners and requirements to cover her head and wear modest clothing. She also struggled to hide what she described as her 'true self'.

On coming back to the UK, she started reading extensively on the region, attending Somali cultural events and, for the first time, making friends with other Somalis. Yet this engagement was difficult and exhausting to sustain as she often found herself having to hide aspects of herself. 'Every time I'm with Somalis an aspect of me dies or fades away,' she said at one point. On the one hand, she desired a connection with her Somali origins and felt that the history of the region was inevitably a part of her sense of self. On the other hand, she realized she would never be able to live in the region or to continue to interact publicly with Somalis, particularly if she revealed her queer identity. 'I'm also a Londoner, I've grown up here and ultimately that's where I feel comfortable. That's where I'll stay and I can feel I can live fully,' she stated, pointing to her decision to maintain a physical and critical distance from the Somali regions and from mainstream Somali community and cultural activities.

Xafsa experienced being Somali as oppressive, partly because she felt excluded by other Somalis who she assumed would view her as unSomali and marginalize her because of her sexual orientation and lack of faith. The exclusionary nature of hegemonic notions of Somaliness was also raised in a discussion on the 'Boundaries of *Soomaalinimo*' in a *Mandeeq* podcast from late 2015, chaired by the writer Hawa Mire and involving several other young scholars.[14] Set up by a group of young 'Somali-demics' following the #*Cadaan*Studies (White Studies) controversy of 2015 (see Chapters 1 and 9) and inspired by debates in critical race and post-colonial theory, the *Mandeeq* website features regular blogs and a monthly podcast on various topics ranging from Somali pop culture to diaspora privilege. I reproduce parts of the conversation from the podcast here to elaborate on how this young group of intellectuals are seeking to challenge the objectification of Somaliness, and to critique claims to authenticity and hegemonic notions of being Somali.[15]

Hawa Mire, a Toronto-based writer and storyteller, began the programme by presenting the founding myth of Somalis, one that she had also reproduced in a recent blog post on the website (Mire 2015). The myth features two sons who are sent by their father in search for water. Prior to their departure, the father instructs them that, should they run out of food, they are permitted to eat a dead animal. However, should they find food immediately after, they should throw up what they have eaten. The brothers set off on their journey and eventually run out of food. They stumble on a dead animal and eat what they can. However, they soon reach a place with food and water and the younger brother throws up the dead meat. The elder brother refuses to do so. Mire (2015) concludes: 'From that day forward, the brothers were separated, the elder brother disowned by his family and his descendants were from that moment forth known as the *Midgaan*.[16] The *Midgaan* can be found scattered across the territories, are often poor but are good workers.'

Mire presented this narrative as an invitation to unpack the power of oral stories in delineating the boundaries of who is and is not Somali. As she argues in the blog: 'To be Somali is to be Muslim, which requires a particular kind of cleanliness, therefore the *Madhibaan*, having engaged in unclean behaviour and practices, cannot be considered Somali' (Mire 2015). The story, however, is not only about so-called 'minority' groups in the Somali regions but can be extrapolated to question the ways in which Somaliness is defined in fixed and bounded ways through distinct sets of characteristics. As Mire elaborated further in the podcast:

> If you're a woman, if you're *madhibaan*, if you're not Muslim or you don't practice what in the eyes of everybody else are the tenets of what it means to be Muslim, if you don't speak Somali ... if your clan isn't connected to this founding family ... all of a sudden your access shifts according to where you've fallen in answering all these questions. (Mandeeq 2015)

In a similar way to Leyla, who felt she was being cast as 'unSomali' for not wearing a *hijab*, Hawa Mire was challenging the meaning of Somaliness. Rather than drawing on an authentic notion of a past nomadic tradition or defining Somaliness through certain practices and values, however, Hawa was questioning the existence of an authentic notion of Somaliness itself. 'No one can hold up "this is the real Somali,"' she claimed.

The other young participants in the discussion suggested that ideas of being Somali had emerged not only in relation to a fixed notion of Somaliness, captured by the myth of origin, but also in relation to a discourse of racial and ethnic minorities produced in the West, and particularly in Britain. Mohamed, one of the young men on the programme, described how when he lived in Sweden he didn't feel Somali as he was 'just a black kid'. But in coming to the UK and dealing with different people who defined themselves according to ethnicity and nationality, he suddenly found himself having to 'deal with ... [his] Somaliness', something he had never had to do before. In being asked to define who he was in ethnic terms, Mohamed suddenly found himself making sense of Somaliness through multicultural frameworks.

Acknowledging the ways in which Somaliness has been shaped by both male elders and political elites in the Somali regions and British policy frameworks, some Somalis are seeking new ways of disrupting these forms of power. 'Being Somali is a contested space. It's not important who's in or who's out ... it's not for us to say who's Somali,' Kinsi, an artist and activist explained to me. I had known her for years, but we met to discuss her work one October afternoon. She was dressed in a beautiful African print dress with a colourful shawl placed casually around neck and large gold earrings tucked under her short, curly and voluminous hair. Kinsi is the founder of Numbi, an ongoing research project that explores art practices from pre-civil-war Somalia to the present-day diaspora. *Numbi* was the last film made in Mogadishu before the war, but the word is also the name of a healing dance during which one lets go of one's inhibitions. The name captures Kinsi's appreciation of art as a liberating and critical force. A collaborative space for artists and writers who organize workshops throughout the year and publish the *Scarfmag* annual magazine, Numbi attracts Somalis from all walks of life. Kinsi describes it as 'Somali originated', African 'diasporic' and cross-cultural, but prefers not to define it through a fixed category of ethnicity or faith. Rather, she sees Numbi as an inclusive and expansive space that goes beyond a static and narrow notion of Somaliness. This gives her more freedom, she explains, to be who she is and to discuss issues such as 'faith, queerness and borders' – the topic of her forthcoming issue of *Scarfmag*. When we met I asked her quite bluntly what it meant being Somali, but she turned the question I posed on its head. Initially I struggled to follow, but I later realized this was part of who she was and was a crucial component of her self-presentation. Like the Somali-demics, she was not only seeking to expand the definition of *Soomaalinimo* but was also opting to transcend the category altogether. 'But do you consider yourself Somali?' I insisted, perhaps wrongly, when I couldn't make sense of where she was taking me. She offered an answer to my query: 'I'm Somali, I'm Muslim ... Somaliness is just a part of me ... I'm black, but I don't see why people have to go around raising banners on who they are.' Somaliness was an embodied dimension of herself, but she was more complex and multiple than these categories. She preferred not to identify through problematized questions of Somaliness, Islam, race and nationality, but rather to explore her own way of narrating herself.

Conclusion

I began this chapter by suggesting that culture has become problematized in the contemporary moment, giving rise to a series of questions around the make-up of culture and people's engagements with it. *The Muted Cry* play, the *Niiko* dancing incident, and the Miss Somali event all raise a set of queries around young women's engagements with culture, the relationship between culture, religion, and modernity, and the delimiting of the boundaries of *Soomaalinimo*.

As we saw in the previous chapters, since colonial interventions within the Somali regions, the notion of Somali 'tradition and culture' has been increasingly transformed to a set of values, practices, objects and attitudes. More recently, however, religious knowledge has been prioritized and has come to provide a moral framework informing the process of selection among a set of cultural elements. This has become embroiled with liberal discourses and forms of governance in the UK, which posit culture as determining and constraining. Young second-generation women have employed these forms of knowledge to argue that the 'bad parts' of culture (clan ideology, FGM, etc.) ought to be discarded, and the 'good parts' (clothes, food, kin values and obligations etc.) retained. Whether some parts of culture (e.g. music and dancing) ought to be retained or abandoned remains a source of contention.

Culture has become increasingly objectified, and being Somali is treated as a set of elements not only to recognize within the self but also to externalize as an identity. In contrast to their parents, however, young Somalis have also sought to rejuvenate and rework Somali culture in distinct ways, leading older Somali women to question the authenticity of these claims and to criticize their daughters' lack of attachments to culture. Questions around authenticity have led some young people to inquire whether there is such a thing as Somali culture, and ultimately to push the boundaries of who is and is not considered a Somali. Others, I have shown, have preferred to present themselves in more fluid ways, transcending and challenging problematized questions around culture, religion and nationality. Together, these women are appropriating the authority to decide the meaning of Somaliness, taking it away from those in power and into their own hands.

These transformations, I maintain, reveal the younger women's historically specific engagements with the ethical imagination. As I have shown, young women appropriate liberal concepts of personal autonomy and authenticity, alongside ideas about culture drawn from multicultural discourses and policy frameworks, reified notions of Somali tradition and culture, and critical and anti-essentialist theories to reformulate their own understandings of themselves and their relations with others. Debates about culture become a means through which these women engage in processes of self-making. The meanings attached to culture are malleable and constantly shifting because the women's relations to culture constitute constantly refracted subject positions. Culture cannot therefore be taken as a descriptive term or analytical entity precisely because it constitutes a historically specific means of engaging with the world and with others. As I have shown throughout, engagements with Somaliness are inseparable from young women's imagined relations to Somali kin, and pious and non-pious Somali friends in London, as well as to distant kin back home, and to policymakers, or a mainstream British public.

In this chapter I have introduced the perspectives of young, not necessarily pious, Somali women who hold contrasting answers to the problematized questions around culture. For Leyla Hussein and Idil, culture is a set of values, characteristics, practices and objects, some of which are 'backwards' and can be abandoned, and some of which can be appropriated, celebrated and, in Idil's case, modernized and repackaged. Both young women emphasize liberal concepts of choice and conscious awareness as modes of subjectification. Their ultimate aim – or *telos* – is to construe themselves as autonomous and authentic subjects vis-à-vis kin, a Somali past, notions of culture and nationality and, importantly, Islam. In order to differentiate themselves through processes of dis-identification and disavowal, they associate older Somali kin with the past, but also construe them as determined by culture and as unconsciously inhabiting culture.

In contrast, for Xafsa, being Somali is not necessarily a choice, but an aspect of herself that she needs to uncover, make sense of, and either embrace or reject. Unlike Leyla and Idil, who are able to liberate themselves from the constraints of culture, being Somali is experienced as constraining for Xafsa. Somaliness constitutes a connection to her origins, place of birth and personal biography; it is an aspect of herself she feels she needs to recognize and learn to relate to. She maintains a critical distance to Somaliness, positioning herself vis-à-vis imagined relations with Somali elders and kin back home, and recognizing the fact that her relationship with Somalis and the Somali regions will always be ambiguous and fraught with tensions. Xafsa's experience reveals that being Somali is also about discovering what it means to her in the present. This may result in a realization that the Somali regions are not really 'home'. As the poet Warsan Shire stated in an interview: 'Maybe home is somewhere I'm going and never have been before.' (Shire 2012) In similar ways, Kinsi evades the question of culture and instead positions Somaliness as a category to be queried, questioned, unpacked and transcended. While Leyla and Idil's processes of self-fashioning reverse British public views of Somalis and Muslims as constrained by culture, presenting them as autonomous agents in relation to a bounded notion of culture and Islam, Kinsi critiques these essentialized and reified constructions of culture and religion.

In the next chapter I turn to another group of young women who, in contrast to Leyla, Idil, Xafsa and Kinsi, define themselves as 'practising' or 'pious'. While many of these young women also seek to engage with culture through notions of choice and autonomy, they differentiate religion from culture in ways that differ to the women presented in this chapter. Like *The Muted Cry* play they draw on reformist notions of 'religion versus culture', but they also reconstitute their relations to Islam through notions of choice, submission and affect. Their engagements with faith are embodied and affective, as well as reasoned and imagined. Contrary to dominant discourses on multiculturalism, which equate religion with culture and community, they separate religion from culture, and understand themselves differently in relation to each.

Notes

1   The campaign used the term FGM and I shall from here on employ this term. The project was implemented by the Ocean Somali Community Association (OSCA), one of the largest Somali associations in the area, and funded by the Esmeé Fairbairn Foundation and the Rosa Fund.

2 The play was written by Abdirahman Yusuf Artan and translated by Zahra Jibril. Since the original production of the play, the organizers have recorded it on film and added Somali subtitles. It has been screened on several different occasions and employed as an awareness-raising tool in workshops across London.

3 Although campaigns to eradicate FGM were also present throughout the 1980s in the former Somali Democratic Republic, these were articulated through a discourse of tradition versus modernity. Here, we can see how this has now been replaced with reformist ideas that stress religion versus culture and tradition.

4 See Johnsdotter (2007) for a discussion of female circumcision among Somalis in the diaspora.

5 I refer to Leyla with her surname 'Hussein' in order to distinguish her from Layla M who I introduce in the following chapter.

6 The term *hooyo* (mother) is used by children to refer to their mothers as well as by mothers to refer to their children.

7 When I raised this issue with Leyla Hussein, she suggested that there was hardly any point talking to old Somali men and that engaging on their terms was a futile exercise which ultimately placed their rights above those of women and girls.

8 Younger Somali women often ridiculed their mothers for considering themselves ethnically different and morally superior to other African women.

9 Somalis have tended not to intermarry with the minority Bantu and the latter have largely been socially and politically excluded and marginalized within Somali territories.

10 Somali Sideways, for example, is a social media platform set up by Londoner Mohamed Mohamud, which encourages young Somalis across the globe to share their stories alongside a photograph of themselves standing sideways. Another initiative, Elmi Magazine, has headquarters in Wandsworth, South London and aims to connect Somalis around the world and to encourage them to share success stories and inspire each other. Warya Post is also a left-leaning progressive media initiative which covers issues affecting Somalis across the globe.

11 Because some *dirac* are made of semi-transparent fabric, practising women prefer not to wear it outside female-only events.

12 The Republic of Somaliland, which declared independence in 1991, remains internationally unrecognized. The issue of independence is hotly contested among Somalis in the diaspora.

13 Interestingly, however, as the Miss Somali event revealed, national divisions (between Somalia and Somaliland) are not viewed as being as 'backwards' as clan divisions, which are often seen as traditional and incompatible with being modern.

14 Mandeeq is the name of the she-camel that symbolically represents the Somali nation in Somali poetry. (See http://themaandeeq.com/about-maandeeq/).

15 While similar arguments have been made by academics (Besteman 1995, 2012; Eno and Eno 2008; Ahmed 1995), rarely have they been heard outside of these circles.

16 The *madhibaan* (also referred to derogatively as *midgaan*) are considered a lower clan by majority clan Somalis and, like other 'minority clans', they have been hugely discriminated against within the Somali regions.

CHAPTER SIX

Mosque hopping: Seeking Islamic knowledge in London

As we waited patiently for Layla M's mother to make her way down from the flat, Quranic recitation blared out of the car stereo, drowning out the children's bickering.[1] Layla sat behind the wheel, her head resting against the car window, with me and her three younger siblings squashed into the back seats. It was a warm summer evening during Ramadan 2010 and, having filled our stomachs with samosas and plenty of spiced rice and meat and cleaned the kitchen following a long afternoon of preparations, we were running late, as usual, for *tarawih* prayers.[2] Because Layla was the only licensed driver in the family, her filial duties often required her to taxi around different members of her large family to mosques, weddings, tuition classes or the homes of friends and family. Luckily, that day we were only dropping them off at the local Al-Huda Somali mosque, a few minutes' drive from their flat (Figure 7).[3] When Layla stopped her car in front of the mosque, her younger siblings jumped out excitedly, ran and waved goodbye while their mother struggled to catch up. As we sped off to the East London Mosque (Figure 8), I glanced back to see them slipping in with many other latecomers. Layla and I picked up a couple of friends on the way and finally parked the car in front of the mosque. The prayers had only just begun and we squeezed in among the crowd to find a spot to stand in, touching shoulders with strangers as we joined the prayers. Throughout Ramadan, Layla and her friends – a group of young newly practising Somali women in their mid-twenties and early thirties – prayed in most of the large mosques in London with a diversity of other Muslims of different ages and ethnicities. This, what they called, 'mosque hopping' took them to some of the more popular mosques, including those at Goodge Street, Finsbury Park, Regents Park and Brixton. After *iftar* (fast-breaking meal) on most evenings, I drove around with Layla as she picked up her friends on the way to various mosques; this sometimes meant driving from Tower Hamlets to Newham and then into the city centre. Most evenings, we experienced a new style of recitation, a different form of prayer or a new setting. Rarely did the women consider attending the local Somali mosque, which was a familiar and regular space of worship and sociality for their mothers and younger siblings. Layla preferred not to attend these gatherings; she didn't like being recognized by her kin, as this distracted her from her worship. 'Everyone's like, "oh you're the daughter of so and so". ... They judge me and ask me why I'm not wearing the whole black *jilbab* thing!' she explained. The last time she had attended she had done so solely to please her father, who was eager for her to listen to a Somali talk, but she had decided to wear the *niqab* (face veil) so as not to be recognized.

Layla and her mother were not unique in having different preferences, nor was Layla's Ramadan routine exceptional. In fact, most young second-generation practising Somali women rarely attended classes or lectures at the local Somali mosques, choosing instead to drive round London to attend a wide range of events and classes organized by independent organizations or mosques. Such sessions were delivered in English and aimed at younger Muslims. This 'mosque hopping' was a regular weekend activity for many young Somali women, and 'seeking knowledge' was characterized by a relentless search for what they deemed authoritative knowledge.

The following two chapters examine the experiences of young women like Layla who are, in their words, 'seeking knowledge' with the aim of 'practising' Islam. Unlike the women in Chapter 5, these young people have recently begun to engage with Islamic forms of knowledge available in London, with the aim of implementing it to the self. This chapter explores how 'mosque hopping' is indicative of these young women's shifting modes of engagement with religious knowledge, changing ideas of what constitutes authoritative knowledge, and transforming expectations of what knowledge is expected to provide.

The chapter is organized as follows. It first presents these young women's narratives of seeking knowledge and becoming more active in their faith, exploring how these develop in reaction to their mothers' engagements with Islam. There has been a tendency in the literature on Islamic reform to portray young Muslims as engaged in a reflexive, self-conscious and rational form of Islam, whereas their parents are bound by a non-reflexive, embodied engagement with knowledge (Jouili and Amir-Moazami 2006). This juxtaposition, however, does not fully capture the experiences of both the older generation (as we saw in Chapter 4) and the younger group, for whom reason constitutes only one mode of engagement. Furthermore, rather than viewing young people's emphasis on reasoning and self-conscious reflection as indicative of generational differences, I suggest that it should be treated as a strategy of 'authentication' that is a constitutive part of a tradition of renewal and reform (Deeb 2006). This strategy is employed by young people to differentiate themselves from their mothers and from older 'traditional' kin.

The second section describes the varied landscape of Islamic knowledge in London, and unpacks the processes involved in 'hopping' or selecting among mosques, scholars, classes and institutes. I elaborate on three intersecting modes of subjectification (Foucault 1985: 26–8) that are crucial to these women's engagements with knowledge: (i) a concept of choice and autonomy; (ii) a submission to Islamic forms of reasoning and to structures of authority; and (iii) an experience of affect. The ability of particular forms of knowledge to facilitate or transmit these modes determines whether these young women consider them authoritative. An experience of affect, I argue, is crucial to establishing a sustained and committed engagement with knowledge. However, this experience is difficult to sustain and often results in short-lived engagements with a particular source of knowledge. In examining one of the young women's most popular scholars, the UK-based *Sheikh* Ibrahim, I suggest that authority rests not only on his ability to draw on Islamic scholarship and on what these young women term 'Western' ideas of knowledge, but also on his skill in engendering affect and a feeling of potential self-transformation.

FIGURE 7 *Al-Huda Mosque in Stepney Green, East London.*
Photograph taken by the author.

Finally, I elaborate on the intersections between these three
modes of engagement by drawing out the ways in which these
young practising women debate different criteria for assessing the
validity and authority of knowledge. 'Mosque hopping' is ultimately
structured around these three modes, but the relationships between
them are often a source of disagreement and negotiation. Through
debates with like-minded friends, these young women reinforce
normative ideas about Islamic knowledge while including and
articulating a range of new criteria on which their assessments are
based.

Recent sociological and anthropological scholarship on Islam
in Europe has argued that, with the growing objectification,
fragmentation and pluralization of authorizing discourses and
institutions, Islam has become increasingly individualized. Scholars
have treated individualization as an indication that Muslims are
engaging in debates, asserting their interpretations and hence
integrating and adapting to European structures (Cesari 2003;
Mandaville 2001, 2003). Others have investigated individualization
as a dimension of agency, as a social fact to be observed and
measured. Roy (2004), for example, has argued that globalization
and Westernization, and the concomitant loss of social authority

FIGURE 8 *East London Mosque and Maryam Centre in Whitechapel,*
East London. Photograph taken by the author.

and a system of social and juridical coercion, has resulted in the
task of seeking knowledge falling to individuals. A democratization
of the religious sphere, Roy cautions, does not, however, necessarily
result in 'critical' liberal or secular discourse. Nonetheless, it has
led to a privatization of religiosity that stresses the individual and
the inner self and a shift from a focus on norms to an emphasis on
ethics and values (ibid.: 191).

My interest is not in unravelling whether young practising
Somalis are becoming more individualized, liberal or European.
Rather, following recent scholarship, I would argue that knowledge
is a condition for becoming pious, and engagement with knowledge
is, therefore, both deliberative and disciplinary (Hirschkind 2006;
Jouili and Amir-Moazami 2006). As Jacobsen (2010: 293–4) notes
in relation to Muslims in Norway, the fragmentation of authority
structures does not result in the autonomous appropriation of

the Islamic tradition, but in 'a complex and structured process of contestation' in which authorities are simultaneously subjected to, challenged and resisted. Processes of individualization are, thus, modes of engagement that should not be divorced from, nor juxtaposed with, institutionalized Islam (Peter 2006; Amir-Moazami and Salvatore 2003). In a similar fashion, 'mosque hopping' and the practice of selecting from different forms of knowledge in London should not be seen as disembodied from authorizing discourses and Islamic structures of authority. Building on these insights, I suggest that seeking knowledge entails drawing on orthodox Islamic texts, teachings and structures of authority, but also on forms of knowledge drawn from, for example, university experiences or public culture. These engagements with new forms of knowledge, I argue, enable these young women to reimagine their relations to self and others, and to articulate new ways of being.

The anthropological study of religious authority has tended to prioritize the views of preachers, scholars and figures of authority (Hirschkind 2006; Gaffney 1994; Hoesterey 2016) at the expense of investigating how ordinary people engage with, negotiate and make sense of figures and structures of authority. By contrast, this chapter prioritizes young women's own modes of assessing and attaching themselves to authoritative knowledge, and explores the possibilities that these processes provide.

New beginnings: Layla and Saynab

Layla was a small child when her family travelled from present-day Somaliland to the UK and settled in East London. Having attended a local secondary school whose students were predominantly Bengali Muslims, Layla went to a university outside of London that had a largely non-Muslim student body. She often found herself having to 'defend Islam and explain about Islam ... especially against Islamophobic comments'. It was then that she started, in her words, 'seeking knowledge' – that is reading Islamic texts, listening to online talks, and attending classes, lectures and events organized across the city.

In retrospect, Layla felt that, as a teenager, she had learnt a lot of facts but had never been taught 'what Islam was all about'. In her opinion, her knowledge had been superficial, focused around rules and obligations rather than on the reasons why certain practices were necessary. 'I used to go to madrasa as a child, but I don't think I was taught Islam properly. It didn't make me understand the religion at all ... reading Arabic, a language I didn't even understand!' she explained. After leaving university and deciding to re-engage with her faith, Layla began distancing herself from the mosques she had attended as a child.

As we saw in the initial vignette, she preferred not to attend the local Somali mosque with her mother but instead drove with her friends to the larger, more diverse, mosques across the city. She did not find the forms of learning in Somali mosques particularly engaging or relevant to her life. Often delivered in Somali, she felt the language, style and content did not suit her 'Western' tastes. She also thought that the women in the mosque were 'cliquey', not welcoming to non-Somalis, and excessively preoccupied with cultural concerns; they spent too much time judging each other and discussing clan and family matters – all things Layla found irrelevant and distracting. In short, Layla claimed, Somali mosques had a different notion of religious knowledge to her own, and tended to confuse religion with Somali culture. In contrast, many of the sessions she began attending were organized by independent institutes in rented spaces across London, and were managed and led predominantly by young second-generation Muslims. It was during these sessions that she met newly practising women like Saynab. These young women were brought together by their mutual interest in seeking knowledge, but they were also at similar stages in their lives and they shared experiences of generational differences.

Saynab was also originally from what is now Somaliland, but she had also lived for some time in Ethiopia, where she had learnt to speak English fluently. She arrived in the UK as a teenager and settled with her mother and siblings in East London in the mid-1990s. She completed her degree in London, began working as a consultant and soon moved out of the council flat she shared with her family in a working-class area of East London to live in an upper-class neighbourhood in West London. She explained: 'I used to think all I wanted was a good job, loads of money, a car and beautiful clothes.' But this life outlook changed on one of her shopping trips with a friend. She was walking around the designer section of a large department store when she suddenly felt dizzy and collapsed. When Saynab regained consciousness, she realized that an ambulance had been called, but it was not there to rescue her. Rather bizarrely, another woman had also collapsed in the shop at the same time, and was in a far more critical condition. 'I thought I was going to die,' she explained, 'but I was saved, I'd been given a second chance.' Although she never explained the reasons for her collapse, Saynab interpreted the incident as a near-death and life-changing experience, which forced her to reflect on her self and move back to live alone with her mother in East London and in close proximity to some of her siblings. At that point, her consultancy was no longer as lucrative as it had been initially, and she was beginning to doubt whether she had made the right career decisions. She was also in her late twenties and was beginning to think seriously about marriage (see Chapter 8). Soon after, she began praying and donning the *hijab*: 'I had to give up my friends, my life ... I changed completely ... I used to think success was working hard, making money, but it's different now. I don't regret a thing and I don't miss it at all.'

Like other first-generation Somali women, whose experiences I described in Chapter 4, Saynab's mother had become more religious since moving to the UK. She had begun reading the *Qur'an* in Somali on a regular basis and donning the *jilbab*. When Saynab returned home, her mother welcomed her with open arms, delighted that she had at long last embarked on the religious path. Together they started attending *Qur'an* classes in Somali at a local mosque. However, Saynab soon began to attend classes that were run in English and aimed at young multi-ethnic Muslims, thus distancing herself – like Layla – from her mother's approach to Islam.

The differences between her engagement with knowledge and that of her mother were captured by the following comment: 'My mum is very disciplined; she goes to talks at 8:30 am, fasts every Thursday. But we're also very different. My mum works from the outside-in. She's more about doing things, praying, *hijab*, actions, and all about the *haram* and *halal*.' In Saynab's eyes, her mother had learnt to correct her practice of Islam but had not worked on her spiritual and emotional connection with God. Nor was she concerned with understanding the reasons behind certain practices, which was crucial to Saynab and her practising friends. This emphasis on exteriority, on rules and regulations, was seen as lacking the reflexivity, choice and reasoning necessary for a 'proper' engagement with Islam. This uncritical adoption of rules and norms was also often described as 'cultural'.

A similar sentiment was expressed by one of Saynab's other Somali friends, Xamda, who explained how she had recently started encouraging her mother and younger sisters to practise Islam more seriously and to pray regularly. However, she continued to experience a divergence in the way she and her mother practised:

> I think for my mum and her generation it is sometimes a by-product of who they are. It's a given. It comes with the culture. She didn't start wearing *hijab* until she came here. So I think when she came here she made more of an effort to practise her religion. But with our generation we made an active intent to go to lessons, classes, to learn the *Qur'an*, the meaning. That's not present in my mum and her generation.

Xamda's mother practised not because she intellectually, critically and spiritually engaged with knowledge, but because she had inherited it from her culture on arrival in the UK, where she unquestioningly accepted knowledge from Somali religious authority figures. Xamda contrasted her mother's 'effort to practise' in London with her own 'intent to understand'; her mother had begun implementing practices without fully and consciously reasoning about the meaning of scriptures. Xamda was, in fact, downplaying some of the changes experienced by the older generation (which I described in previous chapters) in order to position herself as engaged with Islamic knowledge in a reflexive and authentic way.

In furthering these critiques, these young women employed a global discourse of 'religion versus culture' that separates an authentic and universal Islam from tradition and culture (Deeb 2006; Ewing 2008; Jacobson 1998). As we saw in Chapter 5, young Somalis use the discourse to distance themselves from their kin by claiming that the latter engage with culture and religion through habit rather than informed choice and reason. In this chapter, I expand this argument further and explore how young pious Somali women use a similar discourse to critique their mothers' engagements with *religious* practices, in particular, their failure to prioritize a personal relationship with God. For example, these young women criticize their mothers for attending Somali mosques on the assumption that they do so out of habit rather than reasoned choice or a proper connection with God (see also Chapter 7).

The criticism directed at the older generation is also a reaction to the public and political discourse around the demise of multiculturalism that has come to dominate debate on migration and diversity in Europe. In contrast to the women in Chapter 5, who seek to establish a choosing relationship with regard to both Somaliness and Islam, these pious women prioritize religion over culture, and consider these categories as qualitatively different. As I described in Chapter 1, multiculturalism has come under attack for its supposedly 'divisive character': for separating communities, undermining social cohesion, and fracturing national identity (Grillo 2007: 985). By emphasizing 'mosque hopping', these young women are engaging with these ideas and demonstrating that they are not 'segregated' but are, in fact, able to move freely and independently across the city, and participate in religious education with Muslims from a range of ethnicities. Saynab's return to East London is presented as a choice that by no means precludes her from travelling beyond the East End. By contrast, these young women's mothers are positioned as 'ghettoized' within Somali mosques and unable to move beyond the confines of their ethnic and cultural group. They are seen to be determined by, and imprisoned within, their culture.

New forms of knowledge

As Layla and Saynab's narratives reveal, becoming more actively Muslim involves first and foremost seeking knowledge with newly forged friends. Stories and experiences of 'practising' are voiced and shared within these new contexts, enabling these young women to insert their own personal narratives within a larger collective narrative of the *umma* (community of believers). Young practising women often speak about 'seeking knowledge' as a driving force behind their quest to practise Islam at a particular stage in their lives. The phrase is employed to refer to a range of practices – from reading or listening to Islamic sources, to attending classes and lectures – as well as to differentiate their engagement with knowledge from that of their parents. Education has been central to Islamic reform and, as I elaborate below, knowledge (*'ilm*) in the Islamic tradition is inseparable from faith and action. Studying is seen as a means of cultivating faith, and faith emerges and can grow through knowledge.

Sheikh Ibrahim – a particular favourite of the young women – described the essence of 'seeking knowledge' in one of his lectures:

> The first words that *Allah* revealed to the Prophet were the words, 'to recite'. And not a recitation that is based on custom or culture, but read in the name of Your Lord. ... The Prophet has stressed the importance of knowledge. We're an *umma* of knowledge. We're an *umma* of learning.

The *sheikh*'s statement encapsulates the important connection between knowledge and the transcendent *umma*. It echoes many of these young women's critiques of their mothers and their emphasis on abandoning culture or custom for a transcendental form of knowledge.

As I pointed out earlier, many young women found the learning they received as children – with its focus on the recitation of the *Qur'an* and on rules and regulations – unsatisfactory. These teachings had taught them to perform certain obligations, but had not encouraged them to fully comprehend their faith. For many other young women, 'seeking knowledge' signifies a jettisoning of Somali culture and their families as sites of learning in favour of learning through the medium of English among young Muslims of a similar age in a wider transcendent *umma*. In so doing, they turn religion into an object of intellectual inquiry (Jacobsen 2010; Roy 2004). As Khadiija – a young Somali woman who had been practising for over seven years – explained:

> With Somalis, when you ask questions to the elders they answer in a very rigid way. They say: you have to do it cause you'll go to hell. That doesn't do it for me, so I got in touch with other Muslim friends and started going to conferences, lectures, reading books ... and that's when I discovered that there were Islamic books written in English. Tapes, DVDs, videos, everything.

It is the importance attached to choosing from a diverse range of forms of knowledge and modes of argumentation and interpretation that most notably distinguishes these young women from their mothers. Most of them 'hop' around the 'field' of Islamic education within which, as Bowen (2010: 108–9) describes, teachers and institutes differentiate themselves by degree of professionalization, choice of language and choice of sources. They experiment with different forms and styles of learning, arguing that each fulfils a different need and attends to a different aspect of their self-development. I elaborate each of the different forms of Islamic education in turn.

First, and most importantly, these young women have benefitted from the recent surge in independent institutes and organizations that have flourished in London in the last decade. Like many young practising women, Khadiija began attending conferences, lectures and classes run mostly by independent Islamic organizations, which she discovered thanks to her newly acquired network of friends. Most young Somali women do not understand Arabic and therefore attend places of learning which emphasize the English medium. These organizations – which are based across London in places that range from rented conference centres to privately owned buildings – are becoming increasingly popular among a range of young second-generation Muslims in the UK. Although the South Asian *Deobandi* and *Barelvi* traditions of reform are the most prevalent in East London, these organizations represent a wide range of Islamic 'schools of thought' and scholarship from across the Muslim world (Birt 2005a; Werbner 2004; Bowen 2016). Teaching styles and methods are diverse and include learning directly from Islamic scriptures, approaching the Islamic sciences from a range of religious texts, and employing texts to focus on a particular theme or problem usually relevant to the lives of Muslims in the UK. The latter form of teaching and learning is becoming increasingly popular among young Muslims. Employing an approach similar to that found in British higher education, these independent organizations emphasize critical evaluation, self-directed learning and topic-based teaching that utilizes a variety of sources (Gilliat-Ray 2006: 63). Many of the young women attend institutions in which teaching is action oriented and generalist, with an emphasis on self-improvement and *da'wa* (spreading awareness of the faith). Most of the young pious women I observed were concerned not with gaining an official qualification but with learning in order to further their own personal development. It should also be said that many of these young women do not have extensive knowledge of the differences between reformist movements or schools of thought and, as I explain below, categorize knowledge according to a different set of criteria.

Second, young women may also occasionally attend mosques or institutes that provide traditional teachings in Arabic and the Islamic sciences.[4] Many of the young practising women I interacted with during my fieldwork were attending a *tajwid* course and a couple were learning Arabic in order to engage directly with Islamic texts and scriptures. Only one of the young women I encountered was training to become a recognized scholar (*'alima*); she had signed up for an intensive evening course with an independent institute in East London.

Third, while formal lessons provide much of the initial knowledge for newly practising women, young pious women often organize *halaqa* (Islamic study circle) sessions as an informal means of sharing Islamic knowledge with, and learning from, like-minded individuals. These sessions also strengthen the idea of gaining authentic knowledge by engaging with other young Muslim friends, which is in contrast with the experience of the older generation who learn from other Somalis or from kin. Habibah, a twenty-year-old Bengali woman, for example, organized a fortnightly circle in her local community centre for two months. She invited most of her practising and non-practising friends, including many of my young pious Somali friends. She hoped that in inviting non-practising friends she might encourage them to begin seeking and implementing knowledge. Every fortnight, a different young woman would chair the session and give a talk based on lectures or courses they had recently attended: Layla spoke about knowledge and prayer; Saynab about the diseases of the heart; Habibah about *iman* (faith) and the difficulties of practising. 'These sessions are great, cause we can discuss the issues we face as British Muslims practising our faith,' Habibah explained. Her comment highlights the differences between these sessions and those of their mothers; these *halaqa* sessions were based around a particular topic that was relevant to these young women's everyday lives and addressed the challenges of practising Islam in the UK.

Similarly, another young practising woman in her thirties, organized *sira* (the study of the life of the Prophet) sessions at her house on Sunday afternoons. These sessions consisted of reading and taking notes on a passage from *Muhammad: Man and Prophet* by Abdil Salahi, relating it to one's own life, and discussing how best one could apply and embody the Prophet's behaviour and characteristics. These sessions lasted less than an hour, but the rest of the afternoon provided an opportunity for socializing, relaxing and, often, sharing food and watching television.

Fourth, independent study is also crucial to the process of 'seeking knowledge', and many of my interlocutors shared and circulated MP3 recordings of various scholars, YouTube and Halaltube videos, Internet sites, books and DVDs. Layla, for example, would often fall asleep at night listening to Hamza Yusuf's talks, whereas her friend Aniiso would walk around the streets of East London with the words of Anwar Awlaki in her ears, and Saynab did the housework listening to Quranic recitation.[5] Through this media, these young women listened to English-speaking scholars from places as diverse as America and Saudi Arabia, reinforcing a feeling of connection to a wider transnational community of knowledge. Carrying electronic recordings on their phones and iPods allowed them to select whichever speaker they found most emotionally engaging at a particular moment in time, thus enabling them to switch easily depending on their personal moods and tastes.

Finally, many also consumed non-Islamic sources of knowledge and applied them to their practice of Islam. On one occasion, Khadiija explained to me how she had recently taken to attending self-help courses on commitment, discipline and adventure. 'I don't think they clash with religion at all for me,' she explained, highlighting how different sources of knowledge could be employed as long as they were used with the ultimate purpose of disciplining the self and inculcating pious dispositions. Similarly, Ifraax, a young 26-year-old practising woman, often consulted self-development blogs. One of these was *The Change Blog,* which offers advice on how to go about leading a 'radically different' life. These practices indicate that what is at stake is not solely related to Islamic reform but is part of a broader process of striving. Engagements with reformist knowledge are appealing precisely because they offer a means for radical change. Knowledge is meant to assist these young women, at least temporarily, in their processes of aspiring for new possibilities and ways of being.

In the following section, I elaborate on this theme by exploring in detail the content of the most popular set of classes attended by these young women: those offered by *Sheikh* Ibrahim. I point to the importance of the experience of affect, which is grounded in but not determined by the Islamic tradition, in the women's engagement with what they deem to be authoritative knowledge.

Sheikh Ibrahim: Affect and self-transformation

A few days after *Eid-al-Fitr* in September 2010, news spread that a new institute (Institute A) was opening a new academy in London. Institute A is known for its close connections with Sufi centres of Islamic learning in Tarim, Yemen, but its teachers in the UK are associated with a number of different schools of thought. The lessons offered in London were free, although course material cost a single payment of £50. As part of a three-year course aimed at young professionals, the academy was running weekly evening lessons on the Islamic sciences from 7.00 to 9.00 pm in a rented building in central London.⁶ Advertised by a professional website and a Facebook group, the course was based around Islamic scholarly texts and traditional styles of learning. It was intended solely for the acquisition of personal knowledge and offered no final qualification. The timing and venue were convenient for my friends, who had been searching for a regular course that would fit around their work schedules. When they learnt that *Sheikh* Ibrahim Osi-Efa would be delivering some of the classes, they jumped at the opportunity to sign up.

The *sheikh* was well known and respected not only for the depth of his knowledge and his personal piety but also for his charisma. Born and raised in Liverpool he has also studied in Yemen, Syria and Mauritania and is the founder of several Islamic initiatives in the UK. Renowned for his knowledge of the Islamic sciences, he was a source of inspiration for many of these young women, who often travelled across London to attend his talks or exchanged online videos and recordings of his lectures. Every week for a year, I made the car journey from East London to Euston with Layla and her pious Somali friends. With *nashid* (Islamic vocal music) playing on the car stereo, these journeys to and from *Sheikh* Ibrahim's classes provided us not only with an opportunity to socialize but also with the chance to share our personal experiences and opinions of the classes.

On arrival at the first session of the course, we were directed to the basement. There, the main classroom was bustling with activity: some were finishing off their *maghrib* (sunset) prayers, while others were catching up with friends they hadn't seen since the start of

Ramadan. As was typical of these events, the room was split in two by large boards that separated the women from the men. Rows of chairs on both sides faced a stage furnished with a table, chair and microphone for the teacher and, at the back, a large projection screen. We signed our name at the entrance and moved swiftly past the men's section to sit in the final rows of the women's area. Many of the women were between the ages of twenty and thirty and from a range of different backgrounds, including British converts. We exchanged a few brief greetings with some of the female attendees from other talks organized by Institute A that I had attended earlier that year, and the class started promptly at seven o'clock.

Sheikh Ibrahim's classes took place every fortnight and were the most popular and best attended of the classes on the course. The *sheikh* dedicated each class to one or more chapters of the *Book of Numbers*. Written by Al Imam Muhammad Umar Bahraq al Hadrami, the book touches on various aspects of Islam, ranging from jurisprudence (*fiqh*) to spirituality (*tasawwuf*). The chapters are based around a poem and are arranged in numerical order to aid memorization of the text – something the *sheikh* encouraged the students to pledge to do throughout the course and about which he circulated a weekly email reminder. Throughout the class, most of the women took extensive notes and some recorded the lectures on their phones.

On the first day, the *sheikh* sat behind the table, his PowerPoint presentation projected behind him, and began by reciting the *basmala*[7] and a couple of verses from the *Qur'an*. His introductory class started by outlining the importance of knowledge: 'Knowledge comes with responsibility to teach and practise ... it is concomitant with action,' he explained before going on to contrast secular education with religious knowledge and critiquing the Islamic studies courses offered by British universities:

> The problem with studying Islamic knowledge at places like SOAS is that their mission statement has nothing to do with creating God-fearing people. This is not religious knowledge. Before you study subjects like the natural sciences, you must study the sacred. This will protect you from incorrect interpretations of the universe.

The *sheikh* then proceeded by supporting his statement with textual evidence from the *Qur'an* and *hadith*, citing the chain of transmission which is crucial to establishing the authenticity of Islamic sources of knowledge. According to the *sheikh*, religious knowledge is different to secular knowledge. It does not entail an accumulation of facts or the development of particular skills but involves cultivating a 'religious intelligence'. Knowledge creates 'God-fearing people' and thus facilitates the individual's connection with God and with the transcendence of the afterlife and the *umma*. If applied appropriately, it provides the 'protection' and 'sustenance for the soul' that can lead one to paradise; those who 'seek knowledge' are ultimately rewarded. Furthermore, knowledge enables the believer to accept the volatility of this life and project himself or herself into the future.

In the subsequent session, the *sheikh* moved on to a discussion of *wa'ad* (admonition). As the course outline informed us, this class aimed to 'nurture and create an environment which arouses heedless hearts and invigorates the resolve of the slothful'. One of the purposes of studying, the *sheikh* explained, was to 'place knowledge inside the heart … in order to motivate, to create sincere intentions'. The purpose of *wa'ad*, he explained, was to dilate the heart and make it more receptive to receiving knowledge. Drawing on Islamic traditional pedagogical models, which presume a particular relationship between emotions, virtues and actions (Mahmood 2005: 140), the *sheikh* proceeded to instruct his audience on how to experience knowledge:

> One of the signs of the affected heart is the heart that begins to tremble, that is shaken by words. When the eyes fill with tears, the words inspire love for *Allah* and fear and hope for the afterlife. Knowledge should hit you inwards in the heart, and the eyes will start to swell as an outward sign.

Again, this statement was followed by textual evidence from the *Qur'an* and *hadith*, which he projected on the screen, allowing the students to note down the references. He then delivered his own *wa'ad* (admonition): 'Humans live in hope and fear of staying in this world, and are never ready to let go. But we need good deeds. We need metaphysical provisions for a long journey ahead. But time on this *dunya* (this world) is short! Death is near! Don't procrastinate!' After giving this warning, the *sheikh* proceeded with a long, captivating and emotionally charged description of the Day of Judgement. The tone and content of each sentence were measured carefully so as to generate tension. His voice gradually ascended in some sentences, but he interspersed this technique with a sporadic peppering of bellows, often causing jolts in the women. His eyes widened, and he became visibly more agitated. He used his hands wildly to emphasize points, even banging the table for issues of particular pertinence. His imagery also created stirrings in the audience, which were to be expected given his vivid depiction of the numerous disbelievers and sinners who would slip into the depths of hell as they cross the *sirat* (bridge or road) that traverses the summit of hellfire: 'Some will cross in a wink of an eye, like lightening, or a tornado. ... Others will slip before they even set foot on it, with the dogs at the bottom, commanded to catch those who fall! All this relates to how quickly you implement knowledge here on earth!' His deep solemn voice, echoing across the room, made the audience shiver.

The talk finished with a long *du'a'* (supplicatory prayer), after which we all packed away our belongings and left in silence, visibly shaken by his performance. 'Wow, that was intense!' Maryan, another practising Somali friend and student on the course, whispered as we made our way out. 'I needed that! It freaked me out alright! It's good though, it makes me wake up and do things ... won't be sleeping through *fajr* (dawn prayer) tomorrow.' Ifraax, her eyes damp from tears, nodded and said: 'That was inspiring, *masha'Allah* ... you really feel you're there on the Day of Judgement, like you've lived it!' As intended, the *sheikh*'s talk had affected their 'heedless hearts', inspiring fear and hope for the afterlife. We walked outside and, as we sat in the car ready to go, Saynab continued to ponder: 'I'm so scared of going to hell. So so scared. I really don't do enough.'

This form of admonitory talk (*wa'ad*) aims to cultivate a sensibility towards death and instil the emotions and virtues of fear, sadness and humility. Hirschkind (2006), in his ethnography of cassette sermons in Cairo, elaborates on the importance that members of the Islamic revival attach to cultivating a sensibility towards death, which they achieve through a series of techniques and practices of 'death remembrance'. Sermons encourage believers to learn about, and reflect on, death in order to live with 'dead eyes', that is, with the constant presence of death. They enable a 'tasting' (*dhawaq*) of death, which involves constituting death as a habit of thought, heart and body. The processes of refashioning one's sensory experience and infusing one's sensibility towards death with the correct emotions of fear, sadness and humility are thought to open the believer's heart to God (*inshirah*).

As in Hirschkind's (2006: 188–92) description, the pedagogical materials consumed by these young women emphasize some aspects of death more than others. For example, these teachings often stress the imminence of the eschatological future by focusing on the cataclysmic events that are thought to precede and anticipate the 'Final Day'. Ifraax explained to me how, having read Al-Ghazali's book *Remembrance of Death and the Afterlife*, she had begun to regularly conjure and 'make real' an image of the afterlife. Her narration remained very close to the scriptures:

> Then the bridge terrifies me, 'as thin as a string and as sharp as a needle'. People will literally be falling straight into hell from there. It's really freaky. Some people won't even make it … and I always think about the *sirat*. Your *iman* (faith) will be your torch, here on your forehead, so the more you have the easier it will be to cross.

Perplexed as to why Ifraax would spend so much time thinking about and visualizing death, I questioned her about it. She replied:

> I want to know. I want to be prepared for it so that I'm not confused when it happens. It motivates me if I know what's going to happen to us. I'm so scared about not knowing what's going to happen to me, about what God's going to do to me. I think about it so much. I read about it, and it freaks me out that I want to be prepared. It makes me scared but that's a good thing. At the same time, it makes me hopeful that I might make it to *janna* (paradise) instead.

Although fear is more frequently emphasized in pedagogical settings, where it is thought to have a strong impact on moral action, as Ifraax stressed, a believer ought to oscillate between hope (*al-raja'a*), fear (*al-khawf*) and love (*al-hubb*). These emotions and virtues should not be assumed to arise spontaneously but may be cultivated as both modalities and motives for pious action (Mahmood 2005: 140).

Sheikh Ibrahim often complemented these admonitory sermons with his more frequent talks on love (*al-hubb*) for God and the Prophet. At one of the many lectures we attended on the Prophet, *Sheikh* Ibrahim explained how learning about the Messenger was a way of immersing oneself in the 'beauty of the divine'. These talks often revolved around the *hadith* of the Prophet's character (*shama'il*) or stories from the *sira* (life of the Prophet). Drawing on traditional Islamic theology, the *sheikh* explained how the Prophet embodied the divine qualities of God: he manifested attributes on earth that were otherwise incomprehensible to the human mind. For the believer, knowledge of the Prophet should, by extension, also entail knowledge of God. A personal connection with, and love for, the 'One Being' could be established through this knowledge, but this connection could also serve as a means of 'knowing Him' better. As the *sheikh* claimed, the faculty of reason (*'aql*) had its limits and one could not comprehend God solely with the use of the intellect. Hence, knowledge of God is not solely an accumulation of facts, but involves the cultivation of emotions (e.g. love, hope and fear) and virtuous dispositions (e.g. humility) that will make one's heart more receptive to God (Hirschkind 2006; Mahmood 2005).

However, as *sheikh* Ibrahim explained as he highlighted the connections between knowledge, faith and action, knowing must result in virtuous actions. Maryan appreciated the importance of moving 'swiftly to good deeds' and was cautious of the responsibilities that come with acquiring knowledge; but this understanding made her wary of attending too many classes. 'I'm not coming to this talk today,' she explained to me one day, 'I just need to implement what I've learnt so far, instead of piling and piling knowledge. You know, I'll be held accountable for this, I'll be questioned on what I did with all that knowledge.'

While the *sheikh* had alluded to the importance of accepting the limits of reason and the intellect (*'aql*), in another class he drew on the work of Al-Ghazali and also elaborated on the value of *'aql*. Reason, he claimed, should serve the purpose of fashioning a pious self by channelling and employing the 'good' to tackle the 'bad forces' within the heart: 'Religion comes from within. ... If good intentions occur within it [the heart], then the body, by extension, will move in a manner deemed appropriate.'

Following the classes on the Prophet, as well as those on admonition, the young women left feeling excited and uplifted. This was a reaction I observed on many other occasions and following classes on a range of different topics. 'Wow I needed that *iman* boost! That was amazing,' Saynab commented. 'That was really exciting, I feel better.' She had been feeling 'low in *iman*' of late, and was certain that attending one of *Sheikh* Ibrahim's classes would help her recover her lost enthusiasm and encourage her to pray more regularly. Another young woman, Nadiifo, similarly commented: 'These kinds of talks, they're good for me, really inspiring. I need the inspiring intellectual side of it, thinking through, working to better myself.' Nadiifo had been among the first to introduce us to *Sheikh* Ibrahim, having persuaded her friends to attend by emphasizing the scholar's ability to evoke emotions of love for God: '*Sheikh* Ibrahim really has that love for *Allah*, for the *diin* (religion), and he transmits it to you. You know, spirituality is so important. Everything else comes easily if you have love in your heart ... things like praying, wearing *hijab*, they'll seem like nothing if you have love for the Prophet and for *Allah*.' Similarly, Layla, with whom I attended a similar class on the Prophet, added: 'The depth of his knowledge is incredible, *masha'Allah*. And he has so much love for the Prophet, and for *Allah*. You can feel it. You really feel it inside you ... the way he describes the Prophet, the way he is.'

Through the idiom of '*iman*', the young women were describing a feeling of potential connection with the transcendent: the visceral, spiritually uplifting affect that they experienced by attending these classes. They often discussed and compared their respective levels of *iman*; 'I'm on a high' and 'I'm not feeling it' were oft-repeated phrases, which corresponded to individual moods as well as varying levels of commitment, motivation or inspiration. Ifraax compared and contrasted this affect with music: 'Music makes you experience highs, you feel so good, positive, like everything's alright. It's like when you feel you're high in *iman*, but it also darkens your heart, and it takes away time between you and *Allah*. You're meant to feel those emotions for the sake of *Allah*, not music.' Although the same emotions were evoked, music – unlike religious talks – did not connect them with *Allah* and was therefore the 'wrong' cause for their feelings. The importance of the transmission of this emotional experience from these classes was captured by Maryan's comment: 'Even if I'm not listening to the talk it's good to come to the classes ... to get some inspiration.' According to *Sheikh* Ibrahim, Islamic knowledge ought to be approached in specific ways: by employing reason 'correctly' and learning to implement knowledge into their everyday practices, thus altering interior attitudes and dispositions.

As I have shown, these young women employ traditional Islamic conventions regarding emotions, actions and reason in their projects of ethical self-fashioning. In particular, Ifraax's comments reveal how she appreciates the importance of inculcating the virtuous dispositions and emotions that motivate her into action and make her more receptive to God. While her experience indicates that she is rehearsing these pedagogical conventions, the affective experience of these emotions differs from the formal understanding of emotions that both Mahmood and Hirschkind develop in their analyses. These young women are taking these conventions from various teachings and texts but merging them with other experiences and vocabularies taken from elsewhere. Ideas of excitement, inspiration and potentiality are, for example, merged with those Islamic conventions so that the women engage with this knowledge in new ways. Furthermore, these affective experiences also become crucial to their decision-making processes. What matters to these young women more than the content of the talks is the *sheikh*'s ability to provide a feeling of potentiality, a feeling of the possibility to understand themselves and their relationships with others differently. Knowledge that creates this excitement is appealing and, therefore, authoritative in the long term.

Islamic scholarship

Thus far I have stressed how the practice of 'mosque hopping' and seeking knowledge from a diverse range of sources is based on whether a particular scholar is able to instil virtuous emotions that open one's heart to God and produce an experience of excitement and potentiality. Here, I elaborate on the ways in which 'seeking knowledge' is embedded in, and limited by, the Islamic discursive tradition and associated structures of authority and forms of reason (Asad 1986). I then turn to explore the importance of pious friendships in shaping the practice of mosque hopping, and the ways in which young practising women debate and contest other criteria for establishing authority, including the extent to which knowledge ought to be 'Western' in its form, style and content.

In the question and answer session of one of the last classes, a student asked *Sheikh* Ibrahim – who had been discussing the life of the Prophet's uncle, Abu Thalib – whether he regarded Abu Thalib as a Muslim. The *sheikh* responded: 'There are multiple *ahadith* that speak about Abu Thalib and the *'ulama* (scholars of Islam) are in difference of opinion. But the vast majority of the *'ulama* are in the opinion that Abu Thalib died as a believer.' The student disagreed with the *sheikh* and the conversation continued as follows:

> **Student:** But there's a *hadith* that says Abu Thalib will have fire on his chest.
>
> **Sheikh:** No, the *hadith* says Abu Thalib will be placed in the shallow waters of the hellfire, and that *hadith* is *sahih* (sound). What does that say? Is it proof of *shirk* (sin of idolatry)? If we want proof of his *shirk*, then show us proof. ... You're not going to find loyalty to that. That *hadith* is actually a proof against ... that is a punishment reserved for disobedient believers.

The *sheikh* was warning the student against accusing others without authentic evidence. By referring to a *hadith sahih,* he was drawing on traditional chains of transmission, which in Islam are used to ascertain the authenticity of *hadith* statements. In doing so, he offered authentic evidence to the student that the punishment awaiting Abu Thalib was one reserved for disobedient believers, not disbelievers. But the student persisted and the debate continued:

> **Student:** But you can't say ...
>
> **Sheikh:** This is not an argument. If you open a book of *'aqida* (creed) you will see that *jahannam* (hellfire, abode of punishment) is the lowest *darakat* (stage or level) of hell. Let's ask *Allah* to open us up to understand the religion, *amin, amin, amin* ...
> So, *jahannam* ...
>
> **Student:** But ...
>
> **Sheikh:** If you let me finish, it's called *adab* (etiquette). [long pause] Eventually *jahannam* will be free of all those who

have been punished. There are different opinions on this topic. [long pause]
No one can stand and accuse others of being wrong, when the '*ulama* disagree! That's a principle of religion, and ... I wish I could do for the Prophet, what Abu Thalib did for him. If you believe that, hold your tongue in *adab*. Tell us of what you did? We all stand before *Allah* with our opinions; let's just hope that our opinions concur with the religion. You take your opinion and hope that you stand in good faith with *Allah*. But whatever opinion you hold, you must have *adab* with that opinion. And especially if you hold opinion against!

On the way home that evening, I discussed the incident with Maryan, Layla and Ifraax. Maryan was amused and shocked by the arrogance of the student and could not believe he had angered the *sheikh*, who was renowned for displaying composure and a virtuous character. 'That guy, he's so rude,' she giggled. The young women often showed great reverence for scholars and the student's complete lack of etiquette and respect troubled them. Layla was particularly impressed by the way *Sheikh* Ibrahim had been able to restrain his anger: '*Masha'Allah* ... he was right to stress *adab*. And instead of arguing he made *du'a*' for the student. That's what we should always do. He didn't attack him, but prayed he can have better knowledge.' According to Layla, the *sheikh*'s comment, 'Let's ask *Allah* to open us up to understand the religion,' demonstrated his knowledge of Islamic teachings and his personal piety, and hence confirmed his authority.

In an article detailing the styles of reasoning that are grounded in Islamic traditions of civic duty, Hirschkind (2001) argues that this public arena of debate is both normative and deliberative; it is a domain of subjection to authority and the exercise of individual reasoning. While participation in this arena involves argument, criticism and debate, ultimately, religious authority provides the foundation on which opposing viewpoints are articulated. The final aim of reasoning is disciplinary in that it is geared towards ethical self-improvement. An argument, therefore, depends on its ability to move the self towards correct understanding and modes of being and acting. The ability to act and speak reasonably and to conduct an argument in a calm and respectful manner rests on an 'evaluative background', on the inculcation of virtues and emotions of fear and humility (Hirschkind 2001: 21–2).

Sheikh Ibrahim had demonstrated this through his knowledge of Islamic scriptures. His argument involved the proper interpretation of Islamic sources and, therefore, as with Hirschkind's interlocutors, religious authority provided the foundation for his debate with the student. In his classes, the *sheikh* always supported his claims with scriptural evidence and displayed referenced quotations from the *Qur'an* and *hadith* on his PowerPoint slides. In the discussion with the student, he corrected the student's understanding of a particular *hadith*, thus demonstrating his superior knowledge of the tradition.

Leyla and her young pious friends often stressed the importance of presenting scriptural knowledge. Citing the source in support of one's argument demonstrated proof of one's interpretation. Habibah, for example, had recently downloaded an app on her phone that enabled her to check for herself the authenticity and reliability of *Qur'an* and *hadith* references on any given topic. Checking references enabled the young women to read the texts themselves, ascertain their reliability, and decide the extent to which they supported the scholar's claims. Nonetheless, these young women were cautious about arriving at their own interpretation (*ijtihad*) and instead relied on those of scholars who, in their eyes, possessed sufficient Islamic scholarly knowledge.

The fact that *Sheikh* Ibrahim had studied traditional Islamic sciences under scholars in Mauritania, Syria and Yemen lent him further credibility with the young women. As Layla described: 'A *sheikh* is usually trusted through scholarship, the chain of narration through which he's learnt, where he has studied.' Similarly, Habibah explained that she always checked 'the background of teachers and looked at whether other renowned scholars accept them'. Scholars who had studied under important scholars or descendants of the Prophet, or in renowned Islamic universities – such as Al-Azhar or the University of Medina – were regarded as particularly knowledgeable. The form of knowledge they had was often termed traditional or 'Eastern' and was considered by some to be closer to 'true' or 'authentic' Islam.

Furthermore, *Sheikh* Ibrahim had demonstrated that 'true' knowledge was more than an accumulation of facts. His tone and manners illustrated that he embodied the virtues of humility and modesty. He was not only a powerful charismatic orator, his actions also manifested his own embodiment of knowledge, personal piety and connection with God. As we continued discussing the *sheikh*'s dispute with the student, Ifraax added: 'These days, people have no idea how to discuss religious matters. He's right that we should not go around accusing people of disbelief. Who are we to judge? It's between you and *Allah*.'

Ifraax respected the *sheikh*'s humble and non-judgemental attitude, exemplified by his reminder to avoid judgement and accusation. The *sheikh* had displayed his own *adab* and his own ability to conduct debate in a calm, respectful manner, in accordance with the virtues of civic debate (Hirschkind 2001). He directed the student to reflect on the unfounded accusation against Abu Thalib he had made in his criticism of the *sheikh*'s lesson, and he explained to the student that this form of criticism was not conducive to the formation of a pious self. Instead of criticizing others, the student ought to reflect on his own intentions and comportment in the eyes of God. Argument and debate are justified only if the ultimate aim is to move others or oneself towards pious action.

Western knowledge

For knowledge to be authoritative it must be situated, first and foremost, not only within Islamic structures of authority but also within orthodox Islamic notions of reason, emotion, knowledge and action. Yet, many of the young women I spoke to also stress the importance of choice and autonomy in reference to a particular source, style or interpretation of religious knowledge. This notion of choice is employed in a number of ways: it is used in relation to ideas of 'choosing to submit' as well as in reformist discourses of 'religion and culture', wherein Islam enables choice.[8] Many also speak of choice in relation to 'Western knowledge', which, they claim, facilitates their exercise of choice through its format, style and content. The extent to which authoritative knowledge ought to be Western is, however, often a source of debate and contestation.

Layla articulated her views by contrasting Western and Eastern scholarship. On one occasion, I heard her discuss with a friend the work of scholars such as *Sheikh* Ibrahim and Abdal Hakim-Murad – a British Ba-Alawi scholar, lecturer of Islamic studies in Cambridge and dean and founder of the Cambridge Muslim College. She claimed:

> Scholars like them, when they talk about a certain issue, they trace debates historically, provide different opinions on an issue, rather than state one point blank. They appeal to a Western intellectual audience. They bring Western scholarship and combine it with Eastern knowledge. They have a Western way of structuring their thoughts.

Layla also pointed out that knowledge should appeal to a 'Western intellectual audience'. The academic format and style of classes such as *Sheikh* Ibrahim's – with their use of a university lecture hall layout, PowerPoint slides, and question and answer sessions – lent them persuasiveness. Khadiija suggested in an interview that scholars should 'modernize' their teaching techniques:

> I think they [scholars] should do workshops, they should use slides, and structure their classes around activities. We should sit in small groups and ask questions … in this day and age you need to keep the principles of Islam but you need to cater to people – the way in which they are learning at the time. No one does workshops. But that's how people learn these days, not the other way that people often find boring.

Lectures and workshops contrast with the traditional lessons delivered in Somali mosques, where emphasis is placed on recitation, memorization or dictation from a teacher.

More importantly, the young women, as Layla had pointed out, appreciated the *sheikh*'s ability to 'structure his thoughts' in a Western way. Xamda, who was introduced at start of this chapter, elaborated on this idea: 'At university I saw many young people, young women and men, who were looking at religion from an intellectual point of view.' According to the young women, a good Western-style scholar ought to provide multiple interpretations and offer guidance. It was then up to the individual to critique different opinions and select an appropriate interpretation that would facilitate their self-transformation.

For example, in the incident above, the *sheikh* had emphasized the plurality of opinions on Abu Thalib and stressed that everyone was entitled to their own opinions as only God knew the truth. The young women appreciated this exposition of multiple interpretations as it provided them with a base from which they could draw their own conclusions and form their own opinions on the issue while remaining grounded in tradition.

On a separate occasion, Layla contrasted this 'Western academic style' of teaching with that of a Bengali female scholar (*ustadha*) who she had asked about the compulsory donning of the *niqab*. The *ustadha* had told her that it was *fard* (obligatory) and elaborated very little on her claim. This answer had been insufficient for Layla, who explained:

> She didn't explain much, or provide opinions. She said it was worn by the Prophet's wives and so it was *fard*. She said the face is beautiful and should be protected. She didn't explain that the Prophet's wives needed to be protected, as they were associated with him. She didn't go into debates about the different interpretations of modesty.

The female scholar had failed to provide the multiple interpretations that would enable Layla to forge her own opinion. This was unlike what she termed the 'Western' form of relating to knowledge, which emphasized the importance of weighing up and choosing from alternative opinions and a range of schools of thought.

This idea of choosing from several opinions resonates not only with liberal modes of engagement based on autonomy, which I described in Chapter 5, but also with what Bowen (2010) has described as a mode of reasoning based on the 'objectives of scripture' (*al-maqasid*). This approach encourages Muslims to assess normative statements against what are seen to be the overall objectives of God's revelations, rather than against a set of rules. This approach, Bowen argues, 'offers a term that resonates with the history of Islamic scholarship and at the same time offers a mechanism for justifying innovative practices, for mediating between a practical exigency and a system of Islamic norms' (ibid.: 82). Layla was, in the above statement, criticizing the *ustadha* for not providing her with multiple opinions, but also for failing to contextualize the *hadith* and prioritizing the overall objective (guarding modesty) above the prescribed form (*niqab*). According to Layla, *niqab* was obligatory for the wives of the Prophet but might not be necessary for life in the UK today. In a non-Muslim environment, Layla insisted, the *hijab* was sufficient to accomplish the virtue and overall objective of guarding modesty. While some of her friends contested her view (see Chapter 7), this approach enabled Layla to adopt a more flexible and pragmatic attitude to her clothing.

In what follows, I present some of these young women's disputes regarding knowledge, in order to highlight the interconnections between the three modes of subjectification – choice, affect and submission – and show how these are used in establishing what constitutes authoritative knowledge.

Debating knowledge: Sufis, Salafis and the 'bad *imam*'

Sihaan was always quick to voice her views on matters relating to what she defined as 'Sufi practices'. She had regularly attended *Sheikh* Ibrahim's classes for months without expressing a word of discontent. Then, on one occasion, he delivered a lesson on the importance of *dhikr* (remembrance), a practice of collective worship, often associated with Sufism, which involves the chanting of the names of God or verses from the *Qur'an* or *hadith*. As we sat in her car on the way back to East London, Sihaan complained to the others:

I don't get it … isn't it better to worship God by not sinning, by avoiding sins and doing good deeds? What's the point of repeating His name over and over? This wasn't done at the time of the Prophet and there are so many *ahadith* proving that. Reading *Qur'an* to music isn't *sunna* (based on the Prophet's teachings) and the Prophet didn't do it. He didn't play musical instruments.

Layla, who had attended many of these *dhikr* sessions, interjected by emphasizing the importance of intentions and the overall objective of *dhikr*:

> To be honest I don't see the problem with group *dhikr*. I don't agree with *turuq* (paths, schools of Sufism) as I don't like the exclusiveness and I don't understand why we have to have a teacher. But I don't understand what the problem with worshipping God in unison is – if the intention is to worship God, I'm sure you can't be punished for that. It doesn't make sense.

Sihaan continued: 'But it's an innovation (*bid'a*) …'. She had barely finished her sentence before Layla interjected: 'Yes, but there are good and bad innovations and worship surely can't be a bad one.' At that point, Maryan intervened with her own opinion: 'To be honest I don't like referring to someone as Salafi, Sufi, whatever. When I went to the Sufi soul festival, I told one of my Salafi friends and she was so against it. She was saying these people do this and that and it's not even true.'

Layla, who at that point was beginning to get frustrated with Sihaan's accusations, summarized the differences between Salafis and Sufis:

> People say all sorts of things about Sufis – that they think they're at one with *Allah*, so they don't pray … but I've never met someone like that. Salafis place little emphasis on the internal, and I don't like the way they say things, the harshness, they have different manners. They spend half their time saying what we shouldn't be doing, what others do wrong.

These comments reveal the ways in which these young women articulated disagreements on what constitutes 'true' and authoritative knowledge, and the ways in which they categorized different forms of knowledge and attached importance to the three modes of subjectification. They only rarely discussed the differences between different reformist traditions or movements. Many adhered to a *madhhab* out of convenience, but they also often considered and combined the perspectives of the four different legal schools.[9] Furthermore, they very often debated the nature of Islamic knowledge according to a Salafi–Sufi continuum. This distinction is a vernacular categorization that does not necessarily coincide with scholars who, or organizations that, self-identify as either Salafi or Sufi.[10]

This juxtaposition of Salafi and Sufi should also be seen in the context of the growing influence of, and opposition to, Salafi scholarship in London. Saudi sponsorship of mosques, organizations, books and pamphlets has had a significant impact on the forms and styles of knowledge available to young people in Britain (Al-Rasheed 2005). My research confirmed that many young Somali women were drawn, at least initially, to Salafi rhetoric. Imbued with an empowering and simple message of strict, individualized adherence to Islamic scriptures, it is particularly appealing to young Muslims in the early stages of their practice. This form of knowledge is contested by other scholars who defend the centrality of *ijazah* (authorization to teach an Islamic discipline) and the idea that true religion is transmitted through a connection back to Prophetic origin (Birt 2005b).

The Salafi–Sufi continuum is employed to juxtapose knowledge that is based on fixed rules and regulations with knowledge that considers the overall objective of the scriptures and the importance of contextualization and which is ultimately seen as more flexible and pragmatic. For some of the young women, Salafi knowledge – also referred to as the '*haram* versus *halal*' approach (Bowen 2010: 64) – denies complexity and is excessively strict, focusing solely on exterior practices. For others, however, it is attractive because it motivates them to act and provides clear, universal and straightforward rules on how to conduct oneself in everyday life. As Sihaan pointed out, it is considered closer to the Islamic tradition because it avoids innovations (*bid'a*) and emphasizes the *Qur'an* and *sunna* as its sole sources of evidence. Interestingly, this vernacular Sufi–Salafi continuum also maps the tensions between affect and reason; Sufis are considered more emotional and focused on the internal aspects of the self, whereas Salafis are more concerned with implementing rules and reasoning correctly.

Like many of these young women, Maryan experienced ambivalence towards these two forms of knowledge and the choice between prioritizing reason or affect. On the one hand, she enjoyed listening to Salafi scholars. Throughout the winter of 2010, for example, she exchanged with Sihaan, and recommended to others, *Sheikh* Feiz's DVD on death and the grave. 'It's really good for me,' she explained. 'It makes me so scared that I wake up the next morning and start praying on time, stop wearing make-up. Sufi talks don't do that for me.' Having watched the *Sheikh* Feiz DVD, I can confirm that it is, in fact, quite terrifying. Set against a soft and peaceful background melody, the *sheikh*'s shout of 'There's no fleeing from death' made me jump from my seat when I first heard it. Nevertheless, Maryan insisted on watching it over and over again:

> I think I need the shock factor. I like talks about death, the grave and the afterlife. Not because I need to know for the sake of it, but cause it really gives me a kick in the back. I freak out and worry more about doing good things. The Sufis never talk about these things; they never mention death. When I'm with Sufis I'm less on guard cause they're so relaxed.

On the other hand, Maryan also explained to me: 'Sometimes Salafis are too strong. ... You know what I mean, they're a bit judgemental.' This obsession with rules, Khadiija suggested, was similar to the 'cultural' education they had received as children: 'They're not open about things. It's like Somali culture – being told all the time what to do. And there isn't much encouragement to find out for yourself. Your educational scope is limited in that way, I don't like it.'

After watching *Sheikh* Feiz's DVD, Layla, who could not understand Maryan's obsession with the scholar, explained:

> I don't see the point in being so angry. I don't like the attitude of Salafis, they are arrogant and too black and white about things, they always think they're right and tell others they're misguided! I've had so many Salafis tell me I'm wrong, because I go to mixed classes.

For Layla, the Salafi approach paid insufficient attention to aspects of spirituality and to the 'internal' dimensions of faith (Chapter 7). She summarized succinctly the differences between the two approaches: 'The Salafis are strict about rules, and the Sufis have the spiritual dimension, but sometimes they are missing on the rules and obligations. Islam is the middle way, so we should strive for that.' The Sufi approach was considered not only more inspiring and more likely to cause the type of affect that *Sheikh* Ibrahim's classes transmitted; it also provided more choice and flexibility of interpretation.

Despite these categorizations, Maryan and some of her other friends attended events and classes across the Sufi–Salafi continuum, emphasizing the importance of diversity and choice. For example, Maryan also occasionally attended events organised by the Naqshbandi tariqa. On one occasion, she discussed a gathering she had attended with her friends. As one of the few women dressed in a black *abaya* and *hijab*, she had felt a little out of place. However, she had been 'intrigued' and had enjoyed the 'happy atmosphere' and the 'kindness and sharing vibe' of the event. Participating in these gatherings did not preclude her involvement in what she termed more 'Salafi' events. As she pointed out: 'I prefer to pick and mix. I'm not sure I'd take everything about Sufism, but it was good to experience it and see what it was all about. I'm interested in everything; I'd even go to Shi'a talks. I think once you identify as one thing, it becomes a bit like a cult.'

For Maryan, mosque hopping enabled her to avoid identifying with a sectarian Islam, group identity or cultural affiliation. Instead, the practice emphasized a commitment to a universal, transcendent Islam. It also enabled these young women to articulate 'a middle ground', to balance between affect and reason, and between internal and external aspects of the self. The following example demonstrates how these young women debated and negotiated the importance attached to choice, submission to Islamic norms, and affect.

In early June 2011, Maryan, who had at that stage entirely abandoned *Sheikh* Ibrahim's classes, began attending weekly classes at a newly founded independent institute in Whitechapel. Her friend, Hibo, who had recently started practising Islam, had persuaded most of her close friends to attend in order to gauge their views on the classes. The funding and administration of the organization were not known to Maryan, but the classes were free and the centre ran different courses ranging from the Islamic sciences to more thematic ones on the hereafter, the life of the Prophet and his companions, etc. The first one I attended was titled *Heroes of Islam* and was taught by *Sheikh* Faisal. Maryan had warned us that he was a controversial 'Salafi' scholar,[11] but that his lessons were nevertheless inspiring and insightful provided you were able to 'put aside' his opinions. Although Layla was sceptical about attending, she had been persuaded by her friend's enthusiasm about the course and had decided, on that day, to try it out. Five of us walked in past the men at the entrance and made our way to the top of the building, where a TV link with the room below was set up and a few rows of chairs had been laid out for the women to view the class. There were only six other women in the room and the class had already started. The *sheikh* was discussing a *khalifa* (leader of a Caliphate) and making constant analogies between the historical context and the current situation in the UK. I could tell Layla was not enjoying the class and she looked at me, eyebrows raised in amazement, as he spoke about the UK as the 'land of *kufar*' (non-believers) and instructed his audience to voice their discontent at having to live side-by-side with gays, lesbians and disbelievers.

We walked out of the talk silently, as if afraid to open our mouths until alone. This was the first time we had attended such a politicized talk. As soon as we were far enough away from the building, my friends began debating the content of the talk. Layla was shocked, not only by the content of the talk but also by the violent and angry tone of the *sheikh*; much of what he said, she thought, was misguided, and she strongly opposed any of us attending these talks again. But the other women answered back, with Maryan explaining:

> Ok it's definitely a bit extreme, and it really wasn't like this last time. But you just have to learn to take the good things, the knowledge of the *khalifa* or the Prophet, and then leave the rest. His Islamic knowledge is good, but his opinions not so much … so just leave those. But you know, I'm not stupid, I can choose for myself, think with my own head and decide what I think is good and what is a bit extreme.

Sihaan joked: '*Panorama* will be in here next. This guy is wanted. But Maryan is right, you just leave out the violent stuff.' Hesitating for a moment, she added: 'But also, he has a point. Muslims have become too apologetic these days; we don't stand up for things.' Maryan joined in, adding: 'My *iman* has been so stable since I've been going to these classes. They make me passionate and give me energy. And I stand up for myself. I used to ignore the EDL (English Defence League) and now they make me angry.'

Layla felt alone in fighting her case, but she stated her points calmly and clearly. 'I know you're all smart and can judge things for yourself, but I just don't like the environment,' she explained. She felt his reasoning was not particularly intelligent or insightful, it created rifts between people, and references to Islamic scriptures were employed solely to advocate violence. This was not a message worth listening to, she concluded. Hibo noticed Layla's increasing irritation and stepped in to mediate the discussion: 'It's important to do our own research on this topic. Go home now, research him and what he's saying, and make up your own minds. We don't have to take everything he says.'

This incident brings to the fore the ways in which these young women engage with, and navigate their way around, different forms of knowledge and varying public debates about Islamic knowledge. Sihaan's comment, in which she joked about the BBC news programme *Panorama*, suggests a critical awareness of the discourse of the 'bad *imam*'. As Birt (2006: 693) has noted, in public debates in the UK, the 'good *imam*' has come to be defined by reference to models of 'civic religion' in a policy context of community cohesion and counter-terrorism. The 'good *imam*' must be trained in the UK, must embody civic virtues, have interfaith tolerance and pastoral skills, and must work as an agent of national integration, fighting against extremism. In contrast, the 'bad *imam*' has been defined as foreign trained and an agent of religious and cultural divisiveness.

However, for these young women, such government and popular discourses on Islamic knowledge are irrelevant, if not a source of ridicule; a 'good *imam*' is not necessarily one who promotes integration and community cohesion. What constitutes authoritative and 'proper knowledge' is contested and negotiable. Maryan's comment, 'I'm not stupid, I can choose for myself, think with my own head,' was a direct challenge to a public discourse that treats Muslims as passive receptors of extremist rhetoric by radical foreign scholars. Maryan pointed out how her critical intellect enabled her to 'decide' and judge what she desired to take away from the class, meaning that she could, therefore, ignore some of the more 'extreme opinions'.

Most importantly, this incident is indicative of how these young women establish what constitutes authoritative knowledge. Maryan's comment about choosing points to the way in which she understands herself as being able to dissect different aspects of knowledge: facts, emotions, interpretations and modes of reasoning can be differentiated from one another. It is her knowledge of Islamic scriptures and correct modes of reasoning that enables her to choose from among these different aspects of knowledge. Choice is delimited by the Islamic tradition and affect has no place here precisely because, as Maryan suggests, although the *sheikh*'s 'facts' might be 'good', his interpretations are dubious. Affect can only be experienced if scriptural knowledge and the correct Islamic modes of reasoning are in place. Similarly, choice is dependent on an understanding of the Islamic discursive tradition.

A few weeks after the 'bad *imam*' incident, I learnt that Ayaan, another young friend who had attended the class and who had kept silent throughout the previous debate, had decided to abandon the classes and had recommended that her friends do the same. Her brother-in-law, who she claimed had superior knowledge to herself, had explained how these courses were most likely affiliated with *Al-muhajiroun,* a banned Islamist organization based in the UK. They had a hidden political agenda and even though she could ignore their opinions, he explained to her, they would slowly influence the way she thought. 'He doesn't think I have the tools to argue back yet. And he was right. I went to another class and the *sheikh* kept going off course and bringing in his opinions, so I stopped going,' she explained. She was planning to enrol with Bilal Phillips's Islamic Online University.

According to Ayaan, her insufficient religious knowledge made it difficult for her to dissect the teaching appropriately and hence choose in an informed way. Ayaan began informing her friends about the problems she had with these classes and slowly, following her suggestion, her friends decided to abandon the institute. Ayaan's example demonstrates the fact that, for some, choice is shaped within the boundaries of the Islamic discursive tradition, wherein the ultimate aim is the self-fashioning of pious subjects and the establishment of a connection with God.

Yet, as I demonstrated in the previous sections, a long-term sustained commitment to a particular *sheikh* or source of knowledge is ultimately determined by a personalized experience of affect and a potential for self-transformation. These young women constantly revise and reassess, debate and negotiate ideas of knowledge but they ultimately rely on personal feelings and choices in determining whether they take on board any particular lesson. As Nadiifo summarized:

> I listen to everyone, then do my own research and take what I feel is good, what my heart feels is right. Ultimately it is a personal thing. You need to think about what fits you as a person; you need to judge your intuition. I don't get myself bogged down with things too much and just think: does this feel right to me?

Reasoning and choosing are not exercised in isolation but, as I have demonstrated, they arise through, and are shaped by, debates and contestation with friends. These heated discussions are, in fact, crucial to their quests for knowledge and self-transformation. Should knowledge simply engender a spiritual feeling and connection, or should it motivate or scare believers into action? Should it be political and seek to Islamize the environment, as *Sheikh* Faisal suggests? These questions remain unresolved for these young women as they experiment with, and seek out, different forms of knowledge.

These networks of friends play a crucial role in supporting, discussing and sharing the process of practising. They replace the support previously provided by kin, which diminishes in importance when these young women distance themselves from Somali mosques and their mothers' ideas of learning and knowledge. These relations are based around values of trust, care, mutual responsibility and control. Most of the young pious women I knew formed close friendships as they went looking for knowledge. In fact, it was only by 'hopping' around with them to various classes and borrowing their books and DVDs that I was able to become intimate with them and share their thoughts and feelings as they went on their relentless quest for knowledge. These processes of sharing emotions, debating, advising and, ultimately, aspiring not only are constitutive of their processes of learning and engaging with knowledge, but also connect this network of friends to a larger community of believers.

Conclusion

Young pious Somali women, unlike their mothers, argue that Islamic knowledge is not associated with culture and kin but with establishing a personal relationship with God and the *umma*. It does not promote an uncritical engagement with a set of facts and rules but instead unlocks new ways of thinking, reasoning and feeling, and new ways of understanding one's relationships with oneself and others. These differences between generations of Somali women highlight historical shifts and a reworking of the meaning of knowledge in which it is changing from being a set of facts guiding action to being a means through which cognitive and affective states can be transformed.

As we have seen, practising Islam involves a process of navigating across different forms of knowledge. For example, young pious women combine ideas and concepts taken from Islamic classes with notions drawn from popular culture or from their university experience. They employ these in refashioning and reimagining their relationships with their mothers, newly practising friends and God. They challenge the notions of 'segregation' found in public culture by emphasizing their freedom to move around the city and to socialize with other young Muslims from a range of ethnicities. These engagements provide a means by which they can think of themselves in other ways, and imagine and aspire to something new.

Young pious women engage with knowledge and determine what constitutes authoritative knowledge in three interrelated ways: through choice, submission to an Islamic mode of reasoning and to structures of authority, and an experience of affect. Whether knowledge is able to engender potentiality – that is, an experience of affect – is fundamental in determining long-term commitment to a particular source of knowledge. Authoritative knowledge engenders feelings described as '*iman* boosts' or 'high *iman*'. These feelings capture the potentiality experienced by young women as they imagine themselves connected with God. It is the struggle to sustain a feeling of *iman* that further fuels their continuous quest for knowledge, resulting in their 'hopping around' and choosing between various interpretations, opinions and schools of thought. I have suggested that, although a commitment to structures of authority is crucial to their engagement with knowledge, what ultimately dictates whether they continue to seek knowledge from a particular scholar is the feeling that the scholar is assisting their own personal transformation, that is, that the scholar is enabling them to think about themselves and their relationships with others in radically different ways.

However, this feeling of excitement and potentiality is difficult to sustain in the long run. It is precisely for these reasons that engagements with knowledge are often fleeting; there is always the possibility that these young women might turn elsewhere for knowledge. As we have seen, interest and commitment to a particular source of knowledge was not always sustained over a long period of time. Disagreements regarding authority frequently arose among the women, forcing them to question their commitment to a particular class or course. For example, as the winter months approached, attendance and enthusiasm for *Sheikh* Ibrahim's classes slowly waned. One Monday evening Maryan announced in a text message: 'No more classes for me, I'm free! Not doing it for me!' The classes no longer inspired some of the young women, while others noticed little improvement in their everyday actions. Gradually, they turned elsewhere for knowledge and guidance.

Their experiences indicate that Muslims' complex engagements with knowledge over time are best understood from the point of view of individual actors rather than through the lens of particular reformist groups or movements. Young pious Muslims navigate across different groups or fields of knowledge, and their experiences and preferences change over the course of their lifecycles. During my fieldwork, many of these women were in their mid to late twenties, most were unmarried and some had just finished university or were at critical junctures in their lives. Some, like Saynab, had experienced a particularly traumatic incident that had triggered reflection and a desire to aspire for something different.

Over five years after the end of my fieldwork, however, Layla, Saynab and their group of pious friends no longer spend the same amount of time together. Some have married and have become too busy with their young children to attend classes and lectures or to spend time reading about Islam. Others have moved abroad. Some have found new groups of friends with whom to seek and share knowledge. Maryan continues her relentless search for knowledge and her attempt – as she explained the last time we met – to 'figure out who's good and bad'. She has of late decided that she prefers to study and read about Islam on her own: 'I've got to the point that I don't feel I need a little clique anymore, I just do my own thing. I was drifting around from group to group and never felt comfortable.' She continues to exchange lectures, books and YouTube videos with her friends but is less interested in socializing with particular groups. 'I want to find a place where I feel comfortable,' she explained, 'and I still haven't found it.'

Notes

1 Layla M is a pseudonym and is used to differentiate this young woman from Leyla Hussein in Chapter 5. For the remainder of this chapter Layla M is referred to as Layla unless otherwise stated.

2 Prayers performed in the evening during the month of Ramadan.

3 For a description of the Al-Huda mosque, see Chapter 4.

4 For example, the East London Mosque, Ebrahim College, Taybuun Institute and Ibn Jabal Institute provided such courses.

5 Hirschkind (2006) similarly describes how, among pious Muslims, listening to cassette sermons not solely entails accumulating factual knowledge, but also involves cultivating a set of affective-volitional dispositions.

6 These included *Tafsir, Hadith, Shama'il* of Imam Tirmidhi and *'Aqida,* and were taught by a range of different scholars.

7 The phrase *bismillahi rahman rahimi* (in the name of God, Most Gracious, Most Merciful) is often pronounced before any class, lecture or recitation.

8 For example, the Quranic verse 'There is no compulsion in religion' (2:256) is often used to emphasize the importance of personal choice to practise.

9 Bowen (2010: 65–75) notes how this process of combining different juristic traditions is common among some scholars in Europe, who teach Islam on the basis of a set of Islamic principles.

10 *Sheikh* Ibrahim does not self-identify as a Sufi.

11 *Sheikh* Faisal is linked to the political organization *Al-Muhajiroun.*

CHAPTER SEVEN

Multiculturalism, British values and the Muslim subject

Make Bradford British

In February 2012, Layla M and Ikraan, two young pious Somali friends, advised me to watch *Make Bradford British*, a Channel 4 two-part reality TV show.[1] They had both seen it that week and were looking forward to exchanging opinions on the show, a common event whenever a TV programme featured Muslim participants or characters. A year following David Cameron's speech in Munich on the demise of multiculturalism, the programme is presented as an experiment in multiculturalism – an opportunity to question how individuals from different classes and cultural and religious backgrounds can live together, and whether there is such a thing as a shared sense of 'Britishness'. 'Is this a future defined by difference? Or one which brings us together as a nation?' the programme editor, Heenan Bhatti, purports to investigate.

Set in one of the most notoriously 'segregated' cities of the UK, in the first episode the project managers and 'community and diversity experts', Taiba Yasseen and Laurie Trott, bring together 100 British citizens from Bradford to sit the *Life in the UK* test as a social experiment.[2] Eight participants, representing different ethnic, racial, class and religious backgrounds, are selected out of the ninety individuals who failed the test. Among them is Damon, a white metal sheet worker, who lives in a predominantly white working class area of Bradford, Maura a white former magistrate from a middle-class suburb, and two young British Muslims of South Asian descent, Sabbiyah and Rashid. The participants, encouraged by the organizers to 'be honest' and to display their prejudices, are asked to share a large house, with the aim of recreating a microcosm of a multicultural society. Tension builds as Rashid, a devout Muslim and former rugby league player, insists on participating in congregational prayer at the mosque five times a day. The almost exclusive focus of the episode is on the 'problematic' nature of this Islamic practice; the other inhabitants of the house complain as Rashid's trips to the mosque disrupt vital decision-making processes such as drawing up shopping lists, and Sabbiyah argues with him at the dinner table over his interpretations of prayer. Rashid is shown explaining that 'a person who prays in congregation gets the reward 25 to 27 times more than a person who prays individually'. His commitment to prayer is depicted as not only a barrier to successful integration but as part of a straightforward point-accruing system. The episode ends with a field trip for the group and Rashid compromising on his mosque praying; he prays in a forest instead, a scene that moves Maura to tears.

In part two, the participants are paired up and made to live in each other's homes. Sabbiyah, the young *hijabi* Muslim woman, is paired up with Audrey, a mixed-race landlady of a Bradford pub. On her first day of serving soft drinks in the pub, a white middle-aged man in the pub attacks Sabbiyah. 'How long have you been in this country? Why are you dressed like that?' he asks provocatively. 'I was born and bought up here … it's my identity, it's part of who I am,' the young woman replies, taken aback by the comment. 'If you were born here, why not take up our identity … our wear? When was the last time you dressed in a mini skirt and a low-cut top?' he questions. 'I don't want to wear a mini-skirt and a low-cut top! I'm covering my modesty,' Sabbiyah responds, trying to defend herself. At that point, another woman intervenes on the man's behalf: 'I don't mean no disrespect, but this young lady looks beautiful in what she's got on … but it don't fit in, it's not like us. If you're in England, be like English people.' Intimidated, Sabbiyyah retreats, sobbing quietly in the corner of the pub: 'I've never questioned my identity, never, for the first time I felt myself questioning it. Am I really British? Can I ever be seen as British?' Although Audrey initially struggles to empathize with her, she reflects on the racist abuse she had also received in the past, noticing how this has now shifted to the Asian (Muslim) community.

In the meantime Damon, who subsequently explains that he used to think mosques were 'terror camps' and 'secretive places', is invited to live with Rashid, who makes every effort to 'show good character' and the 'good' side of Islam through his hospitality and his constant references to the virtues of Islam. Damon attends congregational prayer at the mosque, and in one of the final scenes of the episode, he reflects on what he has learnt from his encounter with Rashid: 'Islam is not a bad religion ... the ways of life are the old British ways.' As the programme is brought to a close, this statement stands as a final summary and resolution to the initial tensions and conflicts. This Channel 4 programme's contribution to the multiculturalism debate is a statement encouraging an embracement of difference and a recognition of shared values. Echoing political discourses on Britishness and national identity, the programme suggests that recognition of 'shared British values' will overcome the problems and associated threats of segregation and marginalization.

On a Saturday evening, following the screening of the first episode, Layla whom I introduced in the previous chapter, and her friend Ikraan, who initially advised me to watch the programme, came around for some food. As the conversation drifted from the latest YouTube hit to the Channel 4 programme, Ikraan, a young charity worker, accused the participants of the show of overreacting to Rashid's desire to pray in the mosque. 'Why can't they just tell him what they've decided when he gets back? Why are they making such a big deal of this?' Layla sighed: 'He makes Islam seem so stupid and simplistic though!' The mistreatment suffered by Sabbiyah in the second episode infuriated them further. Their frustration, however, unlike my own, was directed less at the editing and directing of the show, and more at the participants. They worried about the perpetuating of stereotypical representations of Muslims and often criticized the depiction of Muslims in the media and in films. One such example is the Peter Kosminsky series *Britz*, which narrates the story of a young second-generation Muslim brother and sister in Bradford who, soon after the July 2005 bombings, pursue divergent paths: the brother takes up a job at MI5, while the sister trains to become a jihadist. Ikraan had on one occasion expressed her anxieties about *Britz*, which she felt contained unlikely and stereotypical depictions of the Muslim community as segregated and patriarchal, organizing jihadist meetings on university campuses, training in jihadist camps in Pakistan, and so on.

However, *Make Bradford British* pleasantly surprised these young women by the end of the programme, and both commended Rashid's presentation of Islamic virtues and the ways in which he challenges Damon's prejudices. 'It's stereotypical, but at least the end is not the usual stuff about Muslims ... Rashid redeems himself!' Layla exclaimed. Although *Make Bradford British* reinforces the problematic nature of Muslim practices, according to my friends, it falls short of reiterating the 'usual' conventions of other TV programmes. It offers a positive resolution to the question of how to be British and Muslim, stressing interior virtues and values – aspects of Muslim subjectivities that my interlocutors too were keen to emphasize – above the practices of prayer and *hijab*.

The problem of being British and Muslim

This chapter takes recent public debates on multiculturalism as a starting point and treats them as a distinctive field of problematization that centres on the question of what it means to be British and Muslim. Within this general terrain of problematization – of the relation between Islam and Britishness – a set of intersecting domains offer a series of problems and challenges for politics and for self-formation. In what follows, I focus on the problem of what constitutes a Muslim subject, and on a series of related queries that are reproduced in debates on multiculturalism and exemplified in programmes such as *Make Bradford British*: Are Muslims British? What does it mean to be a Muslim? How do we know who is a Muslim? Do external practices make one a Muslim? This chapter is concerned with the ways in which this problem is articulated through a preoccupation with exterior practices, such as Rashid's prayer and Sabbiyah's *hijab*, with the relation between interiority and exteriority, and a series of interrelated tensions between visibility and invisibility, particularism and universalism.

These problematizations are evident in the current shift in public and political discourses and policies, where the notion of multiculturalism has become inseparable from the supposed 'problem' of Islam. Within dominant debates around multiculturalism and the

Muslim subject, certain practices such as the donning of the *hijab* or *niqab* have been singled out as objects of concern and scrutiny; they have come to stand as religious symbols, as markers of authentic Muslim identity (Bracke and Fadil 2012: 49), and increasingly of 'extreme' forms of religiosity. The *hijab* has become 'fetishized' and symbolically overloaded – something Muslim women, as we shall see, simultaneously critique and reinscribe (Tarlo 2010: 75–6).

In his ethnography of the headscarf controversies in France, Bowen (2008) explores similar public debates and unravels the historically constructed reasons underlying the law that led to the headscarf ban in public schools in France in 2004. Republican ideas of citizenship, Bowen explains, require that individuals agree on basic values. State institutions such as public schools are designed to ensure uniformity and neutrality; they have the responsibility to guarantee individual freedoms, such as freedom from pressures emanating from the family, community and church (ibid.: 29). It is for this reason that Islam is seen as a threat to Republican values of *laicité* (secularism), for example, and to national identity.[3] In France, these political discourses have permeated media depictions and popular perceptions around the visibility of Muslims in the public sphere, most recently with the 'burkini ban' in some coastal towns across the country. Muslim practices, such as prayer or the donning of the *hijab*, have come to be treated as signs of one's values, and read as an unwillingness to 'fit' into France (Bowen 2004). As Fernando (2010) argues, legal frameworks and political and public discourses on religious freedom in France, and in Europe more generally, assume that religious practices are merely outward manifestations of religious conscience and religious choice. Public discourses make a distinction between belief and practice, whereby the latter is constituted as 'a second-order contingent expression of belief' (ibid.: 27). According to this logic, banning the headscarf 'does not constitute a violation of religious liberty because it has no effect on the believer's [inner] conscience' (ibid.: 26).

In the UK, the issue of the *niqab*, rather than the *hijab*, entered public debate relatively late following Jack Straw's demand in 2006 that Muslim women remove their *niqab* during consultations in his constituency. Like France, the *niqab* was viewed as a sign of social problems, such as the growth in communalism and a lack of social mixing, the influence of 'Islamism' and the denigration of women (Bowen 2008). In contrast to the French context, however, debates in the UK have revolved not around secularism but around the tensions between the politics of difference and the liberal notion of universal equality (Taylor 1994).[4] On the one hand, visible signs of difference such as the *hijab* have been less problematic precisely because they are seen simply as signs of different, particularist religious identities and beliefs constitutive of a liberal public space where different cultures and religions coexist. On the other hand, as rhetoric has shifted towards a greater concern with national identity, British values and security, Muslim practices have come under scrutiny as potential signs of 'extreme' or illiberal beliefs and ideologies. As the former prime minister David Cameron (2011) argued in his speech at the Munich security conference, Britain needs a 'muscular liberalism' which 'believes in certain values and actively promotes them. ... It says to its citizens, this is what defines us as a society: to belong here is to believe in these things.' Over the last decade, the notion of British values has entered political discourse and policies on diversity. It has been dependent on a liberal language of abstract rights, responsibilities and values, which are presented as universal arbiters of the significance of other life forms (Mehta 1999). As I argue in more detail in the conclusion of this book, this abstract universal language not only masks its own contextual particularities, but also emphasizes the difference, remoteness and strangeness of the other. The 'extreme' Muslim subject is presented in juxtaposition with a set of abstract universal ideals of autonomy and freedom, in need of reform, and as determined by her particularist cultural traditions. She is opposed to the valorized figure of the cosmopolitan who is able to abstract herself from habits and social worlds (Ossman 2013: Chapter 1; Keith 2005) and to transcend the particular.

A programme like *Make Bradford British*, or public culture in Britain more broadly, inserts itself within this political context, offering its own solution, but also contributing to the problematization of Muslims in the UK. As reiterated in the programme, 'British values' and 'Britishness' are often evoked in public discourses in connection with a set of universal values of human rights, gender equality and democracy, and in contrast to essentialized notions of supposedly non-liberal, Muslim values.

In what follows, I shift the perspective to young second-generation Somali women, and the ways in which they understand and make sense of what it means to be a Muslim by reflecting on the questions posed by these multiculturalism debates. In so doing, I unravel different understandings of the Muslim subject that contrast with those proposed in mainstream debates. I investigate the manner in which these women respond to these popular representations, and negotiate their processes of self-fashioning by altering their ideas of exterior practices, such as wearing the *hijab,* as well as interior dimensions of the self. I draw on recent anthropological work, which has also explored how pious Muslims in Europe manage these visibly Islamic practices in environments where they are seen as problematically 'other' (Bracke 2011; Fadil 2011; Jacobsen 2011; Jouili 2009).

Building on this work, this chapter highlights how, through multiple strategies of negotiation, young practising women reconfigure their understandings of interior and exterior, and visible and invisible, dimensions of their selves. In so doing, they also rework the tensions between the universal and the particular. I am interested not only in the different ways these women negotiate what they regard as an over-signification of exterior practices, but more importantly in the ways in which they rework their understandings of themselves by prioritizing interiority (see Jacobsen 2010: Chapter 6). In doing so, they distance themselves from the past, by insisting that they, unlike their mothers, work from the 'inside-out'. Their understandings of the relationship between interiority and exteriority, and their prioritization of interiority are, I argue, indicative of historical rearrangements and generational differences. The problematization of exteriority leads these young women to refashion contemporary Islamic pedagogies that stress the dialectic, mutually constitutive relation between interior and exterior processes of the self, crucial to the fashioning of a pious Muslim subject (Mahmood 2001). By emphasizing interiority, they rework the elements that are being problematized in public debates.

The next section returns to Layla and her personal engagements with the relationship between interiority and exteriority. I highlight how her critiques of her parents' excessive preoccupations with exteriority and her concerns with being 'too Muslim' in the workplace impact on her choice to don colourful skirts and headscarves. I contrast her decision with that of Ikraan's, another practising woman who, following a period of reflection, decides to adopt the *jilbab* as a personal and collective challenge. Finally, I compare both of these women with Cawo, a non-believer, who continues to wear a black *abaya* and *hijab* in order to appear visibly Muslim to her family and friends. These three narratives are woven together throughout the chapter to illustrate the ways second-generation Somali women constitute different, unstable and, at times, contradictory subject positions, and to explore changing notions of interiority and exteriority, faith and practice.

The problem of interiority and exteriority

Layla had had a difficult week when she came around for a coffee and chat. She had been arguing with her parents about her clothing, and her Muslim appearance had also been questioned in her workplace. Troubled and uncertain, she had written a poem in order to share her experiences and solutions with her friends, including Ikraan. This is a paraphrased fragment of her poem *Inside-out, Outside-in*, which she performed to me on one occasion:

> Sister A is dressed in black, covered from head to toe, but she is empty inside. She looks down on people, judges them, and when I smile at her as she crosses me on the street she glances at me expressionless and hands me a book on Islamic rules of modesty. Sister B doesn't even look like a Muslim on the outside, but when our paths cross she smiles and I can feel the warmth of her heart, the goodness emanating from her soul. We exchange greetings and part ways. But what if sister A merged with sister B to make Sister C? Someone who is God fearing, who strives to act and refuses to give in to desires and temptations, whose warmth of the heart and whose *iman* are visible on the outside. Sister C covers herself to please her Creator; she is beautiful not because of the curves of her body (because these cannot be seen by other men except her husband) but because of what she is inside.

Following the performance, Layla explained:

> Islam is about the middle way, that's why I say inside out, outside in, ultimately I think it's better to be a good person inside, but it's about balancing the two. ... I think the inside is most important, but I've also seen how the outside works

to make people more aware. If I'm wearing a *hijab* I'm less likely to shout, be loud and aggressive, swear. ... My behaviour changes as well because I'm representing Muslims, so I have an obligation in that sense.

Layla was questioning and problematizing the relation between interiority and exteriority and what it means for her to be a Muslim; the poem captures her attempt to reconcile parental pressures, Islamic ideals and a public gaze. The 'sisters' in the poem capture some of the different subject positions available to Layla, which I will analyse in more detail throughout the chapter.

Layla explicitly sets out to attempt to define and make sense of 'the middle way'; she seeks a Sister C who can adequately balance the 'inside' – a 'warmth of heart' and emotional connection with God – with external practice. This recognition of the mutually constitutive relation between exterior and interior dimensions of the self is informed by contemporary Islamic reformist teachings that emphasize the ways in which obligatory acts of worship, such as donning the *hijab,* are techniques of self-fashioning which ought to arise from – but also cultivate – correct attitudes, intentions, and emotions (Mahmood 2001). Modesty, for both Ikraan and Layla, is more than simply donning the *hijab*; it is a moral virtue acquired through the coordination of outward behaviour and inward dispositions (Mahmood 2005: 135). As Layla claimed, the *hijab* works to make her 'more aware' of her behaviour. Similarly, Ikraan explained to me: 'Once you have the *hijab*, it shifts the way you behave, the way you feel. You start being modest in dress and behaviour.' Modesty requires training oneself to cultivate emotions and sincere (*ikhlas*) intentions (*niyyah*) that subsequently motivate one to act. As Jacobsen (2010: 316) points out in relation to young Muslims in Norway, the 'inner' *hijab* relates to consciousness of modesty, and the 'outer' *hijab* refers both to the manifestation of inner modesty and to its disciplinary dimension. Ultimately, as this chapter will demonstrate, what constitutes the 'middle way' is unclear and unstable; while most young second-generation women agree with Layla's insistence that the 'inside is more important', they vary in their negotiations of exteriority with interiority, and the importance of being visibly Muslim.

Sister A: Exteriority as cultural

To return to Layla's poem, Sister A is depicted as judgemental, fixated on rules and regulations and on perfecting external practices, while being 'empty' on the inside. Her attitude to the *hijab* reflects the ways in which Rashid's prayer is depicted in *Make Bradford British*: dogmatic, unreflexive, unreasoned and an obstacle to successful integration. By discarding Sister A, Layla positions herself against a prioritization of exteriority. This could be seen as a distancing from a strict adherence to rules and obligations pertaining to particular interpretations of Islam – labelled 'Salafi' by many of these women – as well as from an Islamic tradition that emphasizes virtuous action above states of mind (Asad 1993: 219). Sister A also epitomizes the cultural attitude towards the *hijab* from which Layla and many second-generation Somali women distance themselves, and attribute to their parents (see Chapter 6).

Layla frequently argued with her parents about her clothing. Although she worked as a secondary school teacher, she continued to live at home with her parents and five younger siblings. Raised in a religious home, as a child she had been strongly encouraged to don the *hijab* by her parents, but throughout her degree, she began to reflect on religion and questioned her reasons for wearing it. 'I started thinking, am I just wearing it because I've been told to?' she had asked herself. In retrospect she wishes she had not been pushed to wear it as a child. 'Children should not be taught rules regimentally, but they should learn to accept them themselves,' she explained to me. Like the other female members of her family, she consistently wore the *hijab*. However, unlike her older sister and mother, she alternated long colourful skirts and loose long-sleeved tops with the occasional *abaya*.

On one occasion, she described an argument she had with her father about a photo he saw of her trip abroad where she was wearing a dress down to her knees on top of her jeans. He disapproved of her outfit and she argued back:

> I was so offended. I told him he was so bothered about exterior appearances and that wasn't what mattered at all. You could have a girl in bikini with the best character in the world. But I guess that's all he sees, the exterior. He doesn't know all the worship and things I do.

I tried to reassure her, reminding her that she was in fact extremely pious, and she replied modestly:

> No I'm not that pious ... but I try and he just doesn't see that. He [dad] doesn't understand that I'm very conscious of God; I know that I will be judged by Him and I try my best to be good. He just sees me as a bad Muslim, I guess it doesn't help that my sister wears *niqab*. ... I was just upset he judged me so quickly. I was upset he didn't trust me, and he doubted me so much. And I don't understand why he's so obsessed with exterior things like that! It's not that *hijab* doesn't matter, it does, and I know that, but it's not the main thing. I know so many people who wear *hijab* but don't practise or anything.

For Layla's parents, only the *jilbab,* commonly worn by many young and older Somali women, was sufficiently modest. Layla thought her sister's decision to wear the *niqab* had been influenced by her father, and on another occasion she made clear that this parental pressure on her was far from sporadic:

> We have an ongoing battle, everyday. 'Why don't you wear *hijab*?' And I tell him 'I am wearing *hijab*, this is my opinion!' I've never really cared about doing things to please my parents, though, if it goes against my religion. Like the *jilbab*, I wasn't going to wear it to please my dad, the intention is wrong and I would have resented it. I do things to please God and so far as it's considered modest that's ok.

When we discussed the reasons why she felt different from her parents, she explained:

> That's the way they were brought up I guess. Exterior things matter so much to them, they always have. It's a cultural thing, Somalis generally are like that. ... I don't know, to me sincerity is really important. I'd rather explain to my parents my opinion and let them understand me and why I do things, show them I am actually doing what's best. I don't want to lie to them, and just please them like that.

Layla's comments reflect an important distinction made by many young second-generation Somali women between the cultural attitude of their parents and their own commitment to an authentic, transcendent Islam. As I have argued in Chapters 5 and 6, the term 'cultural' is employed to refer to a mode of subjectification based on an uncritical acceptance of inherited practices. Similarly, here it is used to refer to a submission to parents, kin or community. According to Layla, her father is cultural because he judges without listening to her reasoning, focuses excessively on exterior appearances and constantly pressures her and her sisters to adopt the *jilbab*. Unlike her parents, Layla and her practising Somali friends adopt a reasoned, but also emotional, engagement with practice, drawing on Islamic pedagogies of self-discipline (Mahmood 2001). Although the *hijab* is an obligatory practice, crucial to her fashioning as a pious self, it is 'not the main thing', according to Layla, but one of many practices that cultivate interior emotions, intentions and dispositions. What matters most to Layla is her internal, sincere and personal connection with God.

These critiques were reiterated by some of Layla's practising Somali friends. On one occasion, as we were having coffee with other friends, Ikraan explained how the Somali youth she worked with had raised this issue with her in a workshop. She accused the older generation of perpetuating the 'problematic' discourses about external practices: 'Generally it's constantly about being *seen* by the Somali community. That's what matters. There's constant talk among women "did you see so and so wearing this, and so and so what she was wearing?"' Her friend, who had heard our conversation, added:

> If you're wearing trousers that's not considered modest. It's too Western for them. But then you get so many Somali women wearing *abaya* to avoid getting glances or comments. But it's ridiculous, you get Somalis who wear it but don't pray! It doesn't make sense! Older women are very strict about religiosity. But they are also aware of how they are seen by outsiders ... *ceeb* (shame) you know? Or maybe because they want to cling on, they're worried they might lose their identity.

For many Somalis, particularly teenagers and older first generations, the *hijab* and *jilbab* have in recent years also become a marker of collective morality and honour, and a symbol of Somali culture (Talle 2008: 65). As I discussed in Chapter 4, for many of the older women, covering one's head and body is articulated in everyday conversation as signifying religiosity; it is unquestionably the 'right thing to do' and is a marker of a 'good Somali woman'. As an external manifestation of moral integrity, women should be seen to be morally sound, and immoral behaviour is deemed shameful (*ceeb*). For older women, ensuring their daughters are visibly moral serves to enhance their own moral integrity and that of their kin, as well as to increase the younger women's opportunities of marrying well. Aamina, a young mother who felt the pressure imposed by other Somali women to wear the *hijab* and *jilbab*, explained: 'If I wore jeans, I would be gossiped about day and night! It's shameful for a married woman not to dress like this. So in a way it protects me, people don't question. Also it looks really bad on my family if I don't wear this.' For younger women, the *hijab* is seen as cultural when imposed by others, and religious when it is adopted willingly and as a consequence of their own reasoned engagement with Islamic texts and teachings. For practising Somali women, modest clothing is not solely about identity, nor about complying with community pressures and judgements. They consider their mothers to be excessively focused on clothing and external markers of piety, as well as inconsistent in their practice.

These young women's criticisms of their mothers' prioritization of the external reflect many of the characteristics attributed to Muslim communities by the media and popular discourse. Interestingly, these young women appropriate the language employed in debates against multiculturalism in order to criticize their mothers' practices. According to the younger generation, older Somali women are wearing the *hijab* because they feel judged by others; they are embracing it out of social pressure to conform, not out of reasoned choice and an internal connection to *Allah*. This cultural attitude towards donning the *hijab* is understood as susceptible to judgements, and therefore a sign of submission to others and to unequal relations of gender, which are seen as incompatible with British values. Their mothers are accused of prioritizing their connections with other Somalis – and hence particularist forms of relating to others – rather than adopting a liberal and universal attachment to a set of values and ideals. As the following example illustrates, the young women present their mothers as 'segregated' and 'different' to mainstream British society.

In April 2011, a few days following the French ban on wearing *niqab* in public spaces, I met with Layla, Ikraan and some other practising friends in Stepney Green. Sauda, a psychologist in her thirties, mentioned the ban and reflected on the UK and on her own situation:

> *Hijab* will never become a problem here. But things are getting tough. ... It's a political ploy, though. In times of recession, low unemployment, they blame it on immigrants who steal welfare money, this ghettoization thing. I don't see it. They just want to target us, but Muslims aren't ghettoized at all, we're all over the place, you get all sorts of Muslims in West London. Multiculturalism is the best thing we have; we can walk around freely, feeling safe, Muslims all want to come to the UK.

Sauda was referring here to David Cameron's Munich speech, delivered a few months previously, and the rhetoric on the failure of multiculturalism, Britishness and supposed segregation of Muslim communities, and a lack of shared values. For Sauda and many of her practising friends, the UK, unlike other countries, was a safe haven for Muslim women, who could wear the *hijab* in relative freedom, thanks to multiculturalism. To these young women, who identified as British, Somali and Muslim, the talk of ghettoization did not make any sense. It applied more to their parents, who had not been raised in the UK, and as refugees had relied significantly on welfare support. As we saw in the previous chapter, these young women accused their mothers of attending Somali mosques, equating religion with ethnicity and culture, and 'segregating' themselves from society. Ikraan explained further: 'A lot of our mothers have come from war-torn places, then had loads of kids, and have always been housewives, that's the culture, the women are at home. They hang out with Somalis. So it's very strange to have to go to work all of a sudden.'

Layla agreed, but compared her generation with that of their mothers: 'Our generation has had loads of opportunities, and there's no excuse for us not to get out there. It's our responsibility to take part, and contribute.' In contrasting their own duties to participate and contribute to the British public sphere with their mothers' struggles to do so, these young women redirected public critiques of multiculturalism at their parents' generation and their cultural attitude to Islamic practice. Multiculturalism assumed that Islam segregated Muslims, but what was in fact to blame was the 'bad part' of culture.

As I discussed in the previous chapter, young women's insistence on a separation between religion and culture is informed by contemporary reformist teachings that stress the purification of an authentic transcendent Islam from cultural practices. This is a rhetoric expressed by European Islamic scholars and actively embraced and reproduced by young Muslims in Europe. For example, during an *Eid* party organized by my Somali friends and acquaintances in a community centre in Bromley-by-Bow, a female scholar argued in a talk delivered on 'Women in Islam':

> Women should get involved in their community in order to voice their own concerns and represent other women. They should support their sisters to ensure that the services needed for women are in place. Women should work to challenge media stereotypes of Muslim women as oppressed. ... It's men who use culture or cultural norms to oppress women. Islam does not oppress them. ... Muslims should go out there, in *hijab* and show what they are capable of achieving.

According to the speaker, Islam offers a solution: it provides a way for women to challenge oppressive cultural and patriarchal norms, to participate in the wider public sphere, and to disrupt stereotypical representations while maintaining their modesty. Unlike media representations, she contends, women are oppressed because of men's appropriation of culture, not because of Islam.

Problematizing exteriority: From sister A to sister B

In the poem, Layla's distancing from Sister A also represents a critique of public representations, such as those in *Make Bradford British,* that overemphasize and problematize practices such as prayer and *hijab* as crucial to Muslim identity. Following the programme, Layla and Ikraan had commented on their frustration with the participants who, in the first episode, portrayed Rashid's prayer as a problem. Their annoyance was exacerbated by the mistreatment of Sabbiyah, who had been portrayed as a victim of racist, anti-Muslim accusations, despite defending herself by stressing the importance of modesty, choice and identity. Layla and her friends shared with Sabbiyah the experience of being judged for their exterior appearance in the workplace. However, they felt that, unlike Sabbiyah, they were able to defend themselves and negotiate the overdetermination of exterior signs of difference in more effective ways. In what follows, I illustrate the ways in which Layla and Ikraan negotiated their exteriority differently, despite sharing a similar conception of interiority. In doing so, I illustrate how their decisions expose them to different forms of exclusion.

Throughout her teacher training course, Layla had experienced and become frustrated by the over-signification and stigmatization of her *hijab*. She explained:

> I get targeted cause I'm a Muslim! Every time a lecturer says something about Islam, he looks at me to justify what Islam says. He's questioned me and so have others on whether I can teach something like religious studies objectively as a Muslim. They think it's impossible cause I carry it on my head. I've never been in an environment where I'm the only Muslim. But I get treated as a Muslim; I really wish they would just treat me as Layla!

Layla resented the way others saw her solely through her religion. 'They see the *hijab* before they see there's a person there!' she elaborated. The presence of this religious symbol made her lecturers doubt her ability to think and teach anything that fell outside of her faith.

On another occasion, following a lecture, Layla had been questioned abruptly by one of her university classmates about her 'background'. Surprised, Layla had replied: 'My parents are Somali, why?' The classmate continued: 'Do you think that if you weren't a Muslim you'd choose Islam?' Annoyed, Layla retorted: 'What do you mean by that? That I'm blindly following Islam? No, I've actually done a lot of study into it, I know a lot about my religion. How am I meant to answer that question? I don't know! I can't tell you.'

As Layla recounted this incident to me, she pointed out: 'She must just assume I wear *hijab* cause that's what I've always done, or that my parents force me!' Frequently, these young women were confronted, particularly in work environments, with non-Muslims assuming the *hijab* was a sign of a cultural, traditional identity imposed by their families and communities. As we saw earlier, hegemonic discourses in the UK often conflate religion with culture (Werbner 2009: 30) and treat these as interchangeable, while positing culture as an imprisoning and determining force (Phillips 2007; Baumann 1996). Her classmate assumed the *hijab* was what Layla would have described as a cultural symbol of patriarchal subordination, not something she had willingly adopted herself.

Sauda, introduced in the previous section, had had a similar experience when she first started wearing *hijab* at work:

When I started wearing *hijab* at work I got asked so many questions, and I don't even wear *abaya*, imagine if I did! People started saying I looked better before, asking me why was I wearing it. One person said to me: 'Oh, of course, you're not allowed to take it off'. And I shouted back: 'I don't want to take it off!' They couldn't sit in front of someone who wears *hijab*, it bothered them! And I was the only one in the office ... but we have Muslim clients the whole time! They just couldn't take it from one of their employees. I should give them a crash course on Islam cause they have clients [who are Muslims]!

As with Layla's example, Sauda's work colleagues had assumed that the *hijab* was a symbol imposed on her by her culture or community. Sauda, instead, had responded by emphasizing she did not *want* to take it off – that it was her choice to wear it. Similarly to Layla, she employed the notions of choice and autonomy to 'talk back' to a dominant narrative that positions the *hijab* as a normative practice, antithetical to autonomy and choice (Bracke 2011; Jacobsen 2011). This strategy echoes Sabbiyah's reply in *Make Bradford British* that she did not 'want' to wear mini-skirts and low-cut tops; she had the 'choice' to wear what she wanted.

These discursive strategies constitute only one way in which these young women sought to negotiate their practice. Following several weeks of feeling judged by her exterior appearance, Layla phoned me one evening to discuss her current coping strategies:

I've really tried to be less Muslim this week! I've tried not to speak about Islam. I'm actually considering dressing less Muslim, maybe wearing Western clothes like jeans and a long top, rather than black *abaya*. Of course I can't take off my *hijab*, so I can't escape the fact I'm a Muslim.

Following this conversation, she began to wear colourful, long skirts and patterned loose-fitting tops, rather than her usual black *abaya*, although she did wear the latter in certain situations and particularly among other Muslims. For her work outfits she shopped for long-sleeved shirts and tops, dresses and shoes in major high street shops, such as Topshop, Debenhams and Primark, and picked up her *hijab* in markets in Whitechapel. She layered her *hijab* in different colours, and adorned her clothing with bright-coloured bangles. By experimenting with a range of styles, and incorporating a concern with modesty using Western clothing, she articulated and realized what Tarlo (2010) has described as an individualized, cosmopolitan approach to 'Islamic fashion'.

Layla hoped that dressing 'less Muslim' would make her less visible and enable her to manage how those around her interacted with her, encouraging them to focus less on her exterior appearance, and more on her virtues and interior dimensions of self. She was recognizing the *hijab* as simultaneously a sign of her interior dispositions and as a religious duty (Fernando 2010). Acting and dressing 'less Muslim' was a way of 're-signifying' her clothing practices, similar to Jouili's (2009) French and German research participants who were forced to negotiate the donning of the *hijab* in restrictive secular environments. Reflecting Sister B in the poem, Layla was placing greater emphasis on interior virtues, dispositions and manners, downplaying the particularist nature of the *hijab*, while emphasizing the importance of abstract values. Her aim was to encourage others to appreciate her 'good character' (*akhlaq*), which she deemed more representative of what it meant for her to be a Muslim. She had, in fact, applauded Rashid in *Making Bradford British*, and his success in bringing the importance of interior virtues and dispositions to the fore.

Layla was also distancing herself from a prescriptive understanding of modesty by focusing instead on the 'inner' virtue of modesty which could be expressed differently in practice: as long as one was revealing only her face and hands, it did not matter how that modesty was achieved in practice. As the following example illustrates, Layla had appropriated this attitude towards practice from European Islamic scholars.

On a Friday evening in October 2010, Layla and I attended a talk delivered by *Sheikh* Babikir[5] during which he spoke, among other things, about how Muslims should avoid creating barriers with non-Muslims. Instead, they should impress non-Muslims with their hospitality and their manners (*adab*). Following the talk, Layla explained:

> I think he's completely right about being a Muslim through manners – through the person you are, not through a uniform. That's the universal aspect of Islam, it's what unites all cultures. I don't think we should wear things that stick out in the West, or that create divisions amongst us.

'Modesty varies with culture,' Layla elaborated. 'Sometimes cultures pass things off as being the only way to be modest, like Somalis with the *jilbab* and wearing black, but that's not the only way to be modest.' Furthermore, Layla felt quite strongly about not alienating others through her dress. In order to do *da'wa* (raise awareness of Islam), she had to present herself as approachable.

Her focus on Islamic virtues and manners also merged with a public discourse of 'British values'. In the above quote she commented on how a focus on manners was also about emphasizing the universal aspects of Islam that transcend cultural particularities. In so doing, Layla was reversing a discourse that positions liberal values as universal in contrast to particularist or communitarian Muslim practices. On another occasion, she explained to me, following a discussion of Cameron's speech: 'Our aims happen to coincide with Western ones; freedom, democracy, justice, equality these are also Muslim values.' The language of values enabled her to position herself as both Muslim and British within debates on national identity. This echoed with the teachings of one of her favourite scholars and academics, *Sheikh* Abdul Hakim-Murad, who argued in a lecture entitled *British and Muslim*:

> Islam, once we have become familiar with it, and settled into it comfortably, is the most suitable for the British. Its values are our values. Its moderate, undemonstrative style of piety, still waters running deep; its insistence on modesty and a certain reserve, and its insistence on common sense and on pragmatism, combine to furnish the most natural and easy religious option for our people. (Hakim-Murad n.d.)

The scholar's claim challenges a dominant discourse which questions the compatibility of Muslim and British values. Rather, his contention is that British values are in fact akin to Islamic values, and thus do not require learning or appropriation by Muslims – Muslims are already British.

Layla's emphasis on values merges Islamic understandings of virtuous conduct with political discourses on national identity and understandings that 'shared values' offer a solution to the problem of how to be British and Muslim. This is reflected in the final resolution of *Make Bradford British*, where Damon accepts Rashid as British because his Muslim values resemble British ways of life. Furthermore, it also represents an understanding of faith as private – a position reflected in Layla's poem with Sister B who exemplifies interior 'goodness' and 'warmth of heart', and prioritizes the universal above the communitarian.

However, these negotiations were far from straightforward and not ones with which Layla was completely satisfied. Articulating a 'middle way' for young practising women such as Layla and Ikraan is both a personal and social struggle which requires negotiating how they think and feel about practice and faith, and managing how they will be viewed by others.

Ikraan's *jilbab*

The threat of being judged and targeted as a result of her exterior appearance was a serious preoccupation for Ikraan. She typically wore the *hijab* and black *abaya* and had, on several occasions, been the target of verbal abuse on the streets or on public transport. She felt that more modest forms of clothing would have further restricted her employment opportunities. 'Especially after the 7/7 bombings we really got targeted. You never see a *niqabi* at work, do you?' She explained to me: 'Of course you can wear it, but you make a choice of not applying for jobs where you can't wear it.' Although she would have liked to wear it, she felt that clothing such as the *niqab* was not suited to her work life.

Towards the end of my fieldwork, I met with Ikraan and Layla for a walk around Tower Hamlets. As we wandered through back streets and alleyways, and occasionally popped into shops to browse the latest Islamic clothing, Ikraan unexpectedly announced that she had decided to wear the *jilbab*. As mentioned, the *jilbab* is occasionally worn by practising women and particularly by first-generation Somalis. It typically comes in dark colours and is considered by some practising women, such as Layla, to be too cumbersome and sombre, making them 'stick out' in London. Layla and I looked at her with surprise, but Ikraan reassured us that she had already thought about designing her own *jilbab*, by adding creative twists to a piece of clothing that was otherwise quite banal in style. 'It's just that I want to keep moving upwards. I think I'm ready for that and I think what was stopping me before was fear. I had real fear of doing it, but I think I can face that fear now, I'm ready for it.'

I asked her what she meant by fear and she mumbled how it was tied to her previous experiences, but she didn't expand further on that occasion, perhaps because the thought of her past evoked bad memories. She had previously told me how the adoption of the *hijab* and *abaya* had been a personal struggle for her. This was not only because of the stigma attached to them, but also because she felt judged by her non-practising friends. As she explained on that occasion:

> It was so hard. The first few months I was properly depressed. I just felt so uncomfortable in *abaya* and *hijab*. People started treating me differently, everyone was staring at me. I noticed when I was with friends they thought they couldn't do certain things around me, like listen to music, or stuff like that. They thought they couldn't say certain things, so they made me feel like the one that sticks out. I didn't feel comfortable; I felt boring, like the crazy side of me wasn't there anymore, like I couldn't be happy and loud and me. I didn't feel I was in my skin. But at the same time I really wanted it and I'd decided it.

Her decision to don the *jilbab* was tied to her idealized and prescriptive understanding of modesty and pious conduct. Unlike Layla, for whom modesty was a virtue that could be practised in a range of different ways, Ikraan envisioned the *jilbab* as the ideal modest form of clothing. She explained to us that afternoon that the *jilbab* was more effective than the *abaya* in masking her shoulders and figure. Furthermore, in the same way that the *hijab* made Layla 'more aware', the *jilbab* would further strengthen Ikraan's interior *iman* and work as a self-disciplining practice to further improve her behaviour.

Initially, Layla struggled to accept Ikraan's decision and the two young women heatedly debated the issue. Ikraan continued to explain her decision: 'I've done a lot of research into it and I've learnt that the ideal is what the wives of the Prophet used to wear, the *jilbab*.' Layla hesitated and then gently challenged this perspective:

But that was the clothing suited to the time. The Prophet's wives had to be protected more than others. To me, modesty can be reached in different ways … if you look at the *hijab* it's practised in different ways across the world, but they're all modest in different ways … and here I think it's important not to stick out but to adhere to social contexts … so to work I wear a shirt and long skirts cause I'm meant to have a professional look.

Ikraan retorted:

But some cultures wear *hijab* and it doesn't cover their shoulders, like the Syrian trench coat. Also, I wear *jilbab* not to fit into social contexts, but to adhere to an ideal and to please God. To get more rewards – that's my only intention. Instead, by trying to fit in you're pleasing others. It's my *jihad*, my struggle, and it really is hard. It's my own personal struggle to satisfy my Creator.

Layla continued to disagree:

But Islam isn't about struggle … you should be happy! I just don't see it that way. Although part of me wishes I did have an ideal because it would make it easier for me, and I'd know what to work on. But I just see character as more important, not exterior clothing.

But Ikraan refused to give in: 'I see character and manners as important, but I think the outer dimensions are also very important'. While Layla insisted on prioritizing interiority by emphasizing the virtue of modesty, the importance of character and manners, and not 'sticking out', Ikraan felt her friend's position was excessively focused on 'pleasing others' rather than 'pleasing God'. She directed at Layla the cultural critique that practising women often employed to distance themselves from their parents: a cultural mode of subjectification involves an uncritical submission to kin, community or social pressure, whereas their engagements with Islamic practices result from a personal and intimate relationship with God. Unlike Layla and older kin, her decision to don the *jilbab* was not motivated by communitarian attachments – to family, kin or non-Muslim friends – but rather by her commitment to a universal faith. Like Layla, however, she was emphasizing the universal dimensions of Islam; yet she was doing so not by emphasizing internal values, but by insisting on the universal importance of external practices of modesty.

Layla initially struggled to accept Ikraan's decision, as she felt Ikraan was exhibiting a cultural attitude by prioritizing external behaviour. However, on another occasion, she explained to me how she was slowly learning to accept Ikraan's motivations: 'I think it motivates her and sends a constant reminder, and she sees it as a struggle, against what people think about her. She feels stronger when people comment and ridicule.' Although Ikraan's decision had initially surprised Layla, she later explained to me how Ikraan's adoption of the *jilbab* did not actually reflect the cultural attitude she attributed to her parents. Unlike her parents, Ikraan was familiar with Islamic pedagogies that stress the connection between exterior practices and interior intentions, emotions and dispositions. In addition, Layla explained, Ikraan was aware of the importance of interiority and occasionally also privileged it above exteriority. Her emphasis on exteriority was a way of motivating herself to be pious. In fact, she had often stressed the importance of being Muslim 'through manners' in a similar way to Layla.

For Ikraan, donning the *jilbab* was also a statement of her inner strength, determination and commitment to faith. It came to represent not only a personal struggle against experiences of marginalization, but also a collective struggle that connected her with the experience of other Muslim women in the *umma*. 'I feel really brave, you know, it was so hot the other day and everyone on the Tube was staring at me. One man moved away when I sat down!' It was akin to her adoption of the *hijab*, which she had gradually begun to see less as a restriction and more as a visual marker of choice and identity:

A *sheikh* once said that the *hijab* is a protection for women as the beard is for men. It's also a symbol of practising. If you're wearing it, men won't bother coming up to you, because they know you're practising. So it makes sense, and you get used to it. But it's not a fashion accessory. You have to be aware of what it means to wear it.

Ikraan employed a discourse of resistance to defend her decision to become more visibly Muslim – one echoed in Sabbiyah's insistence on clothing as a marker of identity. These items of clothing stood as powerful signs of her practising Muslim identity, and offered her protection from both Muslim men and the non-Muslim public. By articulating her decision through a personal and collective metaphor of struggle (*jihad*), she adopted a confrontational stance, rejecting negative images and taking pride in a stigmatized identity (Jouili 2009: 265). The *jilbab* stood as a signifier of legitimacy and defiance.

However, both Ikraan and Layla were aware of the exclusions and restrictions which they faced by wearing Islamic clothing in public places. Layla had sought to overcome these as much as she could, but Ikraan had accepted that her decision would further limit her movements across the city, and particularly her employment opportunities. Ikraan accepted that becoming more visible would also position her as different within public life; her sartorial decision would be viewed as a prioritization of the communitarian over the liberal or universal. Like Layla's decision to be 'less Muslim' Ikraan's adoption of the *jilbab* was a distressing choice negotiated within spaces of exclusion.

'What matters is what I think and feel': Cawo as a practising non-believer

Cawo, like Layla and Ikraan, was a young second-generation Somali woman who had begun to practise Islam during the early years of her university degree. However, in the last few years, after a long period of struggling, hesitating and trying to convince herself otherwise, she had decided that she was no longer a Muslim. The day we met for an interview, I did not have the slightest inkling that I would learn about her non-belief; dressed in *hijab* and *abaya*, she looked like nothing had changed since I had last met her.

One of the first questions I asked when I learnt of her decision was why she was continuing to wear *hijab* and *abaya*. She explained her clothing choice was a pragmatic one that enabled her to negotiate the pressures from her family and other Muslim friends and acquaintances. More so than her non-belief it was the removal of the *hijab* that was incomprehensible to her family. 'I'm not praying and they comment on that, but somehow that's it, it doesn't matter too much. If I ever took off my *hijab*, that would be the end of it, then they would start accusing me of all things. That's culture!' Like Layla, Cawo expressed the critique of a 'cultural' attitude that involves an excessive preoccupation with external appearances. By maintaining her dress she remained, at least to her family and outsider observers, a Muslim.

With very little prompting on my part, she divulged the difficulties she encountered following this drastic change in herself. She differentiated between values and faith, and elaborated on how her understanding of the former remained 'Islamic', despite her lack of faith:

> My feeling of right and wrong is Islamic. It's just difficult to think about these things without referring to religion cause that's what I've always done. And in a way I don't want to fall back into a Western idea of good and bad because I realise how much it influences us without us even knowing, and I don't really agree with it. I have a void in that sense.

According to Cawo, she could continue to be a non-Muslim, yet share Islamic values and participate in Islamic practices. Like Layla, being a Muslim (or non-Muslim) was not about adhering to a set of rules and values, but was instead connected to having, or not having, faith:

> I've decided not to tell people that I don't believe. To be honest, what matters to me is what I believe personally. ... But it's also very weird. I'm not a Muslim inside, I know I don't believe, but everything else about me is Muslim. I don't drink, I dress like this, so people around me think I'm Muslim. My identity for them is Muslim. But maybe that doesn't matter?

Cawo attempted to reconcile her behaviour by separating practice from interior belief, reflecting the distinction Layla made in the poem between Sister A and B. Although others saw her as a Muslim, what mattered to her was her lack of belief. Donning the *hijab* did not affect her non-belief, as it simply stood as a sign of her identity, not a manifestation of her authentic internal self. As she explained later: 'I hate Muslims who think you believe whatever they do. I never again want to be told how to think and feel, what matters is how I think and feel.'

Cawo was prioritizing interior religious conscience and religious choice (Fernando 2010). The *hijab* did not impact on her interior thoughts and feelings, but usefully worked as a signifier in her relation with her family. Her comments also reflect a mode of subjectification which stresses the importance of personal authenticity (Taylor 1994) and the 'expectation and demand that one's acts should express an authentic inside of who I am and who I choose to be' (Jacobsen 2010: 314; see also Fadil 2008: 273). For Cawo, her faith had infringed on her own thoughts and feelings. Her freedom from faith was articulated according to a liberal conception of 'freedom of conscience' – an ability to think and feel as she pleased.

Canab, a young woman in her mid-twenties, justified her decision to remove her *hijab* by drawing on a similar notion. Although she still considered herself a practising Muslim, she argued: 'It didn't feel right anymore, I wore it but I wasn't connected anymore, it didn't feel like it was me.' Since removing the *hijab* she had been frustrated by the assumptions made by both Muslims and non-Muslims that she was not a practising Muslim. 'I don't understand why my religiosity and spirituality need to be assessed by whether I'm wearing it!' she explained. Her prioritization of internal spirituality through the removal of her *hijab* also posed a challenge to the over-signification of the practice in the public sphere.

Inside-out reconsidered

To return one last time to Layla's poem, Layla insisted that interiority alone is insufficient, as her resolution lies somewhere in the middle, with Sister C, who is capable of balancing interior and exterior dimensions of the self. I have demonstrated above how Ikraan and Layla differently mediate the 'middle way' depending on their personal negotiations of family pressures and workspaces. I have also illustrated how both women shift between different positions: on the one hand, exterior practices do not matter and interiority is prioritized, yet on the other, there is a connection between interior and exterior dimensions of the self, and the *hijab* and *jilbab* do impact on the ways in which they act and 'feel' inside.

Central to both women's ideas is their knowledge and application of Islamic pedagogical projects of ethical self-fashioning, as explained by Mahmood (2001; 2005). Layla, on one occasion, advised her friends on how to remain consistent in their *iman* and in prayers. She stressed the importance of 'fake it till you make it' – repeating prayer in order to instil a habit which will, in turn, generate and strengthen sincerity in one's intentions and motivate action. Layla's understanding of prayer requires a particular coordination between emotions, intentions and actions in which practices are constitutive of a self-disciplining process and are both the means, and the ends, to fashioning a pious self. When contrasting her attitude towards external practices with that of her father, Layla emphasized the importance of 'sincere intentions' and the interior dimensions of the self. Her father failed to understand her intentions to wear the *hijab* solely to connect with God and to instil and cultivate interior virtues and emotions. Fashioning a moral self, according to these young women, and in contrast to their parents, requires a careful coordination of outward behaviour and inward dispositions (Mahmood 2005: 135).

Yet despite this understanding of Islamic pedagogies, both women negotiate their practices in different ways, although they both ultimately prioritize interiority and the universality of Islam. According to Layla, 'the inside is most important'. This emphasis on interiority, I argue, indicates a reworking of this Islamic pedagogical model, which results from the problematization of exteriority. It is illustrated by Saynab, another young practising woman, mentioned in Chapter 6, who contrasts her understanding of *iman* with that of her mother who works from the 'outside-in'. This attitude also resembles an eighteenth-century notion of interiority, which I discussed in Chapter 5, whereby morality becomes anchored in one's internal feelings (Taylor 1994). As I illustrate in the section below, for both Layla and Ikraan the interior experience of *iman* is constituted through virtuous conduct, but it is most importantly an emotional experience of connecting with God. These women are both drawing on Islamic discursive traditions, but it is this insistence on interiority, and its shifting and unstable relation with exteriority, that indicates, I suggest, a historical change in understandings of what constitutes a Muslim subject.

Interiority as affect

On one occasion when Layla expressed the problems she faced in the workplace, her friend Latifa advised with the following:

> You need to strike a balance between being social and maintaining your spirituality. You can do *hijra* in your head;[6] it doesn't have to be physical. Just take yourself out of the context. Increase your *'ibadat* (acts of worship), so that these people don't suck it out of you.

Performing *'hijra* in [one's] head' exemplifies Latifa's insistence on interiority, and is ultimately crucial to her negotiation of exteriority and her understanding of what constitutes a 'proper' Muslim subject. Focusing on her personal feeling of connection with God, Latifa suggested, would help her negotiate social relations and avoid isolating herself, without compromising her faith. What mattered ultimately was not necessarily what she did and looked like, but whether she was able to maintain an internal, spiritual connection with God.

Similarly, on another occasion Luul, another young pious woman expressed her uncertainty about how she should negotiate handshakes with men. On the one hand, she knew modest behaviour required her to avoid shaking hands with men. On the other hand, she realized that in predominantly non-Muslim work environments, she may need to reconsider it.[7] She was attending an interview for a job and was uncertain as to whether she should shake the hand of her male interviewer. Prior to attending, she contacted a *sheikh* whom she knew well and trusted to discuss the matter. He advised her that provided her intention was to succeed in the interview, she should shake the male interviewer's hand. Avoiding shaking hands could compromise her success, making her appear unfriendly and 'religiously biased'. By prioritizing her interior intentions and the importance of an internal connection with God, Luul was able to negotiate the practice without feeling she had compromised her modesty.

This understanding of interiority as a connection with God, and an affective experience of faith, was also shared by Ikraan. For example, on the day she announced her decision to don the *jilbab*, Ikraan described the feelings she hoped to achieve: 'When I went on *'umrah* (pilgrimage) I wore *niqab* and I felt so good. I don't think it's a good idea to wear it here ... but I liked the feeling of being enclosed, feeling connected, and the *jilbab* will help with that.'

The *jilbab* accentuated her relationship with *Allah*. It enveloped and 'protected' her, and created a distance from others so that she could focus on her connection with God. The endpoint, which Ikraan achieved through physical withdrawal, was similar to Latifa's concern with doing '*hijra* in [her] head'. The aim for both women was to move away from caring about how the *hijab* affected their relationships with others, to focusing on an emotional connection with God. As Ikraan explained:

> I've stopped caring how people see me, what people think of me. I used to be so worried at the start. Even when I first started practising and wearing this I was worried what my friends would say, but now I know I have *Allah*, so I don't care. Now when people stare me up and down, I look away and I just ignore it. I'm happy and confident with who I am, I have nothing to hide.

The experience of connecting with God enables both Ikraan and Layla to discard 'what others think', and to feel at ease despite judgements from their parents, other Somalis and the wider public. In emphasizing interiority they de-emphasize the importance of being visibly Muslim, and prioritize the universal dimensions of Islam above the particular and culturally variable. As revealed by their comments, it is a personalized experience of affect that enables them to feel confident, whether they are wearing *jilbab, niqab* or *hijab*, and to retreat, at least emotionally, from the public sphere. While Ikraan initially struggled, experienced discomfort with the *hijab*, and feared others' comments, eventually, as she strengthened her connection with God, she stopped caring and worrying about others' opinions of her.

What draws Ikraan and Layla together as young second-generation practising women, and differentiates them from their mothers, is this shared affective experience of faith and of self-transformation. In Chapter 6 I stressed the ways in which these young women experience novel forms of self–other relationships, and particularly those with God, as affective. I noted how they interpret and describe these occurrences as moments of 'high *iman*'. The importance attributed to these experiences is manifested in the manner in which they frequently discuss and ask after their mutual states of *iman*. These comments testify to the extent to which faith, for these young women, is objectified; it becomes possible to refer to *iman*, as denoting an affective state separate from practice.

This understanding of faith as affective is captured by a comment Layla made, following a *halaqa* session that she delivered on prayer: 'I'd say it's a connection between the heart and the mind. You feel it as well, in your heart. But if you only feel it and haven't quite made sense of it, it's not complete and if you think you have it, but don't feel it, that's not enough.' Following the session, I asked her to elaborate more precisely on this experience, asking her to reflect on her thoughts, bodily sensations and feelings:

> It only happens when I'm in a good spiritual state. When my *iman* is high, I feel God. It's like a feeling, like something is surrounding my heart, wrapping it. Sometimes I feel really warm but not always. I feel overwhelmed by something, at peace, and my body feels really good, my thoughts are fixed on Him.

Similarly, Maryan, another young practising woman, contributed her understanding of what it meant to 'feel connected' with God, and to have a 'high *iman*': 'Sometimes I walk down the street and I feel so good, I feel that connection, that feeling of excitement, like something bursting in my chest.'

This somatic experience of *iman* as a feeling of energy, excitement and potentiality is akin to what Birgit Meyer (2014) has described as the 'wow' factor of religious experience. I argue it is produced through, but is also constitutive of, these women's novel embodied engagements with others – in this case with God. Layla's comment, in particular, captures the ways in which her experience involves a temporary moment of warmth and potentiality, which flows through and transcends the 'mind and body split': this affective experience is not independent of thought and language, but can never be captured fully by language (Moore 2011: 185; Navaro-Yashin 2009). These experiences are crucial to these young women's understandings of interiority. Although their emphasis on 'inside-out' draws on Islamic pedagogical models (Mahmood 2001), it simultaneously reworks these around the tensions between universality and particularism. These understandings of interiority, which are also shared by non-believing, young second-generation Somali women, are indicative of broader historical transformations.

Conclusion

This chapter has argued that multiculturalism debates are indicative of a problematization of the question of how to be British and Muslim. As illustrated by the TV programme *Make Bradford British,* this question has emerged as an object of thought and inquiry, giving rise to a series of queries surrounding the Muslim subject. As I argued in Chapter 5 by drawing on Foucault (2000: 118), problematization does not determine the responses, but it defines the elements and questions that possible solutions will respond to. *Make Bradford British* offers a solution, albeit one that reflects popular and normative political discourses on the supposed 'problem' of Islamic practices in British public spaces. Like other forms of public culture, the programme's solution celebrates and valorizes the liberal and universal above the communitarian, and problematizes the visibility of Muslim practices as a sign of particularism, and hence, difference.

This chapter has outlined the ways in which young second-generation Somali women intervene in this terrain of problematization by rethinking the relationship between two *ethical substances* (Foucault 1985: 26–8) – interiority and exteriority. I have shown how these also rework the tensions between visibility and invisibility, communitarianism and liberalism, and the particular and the universal. I detailed how Layla and Ikraan, two practising second-generation Somali women, negotiate exterior practices depending on their experiences of work environments and their relationships with their parents. In so doing, I pointed to their different attempts to find a 'middle way' between interiority and exteriority, and the ways in which these solutions are often unstable and negotiable. In different ways these young women emphasize the universal dimensions of Islam, challenge the ways in which they have been positioned as determined by particularist cultural constraints, and present Islam as part of a British tradition. In a similar way to their 'mosque hopping' in the previous chapter, they disrupt the ways in which Muslims have been positioned as socially and spatially distant vis-à-vis British society.

Furthermore, I have stressed how any negotiation, even if it involves appearing 'less [or more] Muslim', cannot be divorced from the constraints of hegemonic discourses on multiculturalism, national identity and the Muslim 'other'. As Jouili (2009: 467) points out, negotiations occur within a 'field of enabling constraints', whereby any form of resistance is a painful process of making difficult and fraught moral choices. Layla's and Ikraan's choices are also partially constituted within, and constrained by, normative practices and discourses in British public spaces. While they stress the universality of Islam, their practices continue to be viewed as particularist, and their religiosity as different and in need of reform.

These practising young women draw on a heterogeneity of intersecting forms of knowledge with the aim of fashioning themselves as pious subjects, through identifying ethical substances (exterior practice and interior dimensions), and reworking their modes of subjectification (affect, submission, and choice) (Foucault 1985: 26–8).[8] Fadil (2008: 250–1) argues similarly that the Islamic tradition of ethical self-fashioning intersects with liberal notions of autonomy and that the two traditions coexist in 'non-contradictory ways'; for young pious women autonomy is a *consequence* of their subjection to God. My work partly accords with Fadil's claim, and I have shown how autonomy and choice are employed in engagements with culture, and relations with older kin (see Chapter 5). I have also elaborated on how notions of choice work alongside, and are enabled through, submission to God and to an Islamic discursive tradition. However, I have been hesitant to assign choice and autonomy to a liberal tradition, but rather explored how choice as a mode of engagement is employed differently in particular contexts, ascribed to a range of different traditions, including the Islamic tradition, and also used in reaction to public culture or engagements with non-Muslims.

By comparing practising women's insistence on interiority with a non-believer's understanding of non-faith and a practising non-*hijab* wearer, I have sought to emphasize the diverse forms of negotiations employed by what Fadil (2009; 2008) has described as orthodox Muslims, non-Muslims and non-orthodox Muslims. Contrary to Fadil, I have focused on the similarities between these women, in order to illustrate how second-generation Somali women are transforming the relationship between interiority and exteriority. For Layla, Ikraan, Cawo and Canab, exteriority alone does not make one a Muslim, nor does the manifestation of virtuous conduct (although for Layla and Ikraan both are incredibly important). For these young women, the solution is a prioritization of interiority as a personal and private experience of affect and thought. These processes contrast with the practices of older first-generation Somali women who, according to the younger women, prioritize exteriority and emphasize the *hijab* as crucial to their religion. Overlapping with these generational differences are shifting Islamic discursive traditions. Asad (1993: 219) writes that *diin* (translated as religion) 'relates more to how one lives than to what one believes. ... For Muslims ... it is virtues – mastery of the body, the ability to be patient, and the capacity to judge soundly – that matter, not states of mind.' Mahmood (2001), referring to more contemporary reformist traditions, stresses the dialectic, mutually constitutive relation between interior and exterior processes of the self, as crucial to the fashioning of a pious Muslim subject. These young second-generation Somali women, I argue, are further shifting the relationship between interiority and exteriority, and transforming and reformulating what it means to be a Muslim in Britain within a constraining political landscape.

Notes

1 Layla M, who also features in Chapters 2 and 6, is referred to as Layla for the remainder of this chapter unless otherwise stated.

2 A pass on the test is a requirement, under the Nationality, Immigration and Asylum Act, 2002, for anyone applying for British citizenship and Indefinite Leave to Remain.

3 See also Ewing (2008) for Germany.

4 British values of autonomy and gender equality are often evoked in arguments against the headscarf. Despite this, proposals to consider banning the *niqab* in the UK have often come under intense opposition from the mainstream. Former deputy prime minister Nick Clegg stated that a ban would be 'unBritish', impinging on a liberal tradition of autonomy, religious freedom and freedom of expression.

5 *Sheikh* Ahmed Babikir has been working in the UK since the 1970s. He is the *Imam* of Yusuf Islam's Islamia School, and leads weekly *da'wa* circles at Cricklewood Mosque in North-West London. He studied the Islamic sciences in Sudan under *Sheikh* Fatih Qaribullah.

6 *Hijra* means migration or flight, and refers to the Prophet

Muhammad's migration in 622 CE from Mecca to Medina. It is used more generally to denote Muslim migration away from non-Muslim lands, but in this case Latifa is adapting this concept to encourage Layla to undergo a mental migration from a non-Muslim space to a Muslim space inside her head that will connect her with God.

7   Both Fadil (2009) and Deeb (2006) discuss the ways in which Muslims negotiate the practice of hand shaking.

8   See the Introduction (footnote 17) for an explanation of Foucault's ethics.

CHAPTER EIGHT

Imagining an ideal husband

The *halal* marriage event

On a cold afternoon in December 2010, I sat with a small group of Somali women – which included Saynab, Ifraax and Layla M – sipping tea in a café in central London, in front of the venue where we attended a weekly Islamic class.[1] However, that afternoon we had gathered early before the class, not to undertake additional study, nor to catch up on the week, but to discuss the Somali *halal* marriage event[2] that Saynab was planning for the following month.

The idea for the event had come to her a few weeks earlier, the catalyst for which was a growing frustration in finding suitable men for marriage. While there was a time when Saynab had been a keen clubber, and had had plenty of opportunities to socialize with men, her pool of potential partners had shrunk since she had begun to practice Islam. She was now in her mid-thirties and was beginning to worry that she was past the marriageable age. 'These days it's incredibly difficult to find a professional Somali man who is also practising like us,' she explained. The event, therefore, was conceived as a means through which to unearth some appropriate men, and she had contacted like-minded pious friends (and her anthropologist friend) to help her with planning and organization.

The enthusiasm that Saynab brought to the introduction of the event, however, was quashed within minutes of the conversation. She quickly realized that achieving consensus was not going to be easy. Whereas she was keen to limit the event to *Somali* men, and in particular to *professional* men, Layla was intent on attracting Muslims from a range of ethnicities, and was less worried about issues relating to professionalism, status or wealth. For Layla it did not make sense that an event, which was to be first and foremost an Islamic *halal* event, should be open exclusively to *Somali* men. Agreeing with Layla, Filsan, a young teacher in her mid-thirties, was sceptical about narrowing the event to Somali men, not because she necessarily wanted to prioritize faith above ethnicity but because she worried that Somali men were generally lacking ambition. To add further to the tensions, Ifraax had kept quiet during the discussion and had shown little interest in being involved. When I turned to her towards the end of the discussion to gauge her opinion, she replied: 'I'm too romantic for this, it's not for me!' For Ifraax, such a structured event was devoid of spontaneity, love and romance.

For many of the young women who had begun practising Islam more actively in recent years, strategies for seeking out a potential husband had needed to be transformed. Some had begun searching for husbands through Islamic avenues, stressing their preference for a *halal* premarital relationship where meetings were typically arranged in public venues or with a chaperone (Ahmad 2012: 199–204). These more pious women often relied on recommendations from practising friends or relatives of the same age, sought advice from religious leaders or used websites for single Muslims (e.g. singlemuslim.com, muslims4marriage. com). Others, however, struggled with these restrictions and preferred to spend time with a man without close supervision. Many resembled the 'more or less pious' Muslims described by Deeb and Harb's (2013: 136) who employ moral flexibility in their discourses and practices of leisure and dating. In this case, some women were comfortable with attending shisha cafés or bars, mixed weddings or parties, and meeting men in these contexts, whereas others were not.

These women's ideas and hopes for marriage were shaped in multiple ways and by a wide range of sources. Many were avid consumers of romantic comedies, films and novels. Those who had started practising, however, had additionally begun learning about Islamic notions of marriage, by attending Islamic events or courses run by a vast array of independent institutes which catered to young Muslims. The courses were often practical in nature, and provided information on everything from cultivating the correct virtues and dispositions within marital relations, to managing parental expectations, or adhering to permissible sexual acts within marriage. Furthermore, the women often spent their time skimming through the marriage sections of Islamic bookshops or searching for information, videos and podcasts available online through Islamic websites.

Marriage was not only a topic of study or entertainment but also one of intense conversation and debate. Discussions could be sparked by a remark about a romantic film which one of the women had seen, or a comment from an Islamic course they had attended. Anecdotes about their (often failed) attempts at finding a husband could be humorous, but the tone could often shift, and become serious, as they discussed their ideal husbands, the nature of the marital relation for which they longed, and the married life to which they aspired. While these exchanges involved joking and teasing one another, they also involved a great deal of reflection, thought and imagination. Our conversation that December afternoon and the discussions and planning that ensued were one such example.

By focusing on debates about marriage, this final chapter offers a reflection on the making and remaking of subjectivity in moments of social change. Through marriage debates, young women grapple with the politically charged questions of what it means to be Somali, British, young, female and educated. In what follows, I bring together the three previous chapters to elaborate on how different engagements with notions of piety, culture, modernity and Britishness are managed and negotiated in various ways. In discussions about marriage, these young women experiment with different forms of knowledge, some of which are newly encountered, others not. They draw, for example, on Islamic discourses and teachings, and bring these in relation to other moral projects and ideas, as well as to themselves and their relations with others. Marriage provides a space for these young women to reimagine relations with potential spouses; as these new fantasies are articulated, these women's 'relational matrix' (Long and Moore 2013) shifts so that they also reconfigure their relations to kin, friends, an imagined notion of the British public, and God. This process is made possible through discussion and self-reflection, but also, importantly, through the imagination. Marriage, therefore, like other reflective and imaginative moments of change in the life-course, involves the setting of new horizons. This is not to say that all the young Somali women I encountered and interacted with were concerned with marriage; for some, as I explore later, marriage was of little interest. Yet for many, even if they did not eventually get married, the possibility of marriage constituted a significant turning point in their lives. It offered an opportunity to reflect on themselves and reimagine their relations with the world around them. Therefore, drawing on various debates around marriage, this chapter explores changing engagements with the ethical imagination, as marriage debates offer a space for these young women to articulate, contest and imagine new possibilities for the future.

Through marriage I also shed further light on the process of aspiration. As the final unfolding of the event highlights, the organizers were less concerned with the outcome, and more with the process of managing and planning; the event was a space created by and for them to articulate, discuss, debate and imagine their future. In fact, although the marriage event did go ahead thanks to Saynab's hard work and her successful recruitment of several other organizers, it was ultimately unsuccessful in attracting any 'suitable' men. In the weeks preceding the event, the organizers had registered twenty-five men, but on the day, seven showed up, and only a handful arrived on time. Even those who did attend were quickly dismissed by the women who saw them either as too 'traditional', or not sufficiently pious; others were not earning enough money, and several, as one young woman put it, 'just weren't attractive!' Nevertheless, as I show below, the women continued to discuss and debate the issue and – despite the failure of the event – did not abandon the idea of organizing something similar in the future. Whereas this moment of potentiality was unsuccessful, they sought other avenues for striving.

The ethnographic focus of the article is on three discussions around an 'ideal husband'. The first expands on the marriage event and the ideal of a professional, practising Somali man, while the second explores Ifraax's fantasy of love 'Jane Austen style'. The final brings to light efforts to draw inspiration from Khadija, the first wife of the Prophet, in order to emphasize the importance of personal ambition, professionalism and equality in marriage, but also to justify some women's attempts to delay marriage. Analytically, these examples demonstrate how imagined relations with potential husbands entail drawing on various forms of knowledge, which are used to rework these young women's relations with self and others in various ways. They point to the ways in which marriage offers a particular lens onto the imaginative, aspirational, but also complex and contradictory, processes that engage the ethical imagination.

Imagining a professional, practising Somali man

Saynab had not expected that her idea of organizing an exclusively Somali marriage event would have elicited such disagreement among the group. After all, marrying a Somali spouse was a fairly common practice, even among the younger generations in London. Among the households with whom I conducted fieldwork, only four out of twenty younger couples who had been raised in the UK were married to non-Somalis, seven were married among members of the same clan and nine to other Somalis from different clans. As I describe below, for many young women, such as Saynab, marrying a Somali man is a way of maintaining a connection to Somali kin, culture and society. Furthermore, as Saynab claimed, her preference for a Somali spouse was also a way of acting as a 'good daughter', 'respecting' her parents and kin by choosing someone with a shared heritage with whom they could converse and relate. Saynab's family also placed pressure on her to marry a Somali man, but they never sought to arrange or assist a meeting with a potential husband.

For Saynab, the prospect of marrying a 'practising Somali' was a way of reconciling kinship ties with her pious pursuits – her relationship with her mother and kin, and with God. But Layla saw things differently. She was reluctant to attend the event as she was 'completely uninterested' in marrying Somali men. As revealed in the previous chapter by her views on the *jilbab*, she was less concerned with pleasing her parents than her Creator. Furthermore, she was worried that by limiting the event by ethnicity, the young women were in fact 'segregating' themselves. Whereas Saynab was likely to associate with other Somali women regardless of their interest in religion, Layla's friends were all relatively pious, but more diverse in terms of ethnicity. Expectedly, Layla thus preferred to open up the marriage event to Muslims from different ethnic backgrounds. Nonetheless, some groups, such as Bengali men, for example, were considered less favourable because their marriages were seen to be unequal in gender terms, with wives expected to live with, and look after, in-laws – a practice uncommon within Somali households.

Saynab disagreed. She insisted that marrying a practising *professional* Somali man was a way of ensuring that she was not 'segregating' herself. The discourse of 'practising professionalism' partly echoes the notion of the 'pious modern' described by Deeb (2006) in her ethnography of women in Beirut. As with my interlocutors, 'modern-ness' to pious women in Beirut is inseparable from spiritual progress and refers both to an 'authenticated Islam' and to ideas of progress, civilization and material development. Yet the notion of 'professionalism', as I elaborate on later in relation to Filsan, also emphasizes a sense of belonging to a middle- or middle-upper class, white-collar profession, and is, therefore, more closely associated with notions of work, social status, and financial and material aggrandizement. For Deeb's (2006) interlocutors, enacting a pious, modern self entails discarding certain Western practices and discourses such as those of materialism and social status, whereas in the discourse on 'practising professionals' these are not treated as necessarily incompatible with pious pursuits. As I alluded to in Chapter 6, Saynab's aspirations for social mobility were also evident in her move, following university, away from what she regarded as the poorer working-class areas of the city. Seeking a professional job enabled her, like many of these young women, to aspire to an upwardly mobile life. Marriage, she hoped, was another way to achieve this.

Furthermore, the term 'professional' also points to its opposite, in this case the 'abjected subject' (Ewing 2008) of the 'traditional' or 'cultural' Somali man. Whereas for Ewing the 'abjected' man within the German national imaginary is applied to all Turkish men, in this case these young women used the discourse to apply it only to some categories of Somali men, particularly those who embodied stereotypical and undesirable characteristics. These young women project onto these men all the attributes of an undesirable marital relationship. For example, the young women were adamant they did not want to marry cultural Somalis or men who had recently arrived to the UK from the Somali regions, often referred to as 'freshies' – 'fresh off the boat' – as they were considered to be undesirable partners. 'They expect us to stay at home, do the cooking and cleaning … just to be a traditional Somali wife,' Nadiifo, another young woman, explained. Traditional men are thought to be uneducated and thus speak little English, to have 'old-fashioned' manners, ways of speaking, comportment and dress and, furthermore, to hold traditional ideas about marriage and gender equality. They are criticized for not having, or for not desiring, an egalitarian companionate relationship based on mutual choice. Respect for women's equality is employed as an instrument of modernity and used as a sign of a 'professional' man (Butler 2008; Ewing 2008). Moreover, for some women, 'traditional' men are rarely employed in professions that these young women would deem suitable. 'We have nothing in common with a freshie,' Nadiifo explained. 'We want someone who is employed, is ambitious, but also has a good character, is practising, more than just praying … actively learning religion,' she continued summarizing Saynab's and Ifraax's perspectives.

Throughout the organization of the event, the young women put in place several filters in order to effectively spot 'traditional' men. I was assigned the task of registering the participants, and filtering phone calls from potential attendees. During the lead up to the event, I also received regular phone calls from the women, who were curious to know who had called and whether I deemed any to be suitable candidates. I was told to ascertain the level of English of the enquirers by listening attentively to their accent and language skills, and to enquire as to their educational background and current employment status. This would identify whether they were, in my friends' words, 'traditional' men. If the men demonstrated insufficient conversational English, or inadequate employment prospects, I was told to cut them off the list.

Beyond a dysfunctional marriage

This rejection of 'traditional men' was also an effort to distinguish their ideal marriages from those of their parents. Many of these younger women view their parents' marriages as 'traditional' and 'arranged' rather than based on choice,[3] and as 'dysfunctional' due to high rates of divorce and single-parent households. Divorces, which were frequent in colonial and postcolonial Somali society (Lewis 1994: 61–5), continue to be common among the first generation of Somalis in the diaspora (Griffiths 2002; Affi 1997). While this has become a public concern among many Somalis, the trope of the 'dysfunctional' single-parent household has also been problematically linked to criminality and unemployment within public and policy debates about Somalis in Britain[4] (see Chapter 4). As I describe below, Somali men are held responsible for many of these failures. Ifraax, for example, often explained that she had been against marriage until she began practising because she felt that many of the Somali marriages she witnessed were 'dysfunctional'. She explained to me: 'I used to be so anti-marriage before I started practising. Just cause I saw so many divorces around me, I was convinced I would end up as a divorcee; I just didn't see the point in marriage.'

Young people appropriate this public discourse in casting their parents' marriage practices as 'dysfunctional' and 'traditional', presenting their own marital aspirations in contrast to these stereotyped depictions. They project a different view of marriage, based around the conjugal couple, and a nuclear family with limited interference from both natal and marital kin. They also strive for long-term marital stability, employment and families with fewer children. The problematic marital relation is attributed in part to the unreflexive embrace of what they regard as traditional norms within the marriage, as I show in the following example.

In January 2011, I attended a one-day Islamic marriage course led by *Sheikh* Rabbani[5] with a group of young practising women. 'Marriage is the key test of good character, it is half our *diin* (religion) because you are relating to creation (the other half refers to one's relationship to God). No relationship tests like marriage does; it nurtures good character,' the scholar explained at the start, stressing the relational dimensions of marriage. One of the recurring themes addressed by both Rabbani and the participants was the issue of how to deal with parents who disapproved of a marriage with an individual from a different community, cultural background or ethnic group. The *sheikh* advised that while Muslims had an obligation to be good, gentle, respectful and righteous towards their parents, they did not necessarily have to obey them. He went on: 'If parents say no to someone who is of "good character" and good in *diin* (religion), then hold your ground. Don't get angry, speak to them with respect, just address their concerns.'

A few weeks later, when I met with Saynab and several others, a young woman, Shukri, who had been present at the course mentioned the scholar's comments on parental obligations and the importance of respecting kin, and acting in a good way towards them. Virtuous behaviour towards one's kin was testament of one's pious comportment, she elaborated. Since marriage was 'half our *diin*', this included relations not only to husband and children, but also to parents and other kin. While Saynab agreed with the young woman, Layla, who had been listening attentively, disagreed that marriage was only about relations in the *dunya* (this earth). 'Marriage is about connecting with God ... it should be done for the sake of *Allah*', she explained, and not 'for one's parents', reiterating a similar point made in relation to her choice of clothing (Chapter 7). According to Layla, 'religion' ought to take precedence over parental, or what she termed 'cultural', concerns. For Saynab and Shukri, however, religion ought to be paramount, but social obligations and relations with kin are not inseparable from religious norms and a commitment to God. Islamic discourses can be employed strategically to advocate choice and autonomy, as in Layla's case, but also to emphasize respect vis-à-vis one's kin in marriage, as in Saynab's case.

As we saw in previous chapters, the paradigm of 'religion and culture' is not employed solely to refer to sets of practices and values, but also to a particular *attitude* towards both religion and what are deemed to be Somali culture, traditions and values. 'Traditional' or 'cultural' Somalis – both potential husbands and older kin – are thought to be ignorant, acting out of habit, lacking in choice, and unable to engage with cultural and religious norms in an informed and reasoned way. Critiques of traditional men are not therefore a rejection of Somali traditions, but a critique of a particular mode of engagement (Foucault 1985: 26–8) with the notion of Somali tradition. These 'traditional' men, who act out of habit, are juxtaposed with 'educated' or 'professional' Somali men, who are thought to be attached to their culture and religion in a conscious and self-reflexive way. Povinelli (2006) explores how the love relationship based on intimacy and choice is part of a liberal mode of self-governance. The intimate contract is presented as distinct yet always imminently under threat by economic and political contracts. Typical of what she terms the 'autological subject' – the subject-in-love – exists in opposition to the 'genealogical subject', who is governed by the 'drags of descent' and whose actions are dictated by culture and tradition. The liberal subject 'is presumed to become sovereign at the moment she projects herself as her own authentic ground' (ibid.: 46). According to Povinelli, the autological subject cannot exist without its mirror – in this case the 'traditional' husband.

For young practising women, choice and equity are ways of asserting a difference vis-à-vis their parents, older kin and undesirable Somali men. This particular mode of engagement towards religion and culture is also inseparable from ideas of material and intellectual progress. By favouring an 'optional relationship' to culture, these young women establish a novel imagined relationship with their kin and husbands based on choice and equality, intersected by notions of emancipation and material progress, hence their preference for 'professionals'.

However, engaging with piety does not result in a total rejection of Somali 'traditions', but young women actively choose to embrace certain values or practices. Ikraan described her ideal marriage to me as traditional, yet Islamic:

> I'm a bit of a traditionalist. I've always loved a family … so I really want to be the mum who looks after the home, who cares for her husband. … I want to be a caring, supportive wife, looking after home and family. However, this does not mean that I have to have an inferior relationship to my husband. Housework and child work are valued in Islam, not like in the West.

There is an interesting twist here. While tradition is associated with housework, and the 'West' with women's emancipation from the home, these women see housework as devalued in the West. Islam, they insist, unlike the West, places value on it, and recognizes their social and financial contributions, through its commitment to the ideals of gender equity and mutual companionship.

These women emphasize the importance of choice, but for Layla choosing involves separating one's self from kin and traditional others, and prioritizing a commitment to piety. For Saynab and Ikraan, one can exercise choice to maintain an attachment to kin, traditions and norms, and to a Somali identity, by selecting a Somali spouse who has a 'non-cultural' attitude to both faith and culture. These two contrasting ways of negotiating discourses of piety and culture, social obligations, a desire for social mobility, and public discourses on Somali migrants, engage the ethical imagination in slightly different ways. Through the organization of the event, Saynab and her friends cultivate a fantasized relation to the idealized figure of the Somali, practising, professional man. In so doing, they seek to reconfigure new relations not only to a husband but also to kin, non-Muslim others and to God. Some relations are engaged through choice, reason and reflection; others are fantasized and imagined. Some are based on their own experiences, for example of living and interacting with kin, while others are based on abstract ideas and imaginaries gained from public discourses, texts or ideals of professionalism. Marriage, therefore, offers an interesting site from which to view the ways that contradictory or overlapping forms of knowledge are engaged, reconciled or negotiated, and are tied to relations between self and other.

In what follows I turn to Ifraax, and to another conversation about marriage, to show how this also involved reconfiguring her self–other relations, albeit in a different way.

Love Jane Austen style

I introduced Ifraax, a young practising friend of Layla's in Chapter 6. In her mid-twenties she lived in East London and worked in community arts. Whereas a few years previously Ifraax had been uninterested in marriage, as I mentioned above, this changed as she began to take the practice of Islam more seriously. However, she insisted that in order for marriage to last, it had to be based on love. It was for this reason that she had been hesitant about the marriage event proposed by Saynab. As an avid consumer of Hollywood comedies and romantic novels, and like many other young practising women in their mid-twenties, she wanted, and expected, to 'fall in love'.

She frequently spoke of love in relation to Jane Austen's novels and film reproductions. With her close friend Sumaya, another young practising friend in her late twenties, she had seen the BBC production of *Pride and Prejudice* about a dozen times and they had contemplated planning a *Pride and Prejudice* fancy dress party together. On one occasion, I heard the two women discuss how Elizabeth Bennet, the main protagonist of the novel, could have been Muslim, as she embodied all the virtues of a Muslim wife: modesty, humility, honesty and intelligence. They also saw Elizabeth's critical attitude towards social mores and norms as reflecting their own criticisms of older kin's cultural practices. Yet, Elizabeth's continued respect towards her kin echoed the notion expressed by Saynab: that respecting kin was itself an Islamic virtue. Elizabeth is outspoken, not afraid to speak her mind and is certainly not submissive to male authority, particularly in her relationship with Darcy, her future husband. Choice of spouse is paramount for Elizabeth as it is for Ifraax and many other practising women. Furthermore, Elizabeth initially rejects Darcy for his arrogance and disrespect towards her family, despite recognizing his vast wealth, and only accepts him after he apologizes and endeavours to change his ways. To the young women, this reinforced their belief that love was ultimately more important than wealth and social mobility, although of course the latter were not irrelevant to their lives.

Most importantly, Ifraax and Sumaya longed for this kind of love relationship, in which love arose as a spontaneous emotion between the couple, but also developed as a consequence of learning about each other. In the novel, Elizabeth only begins to love Darcy after she has *learnt* to overcome her pride and prejudice and to see Darcy for who he really is, with his 'true' characteristics and virtues. The kind of love relationship envisioned by these young women involved negotiating between idealized notions of romantic, virtuous and spiritual love gained through Islamic teachings. I elaborate on each in turn.

On a late summer evening while sitting in my house after dinner with a few friends, Ifraax suggested that she believed in soul mates – in the idea 'that two people can be so alike and complement each other, and they just know and feel it'. Layla nodded in agreement and was quick in providing Quranic evidence for the existence of soul mates. Saynab, however, looked up from her smart phone and retorted: 'I'm sceptical. Love is overrated and it never lasts. ... Anyway love like it is in the movies doesn't exist.' Saynab rejected the 'fictionalization' of love (Gell 2011) and adopted a more pragmatic approach to marriage. Ifraax, however, responded by pointing out that she agreed that love was typically represented in Western films as superficial or as lustful based on physical attraction, but that this was not in fact *real* love, the form of romantic love found, for example, in other films and novels such as *Pride and Prejudice*.

Spiritual love, which draws on Sufi-inspired teachings, was frequently juxtaposed to notions of Western love. During one of our conversations Sumaya referred to a lecture we had both attended by Yasmin Mogahed, a popular Muslim scholar from the United States, on the topic of Muslim women's empowerment in marriage.[6] Mogahed had contrasted two types of love. The first type, based on what 'you get from them [husbands], how they make you feel', is ultimately unstable and can never be fully satisfied. Another type of love arises between people who love each other for what they are: 'The beauty you see in them is a reflection of the Creator. ... Learn to love in the right way ... for Him, through Him and by Him,' she argued. Ideally, love for one's husband ought to be an extension of one's love for God.

Sumaya felt that Mogahed had accurately represented the notion of spiritual love to which she should aspire. Husbands should be loved 'for the sake of God', as the most important relationship to cultivate on earth was that between self and God, she reiterated. Husbands should serve as a means to help one forge this intimate connection with the transcendent. This point reflected Layla's views on the *hijab*, which should be worn solely to please God and not one's parents.

Furthermore, this love could not always be expected to arise spontaneously. Just as one had to learn to love God by 'seeking knowledge', the same went for one's husband. While praise and worship is reserved solely for God, love can be learnt by appreciating a husband's naturally good traits (*fitra*), and his pious virtues. According to the young women, love was an intense and unique emotional experience, one that did not necessarily arise naturally, but could be 'worked on' or 'learnt'.

This attitude to love, which prioritizes the self–God relationship, draws on Sufi teachings and is similarly reflected in Layla and Ikraan's emphasis on interiority (Chapter 7). An intimate connection with God lies at the heart of these young women's conceptions of the spiritualization of the romantic relationship: love between a man and a woman is seen as a way of accessing divine love (Samuel 2011: 320). It points to a view of marriage that prioritizes one's relation with God and spouse above extended family.

This form of love was considered sufficient for some. Saynab, for example, insisted that by looking to God for inspiration they would find a deeper experience, one based on 'spiritual love'. The marriage event, in their eyes, was not 'unromantic'; it simply required that love be seen as an emotion that arises from a sincere and affective relationship between self and God. Love might not arise spontaneously at the event but, God willing, they would 'learn to love, for the sake of *Allah*'.

Yet for Ifraax this form of love was insufficient, since the *halal* marriage event simply lacked spontaneity. An emphasis on love 'Jane Austen style' was a way of reconciling a notion of a 'Western' spontaneous love with spiritual love. This contrasts with recent scholarship on marriage which has positioned Islamic reformist movements as opposed to, and critical of, romance relationships (Marsden 2007; Masquelier 2009; Schielke 2010a). Here we see how these young women seek to reconcile their quests for piety with ideas of a romantic, spontaneous love. They do so by drawing on films and novels as well as Islamic lectures and texts, and emphasizing certain elements – in this case love, choice and equality – as constitutive of multiple different discourses available to them in the UK.

Furthermore, by drawing on the narratives from *Pride and Prejudice* these young women are further positioning themselves in different ways in relation to 'Western' or 'British' society. In criticizing the moral deficiencies of certain elements of globalized Western love, such as lust, they turn to what is regarded as traditional English culture for inspiration: Victorian values, norms and manners exhibited in the novel. These are deemed to align with Muslim values. Contrary to public perceptions of Muslim women as foreign and different from British society, these young women insert themselves within the history of the nation, presenting themselves as embodying traditional English values and, hence, as already part of the nation (see Chapter 7).

By positioning themselves within English, and hence British society,[7] they are also making social class visible (Edwards et al. 2012: 12). The contemporary moment in Britain has been characterized by a shift away from the politics of social class towards a postcolonial multiculturalism based around notions of ethnicity and cultural nationalism (Evans 2012). Through appropriating the character of Elizabeth Bennet, young practising Somali women such as Sumaya and Ifraax are challenging this de-politicization of social class by inserting themselves, whether intentionally or not, within discourses of class. In so doing, they are also placing themselves within a notion of traditional English society structured around class hierarchies. Furthermore, *Pride and Prejudice* presents a narrative of social mobility through marriage, one that reflects these women's desire for a 'professional' man. These discussions about ideal husbands offer a means of imagining themselves within the class system, while striving for a higher social status.

Ifraax and Sumaya's aspirations for a 'Muslim Darcy' provide another example of how they negotiate contrasting ideals, conventions, aspirations and desires. On the one hand, they seek to reconcile Sufi-inspired teachings with idioms of romantic love, and to manage public discourses on Muslims as well as their aspirations for social and class mobility. Their discussions also point to how romantic love is not necessarily juxtaposed to pragmatic and financial considerations (Osella 2012; De Munck 1996).

On the other hand, in employing these various discourses and ideals, they engage the ethical imagination. Through these ideals, the young women articulate novel imagined relations to potential husbands, but simultaneously rework their relations with multiple others; they forge an intimate connection with God, and reposition themselves within public discourses and debates around social class, multiculturalism and British values.

Khadija as an independent professional

As I mentioned at the start of this chapter, Filsan was not particularly enthusiastic about organizing a marriage event solely for practising Somali men. She claimed that these men often lacked ambition, and would not provide the kind of marital relationship she desired. While she partly agreed with Saynab that the event ought to be limited to professional men, she insisted that they should ultimately give particular weight to these men's educational backgrounds and employment prospects. 'We can't have men without proper jobs,' she reiterated. While Saynab insisted on the importance of advertizing the event through email and social media and among Somali businesses and networks, in order to attract the right people, Filsan was not fully persuaded. As I described above, the young women often associated the notion of professionalism to a modern and educated outlook but also to class, social status and financial and material success. Attracting a man with a good salary, who could guarantee them a comfortable life, financial security and status, was an important consideration. Not only did Filsan desire to engage in 'intellectual conversations' with her future spouse, she also wanted him to materially support the family and to improve their social status.

According to Sauda, the event was problematic because, like other young women, she regarded Somali men in Britain as lacking ambition. This negative perception is tied to the stereotype of the Somali man who lounges outside Somali restaurants and cafés chewing *qaad,* and who is unemployed and unable to care for his family. 'I don't want to get one of those men who linger outside Internet cafes and Somali shops!' another friend told me in a conversation about Somali men. When I questioned Sumaya on her views on Somali men, she replied: 'They have the reputation of being lazy. They look at their relatives who haven't aspired to higher things and they just like to be comfortable, going into IT, bus driver … maybe they haven't seen successful Somali men, so they don't aspire to do much.' Reinforcing the stereotype, these women insisted that young Somali men raised in the UK, when compared to the women, typically tended to perform poorly in their studies and subsequently struggled to find employment.

The aspiration for a modern, educated professional relationship was often raised with reference to Khadija, the first wife of the Prophet and the first female convert to Islam. Khadija was treated as exemplary of the ideal Muslim wife. On numerous occasions I was told about the way she 'comforted, cared and supported' her husband. My interlocutors, who wished to inform me about the gender equity and importance of choice in Islam, reminded me that Khadija worked, was older and wealthier than the Prophet, and that she chose to propose to him. The Prophet did not take a second wife while he was married to her, and he respected and loved her immensely. This, they claimed, was truly a perfect marriage. Equality, monogamy, mutual support and choice were already present in Islam and hence, my interlocutors insisted, there was no need to draw on Western society to find these ideals.

Concerns for 'gender equity' or 'gender complementarity' surfaced frequently in our discussions. Earlier in this chapter I introduced *Sheikh* Rabbani who led a marriage course that I attended in early 2011. At one point during the course, the scholar encouraged both men and women to 'nudge' their spouse into adopting the *sunna* by sharing tasks at home and helping each other out in everyday life. 'The Prophet did the cleaning, the cooking and fixed his own sandals,' he reminded the men. Gender equity is based on a naturalized notion of gender difference, which considers men and women to be naturally different yet equal in the eyes of God – a notion that has become popular in discourses of authentic Islam (Jouili 2015: 118; Deeb 2006). Deeb (2006) notes in her discussion on 'gender *jihad*' among her Shi'i female research participants that the concept of equity relies on feminist textual reinterpretations. These interpretations claim that, if applied correctly, Islam can eradicate many of the problems women face in patriarchal societies. From these women's perspectives, Deeb shows, the notions of gender equity and gender *jihad* also prove to the West that Muslim women can be both pious and modern.[8] My interlocutors similarly claim that gender equity demonstrates the ways in which the Islamic tradition has already incorporated many of the values associated with Western culture. On one occasion, as we discussed her role as a wife, Aamina, a practising young woman, explained to me: 'Western culture has become part of me and so I think everything has to be equal. But actually I have learnt that equity is also part of Islam.' The companionable ideal, therefore, merges both assumed Western and Islamic attitudes and values.

My pious friends often reminded one another of the Prophet's exemplary behaviour. 'He used to help out at home, mend his own clothes, he never used to shout or hit them or anything. He had real respect. Responsibilities have to be shared, a husband can bring the children to school, help out at home,' Ikraan explained. She added: 'Khadija worked, she didn't have the time to do all the housework!' In reference to a passage from *Sura Al-Nisa* (chapter 'The Women') of the *Qur'an*, which was frequently discussed and reinterpreted among these women, Ifraax commented: 'Both husband and wife should obey each other, not in the sense of obeying orders but in the sense that they work together for the same goals, they cooperate and respect each other.' In unravelling the passage, she emphasized the importance of mutual respect, support and cooperation between the conjugal couple.

As others noted, Khadija not only shared responsibilities with her husband, she was also independent and financially successful.

She worked outside the home and was well educated and ambitious. She was the kind of wife with whom the Prophet could have an 'intellectual' conversation, I was told. For example, Latifa, one of Layla's friends, explained how the Prophet did not curtail her own personal ambitions, adding: 'I want a husband who'll let me travel, explore, do things ... and Somali men don't really like those kind of women.'

Hodan, a Somali woman in her thirties, also drew on Khadija's example. Yet she did not emphasize her piety, love or care for the Prophet, but her personal ambition. 'She was aspirational, just like you!' she told me during one of our many conversations. Hodan wore the *hijab,* but was not actively seeking knowledge like the young pious women I introduced in Chapter 6. She also socialized with both pious and non-practising Somali friends. Emphasizing the importance of interiority and a privatized notion of faith, she explained to me: 'For me religion is something personal, private. It's a way of doing good things, helping others.' On one occasion we discussed her business ideas, and she laid out her plans to leave her job, enrol on a Business Masters degree and set up her own business. She had already identified a partner, and they were working on a business plan. 'I really want to do my own thing, and I can't do it in my current job.' She drew inspiration from her mother, she explained, who had always worked: 'It's important for women to stay working, and be successful. ... My mum has always said that.' She then returned to Khadija: 'She had her own business, was independent, and did a lot of good in the world.' Khadija offered Hodan a role model of a successful entrepreneur, and proof that Islam supported women's empowerment, and was also compatible with business and entrepreneurial success.

Furthermore, she added a little later: 'Khadija didn't marry until much later in life but instead remained independent and dedicated herself to her business.' Her exemplary behaviour illustrated that there was no immediate need to marry if one had not found the right person. Hodan, in fact, was still single and was beginning to experience pressure to marry from family and friends. Yet she did not feel ready for marriage, and was more interested in pursuing her business plans. Several more or less pious Somali women I met during my fieldwork were in a similar position; some had not found a suitable husband, others had little interest in marriage and preferred to focus on other things. Latifa, for example, was intent on travelling and exploring the world, while Layla was keen on prioritizing her relationship with God for the time being. The example of Khadija's marriage to the Prophet offered them the possibility to think of themselves as temporarily independent of marriage, while presenting this as a pious or ethical choice. Imagining themselves as 'contemporary Khadijas' enabled them to see themselves otherwise, not only as ambitious, professional, caring and loving, but also as equal and potentially independent of men.

Marriage, piety and aspiration

As we saw in Chapters 6 and 7, engagements with pious teachings and reformist texts are chosen, reasoned, as well as embodied and affective, and are negotiated in relation to public discourses around Islam in Britain and notions of *Soomaalinimo*. In this chapter, I explored how pursuits for piety do not occur in isolation, but are entangled with other ideals, values, discursive traditions and aspirations. Furthermore, ideas and concepts taken from Islamic texts and teachings are not only geared towards the making of a pious self but also infuse other aspects of life, such as marriage prospects or hopes for economic and social mobility.

I argued that discussions on marriage offer a privileged site from which to view not only the coexistence of new and existing moral discourses, ideals, imaginaries and norms, but also the ways in which these are taken up to reimagine self–other relations. In discussing the event, Saynab merged notions of professionalism with pious ideals and social and cultural obligations towards kin, while Ifraax joined notions of romantic and spiritual love. These women drew on a set of discourses, ideals, values and aspirations, or using Schielke's (2010a) term, different 'moral registers', such as discourses of piety, social obligations towards kin, romantic love, professionalism and notions of personal ambition.

Yet these different ideas, values or projects are not necessarily clearly demarcated or coherent. According to Layla, for example, a religious attitude is not only distinct from a cultural one, but religion and culture are qualitatively different, and coexist and contrast with one another. For Saynab, however, certain 'cultural values' are also Islamic and, therefore, religion and culture can overlap and be combined. Similarly, for Ifraax, romantic love is not necessarily incompatible with pious pursuits and with notions of spiritual love, and for Hodan personal ambition and financial success are not inseparable from Islamic norms. Certain values – such as choice and equality – are claimed to be associated with pious projects, notions of professionalism, liberal discourses around minorities in the UK, and ideas on romantic love. By highlighting these common elements across – what are treated in academic discussions as – separate domains or 'registers', the women seek to resolve the tensions between them. They reveal how separations and divisions are always contextually and historically specific. They also actively transform these different discourses and ideas in the process by blurring the boundaries between them.

Furthermore, we have seen how these women might draw on reformist discourses that emphasize authenticity and the correct implementation of religious practices, while also appropriating Sufi-inspired practices of spiritual love. A range of Islamic forms of knowledge inform what 'piety' or 'practice' mean to these young women. They are not only selecting among various jurisprudential interpretations but also among different paths or schools of thought, combining them in new ways, and thus reworking the Islamic discursive tradition from within. As we saw in the previous chapter, Layla might be more concerned with articulating a form of Islam that is compatible with being British, while Ikraan's critique of her sartorial choice indicates that this is not necessarily a concern for her.

As I discussed in the introduction to this book, the anthropological work on the everyday lives of Muslims (Schielke 2010a; Osella and Soares 2010; Deeb and Harb 2013) has importantly shown how pious projects are not necessarily experienced in coherent and linear ways. Rather, they are often fraught with tensions, and negotiated in relation to other ideals, norms and often contradictory projects. This body of work has prioritized the social and cultural constructions of subjects but neglected the formation of subjectivities as structures of thought, feeling, reflection and imagination (Ortner 2005: 37). Schielke's work (2010a; 2015) has focused on how individuals experience and negotiate among different 'moral rubrics' and 'grand schemes', thus presenting the latter as separate and in opposition to the self. Subjectivities, I have argued in this book, are constituted and transformed through shifting forms of attachment to forms of power, as well as to self and other. These forms of engagement are constituted through processes of identification and dis-identification which are discursive, embodied, affective and imagined (Moore 2011: 76). Social and political shifts may initiate these transformations – providing new ideas or ways of being – but subjectivities are made sense of, and reworked, through events and experiences in the life-course. Marriage, as a transitional moment between youth and adulthood, offers young people a space for rethinking their attachments to ideas, discourses and fantasies, as well as for imagining a different future and novel forms of belonging. As I have shown, the self is always part of a 'dynamic relational matrix' (Long and Moore 2013), which comes to be reimagined through debates around marriage. As these women imagine novel relations with potential husbands, they simultaneously transform their relations vis-à-vis Somali kin and God. Shifting one form of self–other relation involves transforming the entire matrix.

I suggested that, for many of these young women, the endpoint is less important than the processes of striving. Finding an 'ideal husband' often proves to be a challenging mission, and many of these young women come to accept the impossibility of ever finding their ideal spouse. What I have illustrated here, however, is that striving continues in other ways, despite the failure of the *halal* marriage event, and the difficulties encountered. Debates about marriage highlight processes that are often missing in accounts of pious self-formation. They shed light on practices of reflecting, imagining and engaging creatively with the ethical imagination (Moore 2011) – processes that propel these women to engage in various projects of the self. Discussions around marriage provide a space in which to articulate and imagine new ways of being, and refashion their relations with self and other. But these debates are open-ended; through discussions around an 'ideal husband' the young women creatively engage with the questions of what it means to be pious, educated, Somali and British, with the possibility that their answers might change with time, and with the prospect that they may never achieve these endpoints. Marriage debates capture the impetus to keep striving towards an 'as-yet-unattained self', with the 'expectation that outcomes are not fully knowable in advance' (Khan 2012: 55).

Notes

1   Layla M, who also features in Chapters 2, 6 and 7 is referred to as Layla for the remainder of this chapter unless otherwise stated.

2   The young women preferred to use the word 'marriage event' instead of 'dating event' to indicate their intention to meet a man only with the aim of considering marriage.

3   These young women's portrayals of their parents' marriages as 'arranged' disregard the ways in which discourses of modern love and marriage based on mutual consent were widespread among the urban middle classes of Mogadishu throughout the 1960s to 1980s (Kapteijns 2009).

4   See Griffiths (2002) and Affi (1997) for a discussion of divorce among Somalis in the diaspora. Most analyses have centred on the first generation, and there is no available data on, or analysis of, divorce rates among the younger generations.

5   The course delivered by *Sheikh* Rabbani was entitled *True Love, Getting Married: Clear and Practical Guidance for Success*. It included an analysis of passages from the *Qur'an* on marriage, advice on selecting the appropriate spouse, the *fiqh* (law or jurisprudence) of marriage, a summary of Al-Ghazali's comments on the ideal characteristics of a spouse, and a final Q & A session. *Sheikh* Faraz Rabbani currently lives in Amman, Jordan but was born in Karachi, Pakistan, and raised and educated in Toronto, Canada.

6   Yasmin Mogahed lives in the United States and is currently an instructor for the New Dawn Institute, and a journalist for the Huffington Post. She travels frequently to the UK to deliver lectures and classes.

7   Interestingly, many second-generation Somali women stressed their identity as 'Londoners' before their national identity. They also preferred to use 'British' rather than 'English'. The reference to 'English values' is a reflection of the dominant role played by traditional English culture in constructions of Britishness and British society.

8   This notion of complementarity is often used to explain how women are considered to naturally embody characteristics that men lack, such as mercy, kindness, patience, generosity and so on. Other Islamic scholars (e.g. feminist Islamic scholars) may, however, use the language of liberal rights to assert gender equality and its presence within Islam. My interlocutors tended to refer to the former concept, but occasionally also employed the language of gender rights and equality.

CHAPTER NINE

Conclusion: Beyond Prevent

Spotting extremists

Case Study 1: Farah

Farah is a seventeen-year-old student of South Asian background, with long black hair parted to the side and a nose piercing. Always regarded as a good student, she begins to struggle with her secondary school GCSE exams when difficulties arise at home. She decides to take time off and shuts herself up in her room for almost two weeks. To make matters worse, she loses her best friend Leyla, who abandons her – and school eventually – for a new circle of friends. 'I was scared, I was alone,' Farah recounts. She strongly desires to be popular like Leyla, but also recognizes that she is different. 'Does being popular mean going out ... getting off your face? It's not me ... it's not my culture,' she explains. At night she begins talking to people online, many of who share similar feelings and concerns. Among them is Jamal, a young man who makes her feel understood. They talk about world issues, which Farah feels are not typically covered in the news, and discuss the struggles of feeling unwelcome in the UK. Jamal tells her of people who have left the country for a 'life with meaning'. 'I felt like an outsider, different,' she describes. Lying to her mother, she attends a meeting – which she describes as 'pretty intense' – and begins distributing leaflets at school. No one is interested and her anger and isolation are intensified.

At school, her sociology teacher picks up on a final paragraph of an essay she has submitted to him that, he claims, 'veered off the topic'. The language, he explains, was angry, accusative, inflammatory and 'out of character'. He raises concern with colleagues at school, and they advise him to discuss the issue with Farah. When he calls her in to his office, she decides to confide and confesses: 'I just wanted to catch your attention.' The teacher recognizes that Farah is 'lost' and 'struggling to fit in' culturally, but he is delighted that she has called out for help. With the support of the safeguarding lead in school, he refers Farah to a counsellor and encourages her to attend a youth group outside of school that debates issues in a 'safe space'. 'She wanted a purpose', the teacher concludes, and 'they are helping her find one.'

Case Study 2: Callum

Callum is a young working-class boy with a passion for football. Bad grades at school, problems at home, and a troubled relationship with his father result in him becoming distant from his family. He begins attending football games with his mate Stu. Thanks to Stu's connections, he meets Tony at the stands and they start socializing together in the local pub before and after games. On one occasion a fight breaks out and Callum uses his rucksack to deflect a glass in order to protect Tony. Out of gratitude, Tony invites him to a 'secret meeting' in the upstairs room of the pub. There, Tony speaks out against Muslims in their town, claiming that the country is 'being sold down the river' and that money is 'being used to build mosques, and change the law to suit them'. Tony tells Callum that they have the right to decide who lives in their town and that he can make a difference. On his instruction, Callum starts managing a regional Facebook page for Young Patriots, and begins to bully others in his school into 'liking' the page.

At school a teacher picks up on his altered behaviour; he was becoming 'cocky' and intimidating, she claims. A student reports Callum's bullying tactics and, with permission from the school head and safeguarding lead, the teacher looks at the Facebook page. The hateful language on the page immediately concerns her and, with the support of the other staff, she calls Callum in for a chat. He shares his views about immigrants and refugees in town using, the teacher notes, the same 'stock phrases'. The teacher decides to speak to Callum's family, and he is referred to the school counsellor. In these meetings he shares his personal concerns for the future, and his fears of not finding a job when he leaves school. Callum is reassured that he is 'in control of his future' and that it is 'time to stop blaming others for his perceived shortcomings'. He is referred to the careers manager and encouraged to attend a youth group to socialize with young people his age from a range of backgrounds. 'Change happened,' the teacher reports, 'he began to see that what he believed before lacked logic or reason.'

Prevent training

These two case studies form part of the Home Office's Workshop to Raise Awareness About Prevent (WRAP), a two-hour syllabus delivered online or face-to-face.[1] The case studies are presented in short black-and-white videos, narrated first from the point of view of the young person and then from that of the teacher while emotive music plays in the background. While these videos are aimed at staff in the education sector, WRAP is available to, and specifically tailored for, a range of front-line staff in various roles in the public sector. As mentioned in Chapter 1, the Prevent strategy, initially launched in 2003, has recently assumed greater legal importance with the passing of the Counter-Terrorism and Security Act 2015. It specifically enlists public sector workers – including those in education, healthcare, prisons and social services – to pre-empt individuals at risk of becoming terrorists, but also to identify those deemed to be 'at risk' and refer them to the government's deradicalization programme, Channel.[2] In what follows I draw on my own experience of participating in some of these training sessions, and my analysis of their training manuals. I illuminate the ways in which these trainings elicit public sector workers to partake in the shaping and reforming of Muslim subjects.[3] The second part of this conclusion reflects on the politically fraught task of writing about Muslims and Somalis and, by drawing on my ethnography, it proposes a number of alternative visions for a future beyond Prevent and securitized Britain.

WRAP training is structured around five overarching objectives. First, trainees are instructed about Prevent and its purpose. The 'iceberg analogy' is used to explain that attacks such as 9/11 and 7/7, or incidents such as the killing of Lee Rigby in Woolwich, are only the 'tip' of the iceberg. These attacks are a threat, but so is the 'greater mass' that works 'below the surface' to support that tip. This 'hidden activity' builds and builds, leading to the attack itself and, while not all of this activity is necessarily criminal, it is nonetheless considered threatening. The training reinforces the belief that front-line staff are not necessarily required to understand the ideologies promoted by extremists, but should instead focus on the way in which extremists 'hook in' vulnerable people.

The second and third objectives of the training, therefore, reflect on what might make individuals 'vulnerable to terrorism' and on how such vulnerabilities might be exploited to manipulate those individuals into committing a crime. These 'vulnerabilities', the facilitator explains, might be emotional or driven by external factors and may include anything from family upheaval, drugs or crime, mental health, isolation, social exclusion, peer pressure, loss, unemployment, sense of debt or guilt, a need for meaning, identity and belonging, anger and feelings of grievance and injustice, to a need for excitement or adventure. Workshop participants are encouraged to listen to the case studies and to identify these vulnerabilities themselves.

Farah, for example, has problems at home and feels overwhelmed by her exams. She also becomes increasingly isolated following her fallout with Leyla and starts to feel that she does not 'fit in' or belong. She feels stranded between her parents' culture and that of her peers and, as a result, feels lost and confused about her identity and sense of belonging. Callum also struggles with his grades at school and, following upheaval at home, he distances himself from his family and succumbs easily to pressure from his peers. Radicalizers Jamal and Tony exploit these young peoples' 'vulnerabilities' by initially making them feel understood and cared for and subsequently feeding them 'extremist ideologies'. Both Farah and Callum are frustrated and angry about the world around them. Callum worries about Muslim immigration in his town and his future employment prospects, while Farah begins reflecting on global events and injustices and questions her sense of belonging in Britain.

The training's fourth objective is to encourage participants to recognize when a vulnerable individual is in need of support. Here they are expected to look for 'changes in behaviour'. These changes may be emotional (detachment or withdrawal, anger, depression), verbal (scripted speech, obsession with a topic, being closed to debate, asking inappropriate questions) or physical (tattoos, changes in routine, new circle of friends). Behaviours and practices are treated as potential signs of extremist beliefs and ideas. 'Open and free speech' is to be encouraged at this initial stage and trainees are advised not to jump to conclusions but to contextualize behaviour in order to gain a broader view. Beginning to don the *hijab*, for example, is not a sign of extremism, but a woman who couples this clothing with an adoption of extremist language might potentially be 'at risk'. Callum, for example, employs 'scripted' speech and adopts aggressive, arrogant and bullying behaviour at school, as well as managing a far-right Facebook page. Farah withdraws herself from friends and family and then writes the provocative sociology essay which catches her teacher's attention.

Workshop participants are then asked to reflect on how young people can be misguided and coerced, and how they can be helped. While circumstances differ, the processes of 'radicalization' are similar. It is these processes, manifested in changes in behaviour and speech, that trainees are instructed to identify and report. Finally, trainees are advised on how they can help or support someone who they identify as being 'at risk'. This help takes the form of three main steps: noticing behaviour, checking this behaviour with a trusted colleague or friend, and sharing knowledge about this behaviour with someone who has the authority to refer the individual so that a 'proportionate response' can be elicited. The workshop concludes with two deradicalization videos, one explaining the Channel programme and the other featuring a discussion with 'deradicalization experts', Kelly Simcock and Manwar Ali.[4]

The videos in the WRAP programme teach participants that these behaviours are 'fairly easy' to spot and that signs of radicalization 'stand out'. 'Apply your professional judgement and common sense' and use your 'existing skills', trainees are instructed. The workbook for facilitators states that participants should not get 'caught up on whether the motivations are terror-related or not', but should 'think about what behaviours would give [them] ... a cause for concern – as simple as a "gut feeling" – about someone's welfare' (Home Office 2016a: 5). During the WRAP training on which I enrolled, the online facilitator repeated the term 'gut feeling' several times. The risk that 'common sense' or 'gut feelings' may discriminatingly target and stigmatize some students (Muslims, working classes) over others, or lead to over-referral, was not addressed, nor was the fact that many of the identified 'behaviours' are normal for many young people and do not constitute unlawful activities.[5]

Prevent and the Channel referral mechanisms are presented in the duty guidelines and trainings as just another part of staff's safeguarding and welfare duties. The WRAP training characterizes 'at risk' individuals as being in need of 'our help' and 'support'. The Channel programme is described as a 'care package' and a 'natural extension' of the duty of care, while the Channel panel as composed of 'people who want to help'. Extremism is compared with grooming, bullying, abuse or coercion. While, on the one hand, this emphasis on safeguarding and welfare is motivated by the concern that those 'at risk' should be effectively supported rather than unfairly targeted and criminalized, it also has the effect of depoliticizing Prevent and Channel. It disguises the fact that these programmes are fundamentally about counter-extremism and deradicalization. Prioritizing safeguarding concerns also turns welfare, and the relationships of trust on which it depends, into a system that serves the interests of state security, rather than those of individuals in need.

Deradicalization

Both Farah and Callum are identified as potentially 'at risk' of radicalization, and the videos provide trainees with a description of how the process of radicalization works in practice. The potential 'causes' of terrorism are reduced to a set of vulnerabilities caused by a range of personal experiences – from family upheaval and social exclusion to bullying. Radicalization is presented as a linear process, whereby preachers, peers or activists exploit vulnerabilities, leading to the adoption of 'extreme' ideologies, which are manifested in a range of behaviours and practices. The educateagainsthate.com government website refers to this as a 'path to radicalization'. As extremist-turned anti-radicalization expert Manwar Ali states in a Home Office training video, 'the recruiter would exploit a person's lack of connection. ... At first the process of radicalization might seem quite benign, developing friendships and passionate discussions.' He continues: 'Radicalizers are normally very successful because they provide that emotional support that a person sometimes misses in life.' In a similar WRAP video, a forensic psychologist explains the push and pull factors and the tactics used by radicalizers: 'At the core it's quite simple ... a need for belonging, purpose, and self-worth are feelings exploited by radicalizers.'

This emphasis on vulnerabilities and changes in behaviour positions radicalization within welfare and safeguarding frameworks and, thus, individualizes and 'psychologizes' the process. Training manuals for WRAP facilitators stress the importance of emphasizing emotions when identifying vulnerabilities:

> Try and steer the responses to emotions and feelings – these are after all what are truly exploited by a radicalizer. ... Keep turning the circumstantial reasons given for vulnerability into emotions or feelings where you can. This will mean you are far more likely to solicit key words such as Isolation; Belonging; Need; Anger; Desire; Frustration; Grievance. (Home Office 2016b: 6)

As Kundnani (2012b: 4) has argued, radicalization emerged over the last decade as a vehicle for policymakers 'to explore the process by which a terrorist was made and to provide an analytical grounding for preventative strategies'. Rather than investigating the complex causes leading to terrorist actions, Kundnani argues, researchers, analysts and think tanks have focused on 'modeling radicalization' and understanding the process of radicalization through theological and psychological processes, thus serving the needs and agendas of counter-terrorist policymakers. Within these studies, 'individual psychological or theological journeys, largely removed from social and political circumstances, are claimed to be the "root cause" of the radicalization process' (ibid.: 5). 'Psychological dispositions', for example, provide state officials with a supposedly scientific basis for 'indicators of risk' (ibid.: 8).

The work and expertise of scholars in the field of terrorism studies – most famously the psychologist and former CIA operations officer Marc Sageman – is used to legitimize these theories of radicalization. 'Experts' such as Manwar Ali reiterate these teachings through case examples and by drawing on personal experience. Researchers at the University of Liverpool

(Cole et al. 2009), for example, were commissioned to produce the 'Guidance for Identifying People Vulnerable to Recruitment into Violent Extremism'. Based on risk assessment and psychometric approaches, many of the 'vulnerabilities' identified by the researchers are those that appear in the Prevent training, and they also resemble the theological or psychological modelling described by Kundnani (2012b); cultural and/or religious isolation, low tolerance for other communities and religious beliefs, isolation from family, negative peer influences, isolated peer group and hate rhetoric are all presented as key vulnerabilities.[6] Rather than addressing the injustices and inequalities that may lead to acts of terror, attention is directed towards the individual and his or her psychological traits and social behaviour and, as we saw above, towards the religious beliefs and ideologies that are thought to be propagated by extremists.

In the videos, the 'problems' with Callum and Farah are portrayed as connected to the individuals and their social groups, and the causes of these 'problems' are depicted as reducible to a set of psychological factors and external circumstances tied to their immediate family and communities. Farah's interest in global inequalities and foreign policy is not viewed as a legitimate expression of concern about social injustice, but rather it is treated as a sign of extremism and radicalization. Callum's worry about future employment opportunities is not connected to the economic and class-based inequalities that exist in contemporary Britain. Instead, he is held responsible for his own failures and told to take 'control' of his life instead of blaming others. These young vulnerable adults are instructed and empowered to regain control of their lives as 'good' self-governing liberal subjects. Their subjectivities are reduced to a set of behaviours and beliefs, disconnected from a broader context, while extremist ideologies are presented as serving a purpose or fulfilling a need.[7] Inadvertently, the white, working-class boy and the Muslim girl – those most likely to be adversely affected by the government's neoliberal policies – are made to stand as the signifiers of current sociopolitical ills. Unsurprisingly, the solutions offered to Farah and Callum are also individualized, involving psychological or counselling support and participation in forums and youth groups where theological or ideological views can be discussed and challenged. The aim is for them to address their vulnerabilities and to abandon 'extremist' views and opinions.

Promoting British values

Another training programme – aimed at leaders and managers in the education sector and provided online by the Education and Training Foundation – begins its Prevent module with the definitions of 'British values' and 'extremism' taken from the Prevent strategy and duty guidelines. Extremism is defined in opposition to 'British values' as:

> Vocal or active opposition to fundamental British values, including democracy, the rule of law, individual liberty and mutual respect and tolerance for those with different faiths and beliefs. We also include in our definition of extremism calls for the death of members of our armed forces, whether in this country or overseas. (Home Office 2015a: 2)

Trainees are asked to reflect on how they will 'ensure that all staff "buy into" this definition' of British values, and on how British values will be integrated into the curriculum and exemplified in the behaviour of staff and students. They are told that inspections by the regulator Ofsted will look for how effectively providers prepare learners for successful life in modern Britain and promote fundamental British values. Yet, despite this emphasis on British values, little clarity or guidance is offered on what teachers are supposed to do in the classroom. The module makes some suggestions, such as teaching about the value of democracy through eliciting discussions on elections, the importance of registering to vote, or on how laws which apply to all – such as speed limits – are decided upon. The childcare.co.uk website suggests that Valentine's Day can provide a way of indirectly teaching young children about British values such as valuing family or making links to their local communities. But how are these values specifically *British?* And, given that the concept of British values is so encompassing, does this mean one can teach British values through racism, colonialism and slavery? Are there any topics that cannot be taught? What should I make of the story I heard recently about a secondary school teacher who was discouraged from teaching about Frantz Fanon's ideas in a class on racism and discrimination in British society? The sheer arbitrariness of these efforts to incorporate British values into the curriculum almost inevitably leaves trainees unclear as to what they can teach, wary of what they cannot teach, and confused as to why these values are specifically *British.*

One of the few clear messages that does emerge from this training is the need to cultivate a liberal attitude among students and encourage them to embrace diversity, develop 'critical thinking' skills, discuss and debate, but not hold too strongly to any single opinion. 'Closed debate' or 'an obsession on a topic' are signs of potential extremist behaviour. The Prevent duty guidelines state that schools should 'forbid political indoctrination and secure a balanced presentation of political issues' (Home Office 2015b: 11). Meanwhile, the guidelines on *Promoting Fundamental British Values as Part of SMSC in Schools* state that 'actively promoting the values means challenging opinions or behaviours in school that are contrary to fundamental British values' (Department for Education 2014: 5). Although, interestingly, critical engagement is encouraged only as long as it is not in opposition to British values.

The duty guidelines for higher education institutions state that events with external speakers should be monitored and, when they are allowed to proceed, speakers with extremist views should be 'challenged with opposing views as part of that same event' (Home Office 2015a: 4). At universities across the country, it has become disturbingly common to hear of Muslim students struggling to book rooms for Islam-related events or being referred to Prevent coordinators for taking part in pro-Palestine protests or engaging in events that question UK foreign policy. A similar pattern is emerging in schools, as evidenced by the infamous incident of a Luton seventeen-year-old boy, Rahmaan Mohammadi, who was referred to a 'special constable' for Prevent and questioned at home by the police for wearing a Palestine badge and handing out leaflets in school about the humanitarian emergency in Gaza (Rights Watch 2016: 35–40).

The promotion of 'British values' has become a key component in the effective implementation of Prevent, particularly in the education sector. As I outlined in Chapter 1, this emphasis on Britishness has been part of a rhetorical and policy shift away from multiculturalism towards greater cohesion, integration and national identity; the promotion of British values has become inseparable from discourses on anti-multiculturalism, Islam and the problems of integration. Under Prevent, British values have become juxtaposed with 'extremist ideology'. In the duty guidance, 'extremists' are said to regard 'Western intervention in Muslim-majority countries as a "war with Islam", creating a narrative of "them and us"' and are accused of holding the belief that 'people cannot be both Muslim and British' (Home Office 2015b: 3). Radicalization expert Kelly Simcock states in a Home Office video that extremist ideologies blur 'fact and opinion', leave no 'place for others', and manipulate faith, history and politics.

Extremist ideologies are presented as ahistorical, inaccurate, biased and divorced from the political context – and importantly from the effects of a colonial legacy and British foreign policy – and hence as originating solely within Muslim groups. This is part of a broader 'culturalization of politics' whereby difference has come to be understood through 'the lexicon of a bland corporate multiculturalism and ethnic pluralism' (Goldberg 2002: 207). Under the current multicultural framework, Islam has come to be seen in cultural terms, as a set of fixed and essentialized ideas and beliefs divorced from context.

While discourses of Britishness and British values have not directly been targeted at Islam, they have served to regulate the presence of the 'bad', illiberal, non-modern and extremist Muslim. This extreme 'other' is silently present in the teaching of British values. Like the 'tolerance talk' discussed by Wendy Brown (2006a), appeals to 'British values' have operated as a discourse of power that constructs liberal and non-liberal subjects, cultures and regimes. Tolerance, according to Brown, has emerged as part of a civilizational discourse, separating the free, autonomous, tolerant and civilized subject from the fundamentalist, intolerant and barbaric one. Tolerance has become synonymous with the West, with liberal democracy and Enlightenment modernity and is a marker that distinguishes 'us' from 'them'.

Appeals for a more cohesive national identity made in the liberal language of universal values such as democracy, freedom and equality, however, have had the effect of producing or reinforcing the 'extreme' Muslim other as different and repugnant. In a study of liberal thought and its emergence in conjunction with empire, Mehta (1999) offers a powerful critique of the effects of liberalism's abstract universal claims.[8] Drawing on Simmel's notion of the 'stranger', Mehta argues that this abstract universal language not only masks its origins in a European tradition, but also has the effect of emphasizing difference, remoteness and strangeness. Citing Simmel's essay he states:

> The consciousness of having only the absolutely general in common has exactly the effect of putting a special emphasis on that which is not common. For a stranger to a country, the city, the race, and so on, what is stressed is again nothing individual, but alien origin, a quality which he has, or could have, in common with many other strangers. For this reason strangers are not really perceived as individuals, but strangers of a certain type. The remoteness is no less general than their nearness. (Simmel 1971a: 148, cited in Mehta 1999: 25)

In a similar way, the language of universal values draws on a civilizing discourse to construe the 'extreme' Muslim 'other' as different, 'backwards', determined and constrained by culture, and hence opposed to liberal values of individuality and freedom (Brown 2006a). A liberal narrative of abstract rights, responsibilities and values – encapsulated in the political notion of Britishness – has turned the Muslim 'other' into a stranger of a certain type. It has emphasized difference by viewing the 'other' as an 'abstract type' and has upheld a progressive notion that the 'other' may be reformed. At the same time, universal values are derived from a British liberal tradition and employed to advocate a particularist national identity.

These tensions have been particularly pronounced around debates on gender and Islam, especially those on Muslim women, who have come to stand as visible signs of difference and as symbols of Islam's incompatibility with universal liberal values and with British national identity. As I analysed in more detail in Chapter 7, the visibility of Muslim practices such as wearing the *hijab* or *niqab* has helped single them out as objects of concern and scrutiny, and linked them to a range of other problems, from segregation to lack of freedom, violence and a threat to national identity. The Prevent duty guidelines for higher education institutions (Home Office 2015a: 4) place an obligation on these institutions to pay due regard to their existing 'responsibilities in relation to gender segregation'. As we have seen elsewhere, gender inequality (and gender segregation at university events) is often presented as a sign of Muslims' incompatibility with, and disdain for, British liberal values and hence as a sign of their extremist views. Respect for women's equality has become an instrument of progress (Butler

2008), a way of identifying, demonizing and reforming some Muslim subjects.

In sum, Prevent has been part of a process of shaping and reforming the Muslim subject, of turning the 'extreme' other into a liberal religious subject. The language of extremism, radicalization and Britishness has entrenched particular ideas about the 'good' and 'bad' Muslim (Mamdani 2004), where the latter is defined in opposition to abstract and universal liberal values. The liberal Muslim is she who willingly embraces a set of practices as a sign of her (apolitical) values and beliefs. Crucially, these beliefs or ideologies are to be approached 'critically'; the individual ought to be able to recognize that they are just one 'opinion' or perspective among many, and not the only truth. Truths must not be held onto too strongly, and individuals must be open to debate and to being challenged on their beliefs. Liberal values are not in themselves seen as a form of ideology, but rather are considered neutral and universal, providing the space for multiple truths to flourish. As we have seen, however, the notion of British values creates an 'us versus them' narrative between the liberal and illiberal subject, but any effort to highlight this process is classified as 'extreme'. The liberal religious subject, finally, is self-governing, not easily influenced or reliant on others. She does not seek to effect radical change in society but rather to work on herself. As a result, the state can only support and empower her to recognize her own struggles and to gain control of her own future.

Writing with Somali women: Future aspirations

How does one write about Somali women in Britain from a knowledge-producing institution that is complicit in this process of reforming Muslim subjectivities? What categories of analysis should one use, and how does one avoid denying Somali women's subjectivities? These are also the sorts of questions that the *Cadaan* Studies (Whiteness Studies) movement has been grappling with over the last year. Young Somali scholars have been engaged in reimagining what knowledge might look like when Somalis become active producers – not objects – of knowledge. This critique has developed in part in reaction to the surge of 'experts' on Somalia in the last few decades as consultants, researchers, academics and journalists have raced to set up institutes, draft recommendations, conduct research and engage in capacity building and development projects. Some have done so without ever having set foot in the region. The collapse of the state in Somalia and the ensuing civil war have created a lucrative field in which careers are forged and CVs enhanced. Funding has also been available for the study of diaspora Somalis and the 'problems' of security, extremism, social exclusion and integration. In 2012–13 David Cameron's government held two Somalia conferences in London, presenting the country as a foreign policy priority. Diaspora consultations were held before the conferences, and the Somalia Unit was given the first and only 'diaspora outreach role' in the Foreign Office. Yet, diaspora subjects have continued to be seen in ambiguous ways: on the one hand they represent potential resources and assets for development and counter-terrorism strategies, on the other they are viewed as biased, divided and lacking in objectivity (Liberatore forthcoming). As a consequence, project funding has tended to privilege non-Somali researchers and organizations, thus reinforcing the 'whiteness' of Somali studies.

In addition, over the last two decades we have seen the proliferation of research projects, grants and teaching positions focusing on Islam, Muslims in Europe and Muslim societies. This is likely to grow with the further marketization of universities; research and teaching topics will increasingly be driven by the interests of students-as-consumers who, with their future careers in mind, will demand courses on 'topical' issues such as Islam and Muslim societies (Deeb and Winegar 2016). Yet, despite this growing surge of interest, anthropological knowledge has tended to be seen by policymakers as less 'useful' than that of other disciplines (ibid.). I have experienced this with my own work. Increasingly, while presenting at conferences and informal gatherings, I have been pushed to say something about integration and, more recently, to comment on extremism and the experiences of young Somali women who have left the UK to join ISIS.

So how do we navigate this terrain, ensuring that we are listened to, while challenging dominant frames and systems of knowledge production that problematize Islam and reify otherness? This book grapples with these preoccupations. It critiques scholarly approaches to Islam that have emphasized difference and foreignness and reinforced static and homogenous accounts of Muslim subjects.

It seeks to disrupt the dominant frameworks around Islam, multiculturalism and national identity in Britain and calls for a repoliticization of these debates and for attention to be paid to the particularities and historical contingencies of the forms of difference produced (Brown 2006a). Throughout I have exposed the historical conditions that have made these understandings of religion and culture appear axiomatic, revealing the ways in which they are shaped by problematizations that have arisen at this particular moment in time.

Most importantly, the book has offered a different starting point and a more hopeful vision that might challenge the exclusionary and abstract liberalism that has come to dominate public debate around Islam in contemporary Britain. In contrast to representations of Muslim youth as a threat, or at risk and vulnerable, I have emphasized youthful aspirations as they shift across time and space and across individual lives. Most of the young people who feature in this book do struggle with fitting in or finding employment, and they do face discrimination and pressure from family and peers. This book has placed emphasis, however, on how, at critical junctures in their lives, these individuals turn moments of potentiality into forms of striving.

For the women in this book, pious teachings and projects offer a way of articulating a new way of being, as do engagements with modern lifestyles, discourses on autonomy and authenticity, and hopes for prosperity, status and social mobility. Many of their aspirational projects are not divorced from the aspiring liberal self-governing subjectivity promoted through government rhetoric and policy. The notions of self-stylization and self-making, and the idea of taking charge of one's future, are features of the contemporary moment, manifest not only in religious projects but also, for example, in financial worlds (Miyazaki 2006). It would be misleading, however, to suggest that the women discussed here are either seeking to conform to, or actively subvert, the liberal policies and debates described above. Rather, they are articulating new forms of sociality and new ways of being, belonging and relating to the world around them (Moore 2011) that do not sit comfortably within a 'liberal versus illiberal' binary nor within the restrictive and dominant subjectivities described above. Taking these ways of being seriously, I have argued, can help us to rethink and challenge the problematized categories of difference that much academic work on Islam takes for granted.

For example, through their efforts to embody a pious self, young Somali women seek to reconfigure themselves as inextricably bound to God. In Chapter 7, Ikraan expresses concern at her friend's attempt to adapt her clothing to be 'less Muslim' in order to 'fit in' and not reinforce the foreignness of Islam. Ifraax accuses her of placing her relationship with others above her relationship with God. For women like Ifraax, Islam is the ultimate truth and God comes first and foremost; her faith is not an 'opinion' or one 'belief' or ideology among many. Similarly, as we saw in Chapter 6, Islamic knowledge can be approached critically, but this 'criticism' remains within existing structures of authority. In contrast to public debates around British values, young, pious Somalis present Islam as universal and, hence, as already British. In so doing, they rework the juxtaposition of British liberal values and 'extreme' Islam that is inherent in public and political discourse. They posit themselves as submitting to a universal faith, but also as willingly embracing aspects of Somali and British cultural values, norms and practices.

In this book, I have offered a critique of current policy, legislative frameworks and political discourses and categories by juxtaposing the latter to Somali women's own categories and experiences. If we were to start with these women's own theories of change, rather than with the categories of analysis that dominate securitized Britain, what might the world look like? I would advocate a complete rethink of the post-9/11 legislative and policy apparatus around terrorism and extremism, with a particular focus on the definitions of extremism and terrorism that are at their core. Current security frameworks, particularly those focused on prevention, are a form of violence that will likely lead to further marginalization, stigmatization and resentment. The language of radicalization and extremism and the assumptions inherent in its use deny certain ways of being and render all Muslims as potential suspects. If we are to have terrorism policies at all, they cannot be divorced from colonial pasts and postcolonial presents or, indeed, from foreign policy in Muslim-majority lands. A more utopian vision would also address the inequalities that underpin social and political conflicts at both national and global levels, and hence imagine and develop a radical politics of redistribution.

I would also hope for a shift away from the rhetoric of integration, cohesion, national identity and British values, and recognition that nationalist sentiment is always divisive and exclusionary. I would hope too for greater historical and political awareness about how categories of difference are produced and reinforced, and a move away from conceptualizing Islam as a 'problem'. I would not advocate a return to the politics of multicultural difference, nor promote a secular public sphere or the universalism of a Rousseau-inspired politics of equal dignity (Taylor 1994) – such projects also regulate and forge minority subjects in particular ways (Asad 2003). And, while I appreciate the empowering force of identity politics, I would envision a public space where varied forms of being can coexist without being categorized, essentialized and legislated against.

I would support Connolly (1999: 8) in his hope for 'a possible world of intersecting publics, expressing a variety of religious and metaphysical orientations, interacting on several registers of being'. This would include forms of difference that are not reducible to identities, and those that are not necessarily recognizable within liberal or secular registers. It would allow the ways of being described in this book to flourish, to be rendered visible without being problematized. Public institutions, which have been co-opted by the state's securitization agenda, should be reclaimed. In schools, students should not be taught *about* British values and instructed on how to cultivate liberal norms and practices, but encouraged to think beyond this exclusionary form of liberalism. Education can provide a space to think critically about colonialism, race and politics, and to imagine new ways of sharing our worlds with others based on solidarity and the transcendence of categories, identities, borders and boundaries.

Finally, within academia, our writing and teaching should be accompanied by advocacy for social justice. I would also echo the *Cadaan* Studies activists in calling for a more profound decolonization and dismantling of the hierarchies of knowledge production. As anthropologists we should be critical of power, questioning research agendas that continue to objectify, problematize and marginalize those they purport to study. And we should aim to dismantle the 'conceptual whiteness', noted by Safia Aidid (2015), of scholarship about Somalis and other minority subjects. We can do this by making space for scholarship that stems from alternative agendas and emanates from other places and outside the dominant knowledge-producing institutions, as well as by prioritizing our interlocutors' perspectives and experiences. Finally, I would follow Eriksen, who in a recent interview with Stein (2017: 236) argues for a different type of 'impact', one that does not necessarily engage in policy recommendations, but instead asks 'surprising questions' and, by taking a step back and slowing down, allows alternative imaginaries to emerge.

Notes

1　These videos are also available on the government's e-learning platform for Prevent (https://www.elearning.prevent.homeoffice.gov. uk/).

2　WRAP is the most commonly used training and is designed for staff in various public sectors (e.g. education, health and local authority, prisons). A list of all Prevent training is available in the Prevent training catalogue at https://www.gov.uk/government/uploads/system/ uploads/attachment_data/file/503973/Prevent_Training_catalogue_-_ March_2016.pdf.

3　I took part in a WRAP online interactive training session aimed specifically at staff in Higher and Further Education in August 2016, as well as in other online training programmes provided by private organizations for staff in the education sector. I also analysed the Prevent training documents, including training manuals and facilitator's scripts leaked by CAGE on www.preventresources.com.

4　Kelly Simcock is the director of Foundations for Peace, which organizes programmes and projects aimed at the prevention and resolution of violent conflict. She is also Labour councillor for Didsbury East. Manwar Ali is an Islamic scholar, anti-radicalization campaigner and founder of JIMAS, a Muslim educational charity. He claims to have formerly fought among, and trained with, Islamist fighters across the globe.

5　Like the Immigration Act 2014, the Counter-Terrorism and Security Act 2015 is pre-emptive and intervenes within a 'pre-criminal' space.

6　The researchers do state that the behaviours identified as 'vulnerabilities' are based on statistical associations and probabilities, and do not necessarily predict future behaviour. This point, however, is often lost in the Prevent and Channel resources.

7　This parallels the argument made by scholars of Islam in Europe that a growth of religiosity among Muslim youth is a result of their social exclusion, and their search for identity, belonging and meaning (see Chapter 1).

8 Mehta (1999) traces a tradition of liberalism that dates back to Locke, which was further developed three centuries later by nineteenth-century theorists such as John Stuart Mill, Thomas B Macaulay and Jeremy Bentham.

REFERENCES

Abdi, C. M. (2007). 'Convergence of Civil War and the Religious Right: Reimagining Somali Women.' *Signs* 33 (1): 183–207.

Abdi, C. M. (2015). *Elusive Jannah. The Somali Diaspora and a Borderless Muslim Identity*. Minneapolis: University of Minnesota Press.

Abu-Lughod, L. (2000). 'Modern Subjects: Egyptian Melodrama and the Postcolonial Difference.' In *Questions of Modernity*, edited by T. Mitchell, 87–114. Toronto: University of Toronto Press.

Adan, A. H. (1994). 'Somalia: An Illusory Political Nation-State.' *Comparative Studies of South Asia, Africa and the Middle East* 14 (1): 99–109.

Affi, L. (1997). 'The Somali Crisis in Canada: The Single Mother Phenomenon.' In *Mending Rips in the Sky: Options for Somali Communities in the 21st Century*, edited by R. Ford and H. M. Adam, 441–8. Lawrenceville: Red Sea Press.

Agrama, A. H. (2012). *Questioning Secularism: Islam, Sovereignty, and the Rule of Law in Modern Egypt*. Chicago: University of Chicago Press.

Ahmad, F. (2012). 'Graduating Towards Marriage? Attitudes Towards Marriage and Relationships among University-Educated British Muslim Women.' *Culture and Religion: An Interdisciplinary Journal* 13 (2): 193–210.

Ahmed, A. J. (1995). '"Daybreak is Near, Won't You Become Sour?" Going Beyond the Current Rhetoric in Somali Studies.' In *The Invention of Somalia*, edited by A. J. Ahmed, 135–55. Lawrenceville: Red Sea Press.

Ahmed, S. (1999). 'Islam and Development: Opportunities and Constraints for Somali Women.' *Gender & Development* 7 (1): 69–72.

Aidid, S. (2010). 'Haweenku Wa Garab (Women Are a Force): Women and the Somali Nationalist Movement, 1943–1960.' *Bildhaan: An International Journal of Somali Studies* 10: 103–24.

Aidid, S. (2015). 'The New Somali Studies.' *The New Inquiry*, 16 October.

Akou, H. M. (2011). *The Politics of Dress in Somali Culture.* Bloomington: Indiana University Press.

Al-Rasheed, M., ed. (2005). *Transnational Connections and the Arab Gulf.* London and New York: Routledge.

Ali, R. (2014). 'The Making of a Modern Africa City.' In *Mogadishu Lost Moderns*, edited by R. Ali and A. Cross, 10–15. London: A. M. Qattam Foundation.

Alibhai-Brown, Y. (2001). 'After Multiculturalism.' *The Political Quarterly* 72: 47–56.

Amir-Moazami, S., and Salvatore, A. (2003). 'Gender, Generaton, and the Reform of Tradition: From Muslim Majority Societies to Western Europe.' In *Muslim Networks: Transnational Communities in and across Europe*, edited by S. Allievi and J. S. Nielsen, 52–77. Leiden: Brill.

Angé, O., and Berliner, D. (2014). 'Introduction: Anthropology of Nostalgia–Anthropology as Nostalgia.' In *Anthropology and Nostalgia*, edited by O. Angé and D. Berliner, 1–16. Oxford: Berghahn.

Appadurai, A. (2013). *The Future as Cultural Fact: Essays on the Global Condition.* London and New York: Verso.

Appiah, A. K. (1994). 'Identity, Authenticity, Survival. Multicultural Societies and Social Reproduction.' In *Multiculturalism*, edited by A. Gutmann, 149–64. Princeton: Princeton University press.

Artan, A. Y. (2012). *The Muted Cry.* London: Kayd Somali Arts and Culture. [Translated by Zahra Jibril].

Asad, T. (1986). *The Idea of the Anthropology of Islam.* Washington, DC: Center for Contemporary Arab Studies.

Asad, T. (1993). *Genealogies of Religion: Discipline and Reasons of Power in Christianity and Islam.* Baltimore: Johns Hopkins University Press.

Asad, T. (2003). *Formations of the Secular: Islam, Christianity, Modernity.* Stanford: Stanford University Press.

Baadiyow, A. A. M. (2010). 'Women, Islamists and the Military Regime in Somalia: The New Family Law and Its Implications.' In *Peace and Milk, Drought and War: Somali Culture, Society and Politics*, edited by M. V. Hoehne and V. Luling, 137–60. London: Hurst & Company.

Barre, S. (1971). 'Let us Follow Islam's Way' In *My Country and My People: The collected speeches of Major-General Mohamed Siad Barre, President, The Supreme Revolutionary Conucil, Somali Democratic Republic 1969-1970.* Mogadishu: The Ministry of Information and National Guidance.

Baumann, G. (1996). *Contesting Culture: Discourses of Identity in Multi-Ethnic London.* Cambridge: Cambridge University Press.

Berns-McGown, R. (1999). *Muslims in the Diaspora: The Somali Communities of London and Toronto.* Toronto: University of Toronto Press.

Besteman, C. (1995). 'The Invention of Gosha: Slavery, Colonialism, and Stigma in Somali History.' In *The Invention of Somalia*, edited by A. J. Ahmed, 43–62. Lawrenceville: Red Sea Press.

Besteman, C. (2012). 'Translating Race across Time and Space: The Creation of Somali Bantu Ethnicity.' *Identities* 19 (3): 285–302.

Biehl, J., Good, B. and Kleinman, A., eds (2007). *Subjectivity: Ethnographic Investigations*. Berkeley and Los Angeles: University of California Press.

Birt, J. (2005a). 'Locating the British Imam: The Deobandi Ulama between Contested Authority and Public Policy Post-9/11.' In *European Muslims and the Secular State*, edited by J. Cesari and S. McLoughlin, 181–96. Aldershot: Ashgate Publishing Company

Birt, J. (2005b). 'Wahhabism in the United Kingdom: Manifestations and Reactions.' In *Transnational Connections and the Arab Gulf*, edited by M. Al-Rasheed, 168–84. London and New York: Routledge.

Birt, J. (2006). 'Good Imam, Bad Imam: Civic Religion and National Integration in Britain Post-9/11.' *The Muslim World* 96 (4): 687–705.

Bjork, S. R. (2007). 'Clan Identities in Practice: The Somali Diaspora in Finland.' In *Somalia: Diaspora and State Reconstitution in the Horn of Africa* edited by A. O. Farah, M. Muchie and J. Gundel, 102–13. London: Adonis & Abbey

Bowen, J. R. (2008). *Why the French Don't Like Headscarves: Islam, the State, and Public Space*. Princeton: Princeton University Press.

Bowen, J. R. (2010). *Can Islam Be French?: Pluralism and Pragmatism in a Secularist State*. Princeton: Princeton University Press.

Bowen, J. R. (2016). *On British Islam: Religion, Law, and Everyday Practice in Shari'a Councils*. Princeton: Princeton University Press.

Boyer, D. (2012). 'From Algos to Autonomos: Nostalgic Eastern Europe as Postimperial Mania.' In *Post-Communist Nostalgia*, edited by M. Todorova and Z. Hgille, 17–28. Oxford: Berghahn.

Bracke, S. (2008). 'Conjugating the Modern/Religious, Conceptualizing Female Religious Agency.' *Theory, Culture & Society* 25 (6): 51–67.

Bracke, S. (2011). 'Subjects of Debate. Secular and Sexual Exceptionalism, and Muslim Women in the Netherlands.' *Feminist Review* 98: 28–46.

Bracke, S., and Fadil, N. (2012). '"Is the Headscarf Oppressive or Emancipatory?" Field Notes on the Gendrification of the "Multicultural Debate".' *Religion and Gender* 2 (1): 36–56.

Braidotti, R. (2008). 'In Spite of the Times: The Postsecular Turn in Feminism.' *Theory, Culture & Society* 25 (6): 1–24.

Brown, W. (2006a). *Regulating Aversion: Tolerance in the Age of Identity and Empire*. Princeton: Princeton University Press.

Brown, W. (2006b). 'Subjects of Tolerance: Why We Are Civilized and They Are the Barbarians.' In *Political Theologies: Public Religions in a*

Post-Secular World, edited by H. D. Vries and L. E. Sullivan, 298–317. Princeton: Princeton University Press.

Butler, J. (2008). 'Sexual Politics, Torture, and Secular Time.' *The British Journal of Sociology* 59 (1): 1–23.

Cameron, D. (2011). 'Prime Minister's Speech at Munich Security Conference.' Available online: https://www.gov.uk/government/speeches/pms-speech-at-munich-security-conference (accessed 8 April 2016).

Carver, N. (2015). '"In Here, Everything Is Questioned": Gender and Divorce.' Paper presented at the Somali Studies International Association Congress, Helsinki, Finland, 19–23 August 2015.

Cesari, J. (2003). 'Muslim Minorities in Europe: The Silent Revolution.' In *Modernizing Islam*, edited by J. L. Esposito and F. Burgat, 251–71. New Brunswick: Rutgers University Press.

Cole, I., and Robinson, D. (2003). *Somali Housing Experiences in England*. Sheffield: Sheffield Hallam University.

Cole, J., and Durham, D., eds (2008). *Figuring the Future: Globalization and the Temporalities of Children and Youth*. Santa Fe: School of Advanced Research Press.

Cole, J., Alison, E., Cole, B., and Alison, L. (2009). *Guidance for Identifying People Vulnerable to Recruitment into Violent Extremism*. Liverpool: University of Liverpool.

Coleman, S. (2013). 'Afterword: De-Exceptionalising Islam.' In *Articulating Islam: Anthropological Appaoraches to Muslim Worlds*, edited by M. Marsden and K. Retsikas. 247–58. London: Springer.

Connolly, W. E. (1999). *Why I Am Not a Secularist*. Minneapolis: University of Minnesota Press.

Davis, F. (1979). *Yearning for Yesterday: A Sociology of Nostalgia*. New York: Free Press.

De Munck, V. C. (1996). 'Love and Marriage in a Sri Lankan Muslim Community: Toward a Reevaluation of Dravidian Marriage Practices.' *American Ethnologist* 23 (4): 698–716.

Declich, F. (2000). 'Sufi Experience in Rural Somalia. A Focus on Women.' *Social Anthropology* 8 (3): 295–318.

Deeb, L. (2006). *An Enchanted Modern: Gender and Public Piety in Shi'i Lebanon, Princeton Studies in Muslim Politics*. Princeton: Princeton University Press.

Deeb, L., and Harb, M. (2013). *Leisurely Islam: Negotiating Geography and Morality in Shi'ite South Beirut*. Princeton: Princeton University Press.

Deeb, L., and Winegar, J. (2016). *Anthropology's Politics: Disciplining the Middle East*. Stanford: Stanford University Press.

Department for Education. (2014). *Promoting Fundamental British Values as Part of SMSC in Schools. Departmental Advice for Maintained Schools*. London: Department for Education.

Dwyer, C. (1999). 'Veiled Meanings: Young British Muslim Women and the Negotiation of Differences.' *Gender, Place & Culture: A Journal of Feminist Geography* 6 (1): 5–26.

Edwards, J., Evans, G. and Smith, K. (2012). 'Introduction: The Middle Classification of Britain.' *Focaal-Journal of Global and Historical Anthropology* 62: 3–16.

Eickelman, D. F., and Piscatori, J. (1996). *Muslim Politics*. Princeton: Princeton University Press.

Eno, M. A., and Eno, O. A. (2008). *The Bantu-Jareer Somalis: Unearthing Apartheid in the Horn of Africa*. London: Adonis & Abbey.

Eriksen, T. H., and Stein, F. (2017). 'Anthropology as Counter-Culture: An Interview with Thomas Hylland Eriksen.' *Journal of the Royal Anthropological Institute* 23 (1).

Evans, G. (2012). '"The Aboriginal People of England": The Culture of Class Politics in Contemporary Britain.' *Focaal-Journal of Global and Historical Anthropology* 62: 17–29.

Ewing, K. P. (2008). *Stolen Honor: Stigmatizing Muslim Men in Berlin*. Stanford: Stanford University Press.

Fadil, N. (2008). 'Submission to God, Submitting to the Self: Secular and Religious Trajectories of Second Generation Maghrebi in Belgium.' PhD thesis, Onderzoekseenheid: Centrum voor Sociologisch Onderzoek [CeSO], KU Leuven.

Fadil, N. (2009). 'Managing Affects and Sensibilities: The Case of Not-Handshaking and Not-Fasting.' *Social Anthropology* 17 (4): 439–54.

Fadil, N. (2011). 'On Not-/Unveiling as an Ethical Practice.' *Feminist Review* 98 (1): 83–109

Fadil, N., and Fernando, M. (2015). 'Rediscovering the "everyday" Muslim: Notes on an Anthropological Divide.' *HAU: Journal of Ethnographic Theory* 5 (2): 59–88.

Farah, C. A. (2014). 'Mogadishu, Pearl of the Indian Ocean.' In *Mogadishu Lost Moderns*, edited by R. Ali and A. Cross, 28–35. London: A. M. Qattam Foundation.

Farah, N. (2000). *Yesterday, Tomorrow: Voices from the Somali Diaspora*. London and New York: Cassell.

Farah, N. (2007). 'Of Tamarind and Cosmopolitanism.' *Halabuur: Journal of Somali Literature and Culture* 2 (1–2): 34–7.

Faubion, J. D. (2001). 'Toward an Anthropology of Ethics: Foucault and the Pedagogies of Autopoiesis.' *Representations* 74 (1): 83–104.

Fernando, M. L. (2010). 'Reconfiguring Freedom: Muslim Piety and the Limits of Secular Law and Public Discourse in France.' *American Ethnologist* 37 (1): 19–35.

Fernando, M. L. (2014). *The Republic Unsettled: Muslim French and the Contradictions of Secularism*. Durham and London: Duke University Press.

Fischer, E. F. (2014). *The Good Life: Aspiration, Dignity, and the Anthropology of Wellbeing*. Palo Alto: Stanford University Press.

Foucault, M. (1985). *The History of Sexuality. Vol II: The Use of Pleasure*, trans. R. Hurley. New York: Pantheon.

Foucault, M. (2000). *Ethics: Subjectivity and Truth* (Essential Works of Michel Foucault, 1954–1984) Volume 1 edited by P. Rabinow. London: Penguin.

Gaffney, P. D. (1994). *The Prophet's Pulpit: Islamic Preaching in Contemporary Egypt*. Berkeley and Los Angeles: University of California Press

Gardner, J., and El-Bushra, J. (2004). *Somalia–the Untold Story: The War through the Eyes of Somali Women*. London: Pluto Press.

Gell, A. (2011). 'On Love.' *Anthropology of this Century* 2.

Gidley, B. (2013). 'Diasporic Memory and the Call to Identity: Yiddish Migrants in Early Twentieth Century East London.' *Journal of Intercultural Studies* 34 (6): 650–64.

Glynn, S. (2002). 'Bengali Muslims: The New East End Radicals?' *Ethnic and Racial Studies* 25 (6): 969–88.

Goldberg, D. T. (2002). *The Racial State*. Malden and Oxford: Blackwell Publishers.

Goodhart, D. (2014). *The British Dream. Successes and Failures of Post-War Immigration*. London: Atlantic Books.

Goth, B. (2015). 'A Jihad against Somali Music in the Land of Freedom' *Horn of African News Update and Analysis*. Available online: http://hanua.blogspot.co.uk/2015/02/a-jihad-against-somali-music-in-land-of_16.html (accessed 16 February 2016).

Griffiths, D. (2002). *Somali and Kurdish Refugees in London: New Identities in the Diaspora*. Aldershot: Ashgate.

Griffiths, D., Sigona, N. and Zetter, R. (2006). 'Integrative Paradigms, Marginal Reality: Refugee Community Organisations and Dispersal in Britain.' *Journal of Ethnic and Migration Studies* 32 (2): 881–98.

Grillo, R. (2007). 'An Excess of Alterity? Debating Difference in a Multicultural Society.' *Ethnic and Racial Studies* 30 (6): 979–98.

Hakim Murad, A. (n.d.). 'British and Muslim?' Based on a Lecture Given to a Conference of British Converts on 17 September 1997. Available online: http://masud.co.uk/ISLAM/ahm/british.htm (accessed 8 October 2016).

Hammond, L. (2012). 'The Absent but Active Constituency: The Role of the Somaliland UK Community in Election Politics.' In *Politics from Afar: Transnational Diasporas and Networks*, edited by T. Lyons and P. Mandaville, 157–78. New York: Oxford University Press.

Hansen, P. (2006). 'Revolving Returnees: Meanings and Practices of Transnational Return among Somalilanders.' PhD thesis, Department of Anthropology, Danish Institute for International Studies, University of Copenhagen.

Hansen, P. (2013). 'Khat, Governance and Political Identity among Diaspora Returnees to Somaliland.' *Journal of Ethnic and Migration Studies* 39 (1): 143–59.

Harris, H. (2004). *The Somali Community in the UK: What We Know and How We Know It*. London: The Information Centre about Asylum and Refugees in the UK (ICAR).

Hassan, D. F., Adan, A. H. and Warsame, A. M. (1995). 'Somalia: Poetry as Resistance against Colonialism and Patriarchy.' In *Subversive Women: Women's Movements in Africa, Asia, Latin America and the Caribbean*, edited by S. Wieringa, 165–82. London: Zed Books.

Hess, R. L. (1966). *Italian Colonialism in Somalia*. Chicago and London: University of Chicago Press.

Hirschkind, C. (2001). 'Civic Virtue and Religious Reason: An Islamic Counterpublic.' *Cultural Anthropology* 16 (1): 3–34.

Hirschkind, C. (2006). *The Ethical Soundscape: Cassette Sermons and Islamic Counterpublics*. New York: Columbia University Press.

Hoesterey, J. B. (2016). *Rebranding Islam: Piety, Prosperity, and a Self-Help Guru*. Stanford: Stanford University Press.

Home Office. (2001). *Community Cohesion: A Report of the Independent Review Team*. London: Home Office.

Home Office. (2002). *Secure Borders, Safe Haven: Integration with Diversity in Modern Britain*. London: Home Office.

Home Office. (2004a). *The End of Parallel Lives? The Report of the Community Cohesion Panel*. London: Home Office.

Home Office. (2004b). *Strength in Diversity: Towards a Community Cohesion and Race Equality Strategy, Consultative Document*. London: Home Office.

Home Office. (2011). *Counter-Terrorism Strategy (Contest)*. London: Home Office.

Home Office. (2015a). *Prevent Duty Guidance: For Higher Education Institutions in England and Wales*. London: Home Office.

Home Office. (2015b). *Revised Prevent Duty Guidance for England and Wales*. London: Home Office.

Home Office. (2016a). *Workshop to Raise Awareness of Prevent: Full Workshop Script*. London: Home Office.

Home Office. (2016b). *Workshop to Raise Awareness of Prevent: Facilitator's Workbook*. London: Home Office.

Home Office (n.d). E-Learning Training on Prevent. Available online: https://www.elearning.prevent.homeoffice.gov.uk/ (accessed 7 November 2016).

Hopkins, G. (2010). 'A Changing Sense of Somaliness: Somali Women in London and Toronto.' *Gender, Place and Culture* 17 (4): 519–38.

Horst, C. (2006). *Transnational Nomads: How Somalis Cope with Refugee Life in the Dadaab Camps of Kenya*. Oxford: Berghahn.

Jacobsen, C. M. (2010). *Islamic Traditions and Muslim Youth in Norway.* Leiden: Brill.

Jacobsen, C. M. (2011). 'Troublesome Threesome: Feminism, Anthropology and Muslim Womens Piety.' *Feminist Review* 98 (1): 65–82.

Jacobson, J. (1997). 'Religion and Ethnicity: Dual and Alternative Sources of Identity among Young British Pakistanis.' *Ethnic and Racial Studies* 20 (2): 238–56.

Jacobson, J. (1998). *Islam in Transition: Religion and Identity among British Pakistani Youth.* London: Routledge.

Jama, Z. M. (1991). 'Fighting to Be Heard: Somali Women's Poetry.' *African Languages and Cultures* 41 (1): 43–53.

Jensen, T. G. (2006). 'Religious Authority and Autonomy Intertwined: The Case of Converts to Islam in Denmark.' *The Muslim World* 96 (4): 643–60.

Johnsdotter, S. (2007). 'Persistence of Tradition or Reassessment of Cultural Practices in Exile? Discourses on Female Circumcision among and About Swedish Somalis.' In *Transcultural Bodies: Female Genital Cutting in Global Context* edited by Y. Hernlund and B. Shell-Duncan, 107–34. New Brunswick: Rutgers University Press.

Johnson, W. J. (1974). *Heellooy Heelleellooy: The Development of the Genre Heello in Modern Somali Poetry.* Vol. 5. Bloomington: Indiana University Publications.

Joppke, C. (2004). 'The Retreat of Multiculturalism in the Liberal State: Theory and Policy.' *The British Journal of Sociology* 55 (2): 237–57.

Jouili, J. S. (2009). 'Negotiating Secular Boundaries: Pious Micro-Practices of Muslim Women in French and German Public Spheres.' *Social Anthropology* 17 (4): 455–70.

Jouili, J. S. (2015). *Pious Practice and Secular Constraints: Women in the Islamic Revival in Europe.* Stanford: Stanford University Press.

Jouili, J. S., and Amir-Moazami, S. (2006). 'Knowledge, Empowerment and Religious Authority among Pious Muslim Women in France and Germany.' *The Muslim World* 96 (4): 617–42.

Kamaldeep, B., Craig, T., Mohamud, S., Warfa, N., Stansfeld, S. A., Thornicroft, G., Curtis, S. and McCrone, P. (2006). 'Mental Disorders among Somali Refugees.' *Social Psychiatry and Psychiatric Epidemiology* 41 (400): 400–8.

Kapteijns, L. (1995). 'Sittaat: Somali Women's Songs for the "Mothers of the Believers".' Boston University African Studies Center's Working Papers in African Studies, 25.

Kapteijns, L. (2004). 'I.M. Lewis and Somali Clanship: A Critique.' *Northeast African Studies* 11 (1): 1–24.

Kapteijns, L. (2009). 'Discourse on Moral Womanhood in Somali Popular Songs, 1960–1990.' *The Journal of African History* 50 (1): 101–22.

Kapteijns, L. (2010). 'Making Memories of Mogadishu in Somali Poetry About the Civil War.' In *Mediations of Violence in Africa: Fashioning New Futures from Contested Parts*, edited by L. Kapteijns and J. M. Richters, 25–74. Leiden and Boston: Brill.

Kapteijns, L. (2013). *Clan Cleansing in Somalia: The Ruinous Legacy of 1991*. Philadelphia: University of Pennsylvania Press.

Kapteijns, L., with Omar, M. A. (1999). *Women's Voices in a Man's World: Women and the Pastoral Tradition in Northern Somali Orature, C. 1899-1980*. Portsmouth: Heinemann.

Kapteijns, L., and Farah, M. (2001). 'Review Article: A Pastoral Democrat: A Study of Pastoralism and Politics among the Northern Somali of the Horn of Africa.' *Africa: Journal of the International African Institute* 71 (4): 719–22.

Keane, W. (2015). *Ethical Life: Its Natural and Social Histories*. Princeton: Princeton University Press.

Keith, M. (2005). *After the Cosmopolitan? Multicultural Cities and the Future of Racism*. London: Routledge.

Khalif, H. (2013). 'Mother of Mogadishu.' *Gabay iyo Gabarnimo*, 8 December. Available online: https://hamdikhalif.com/2013/12/08/mother-of-mogadishu-2/ (accessed 27 January 2017).

Khan, N. (2012). *Muslim Becoming: Aspiration and Skepticism in Pakistan*. Durham and London: Duke University Press.

Kibria, N. (2008). 'The "New Islam" and Bangladeshi Youth in Britain and the US.' *Ethnic and Racial Studies* 31 (2): 243–66.

Kleist, N. (2004). 'Nomads, Sailors and Refugees: A Century of Somali Migration.' *Sussex Migration Working Paper* 23, University of Sussex.

Kundnani, A. (2007). 'Integrationism: The Politics of Anti-Muslim Racism.' *Race and Class* 48 (4): 24–44.

Kundnani, A. (2012a). 'Multiculturalism and Its Discontents: Left, Right and Liberal.' *European Journal of Cultural Studies* 15 (2): 155–66.

Kundnani, A. (2012b). 'Radicalisation: The Journey of a Concept.' *Race and Class* 54 (2): 3–25.

Kymlicka, W. (2007). *Multicultural Odysseys: Navigating the New International Politics of Diversity*. Cambridge: Cambridge University Press.

Laidlaw, J. (2014). *The Subject of Virtue: An Anthropology of Ethics and Freedom, New Departures in Anthropology*. Cambridge: Cambridge University Press.

Laitin, D., and Samatar, S. (1987). *Somalia: Nation in Search of a State*. Boulder: Westview Press.

Lambek, M., ed. (2010). *Ordinary Ethics: Anthropology, Language and Action*. New York: Fordham University Press.

Lambek, M. (2014). 'What Is "Religion" for Anthropology? And What Has Anthropology Bought to "Religion"?' In *A Companion to the*

Anthropology of Religion, edited by J. Boddy and M. Lambek, 1–32. Somerset: Wiley-Blackwell.

Lewis, I. M. (1961). *A Pastoral Democracy*. London: Oxford University Press.

Lewis, I. M. (1994). *Blood and Bone: The Call of Kinship in Somali Society*. Lawrenceville: Red Sea Press.

Lewis, I. M. (2002). *A Modern History of the Somali: Nation and State in the Horn of Africa*. Oxford: James Cyrrey Ltd.

Lewis, I. M. (2008). *Understanding Somalia and Somaliland*. New York: Columbia University Press.

LLiberatore, G. (2018). 'Forging a "good" diaspora': Political mobilization among Somalis in the UK.' *Development and Change* 49 (1): 146–169.

Lindley, A. (2010). *The Early Morning Phone Call: Somali Refugees' Remittances*. New York and Oxford: Berghahn Books.

Lindley, A., and Van Hear, N. (2007) ' New Europeans on the Move: A preliminary review of the onward migration of refugees within the European Union' COMPAS Working Paper, WP-07-57, University of Oxford.

Long, N. J., and Moore, H. L., eds (2013). *Sociality: New Directions*. New York and Oxford: Berghahn.

Luhrmann, T. M. (2006). 'Subjectivity.' *Anthropological Theory* 6 (3): 345–61.

MacIntyre, A. (1981 (2007)). *After Virtue: A Study in Moral Theory*. London: Duckworth.

Mahmood, S. (2001). 'Rehearsed Spontaneity and the Conventionality of Ritual: Disciplines of Salat.' *American Ethnologist* 28 (4): 827–53.

Mahmood, S. (2005). *Politics of Piety: The Islamic Revival and the Feminist Subject*. Princeton: University Press.

Mamdani, M. (2004). *Good Muslim, Bad Muslim: America, the Cold War, and the Roots of Terror*. New York: Pantheon Books.

Mandaville, P. G. (2001). *Transnational Muslim Politics: Reimagining the Umma*. London: Routledge.

Mandaville, P. G. (2003). 'Towards a Critical Islam: European Muslims and the Changing Boundaries of Transnational Religious Discourse.' In *Muslim Networks and Transnational Communities In and Across Europe*, edited by S. Allievi and J. S. Nielsen, 127–45. Leiden: Brill.

Mandeeq (2015). 'Boundaries of *Soomaalinimo*' Podcast Episode 4. Available online: http://themaandeeq.com/podcast-episode-4-boundaries-of-soomaalinimo/(accessed 7 November 2017).

Mansur, A. O. (1995). 'The Nature of the Somali Clan System.' In *The Invention of Somalia*, edited by A. J. Ahmed, 117–34. Lawrenceville: Red Sea Press.

Maqsood, A. (Forthcoming). *The New Pakistani Middle-Class*. Cambridge: Harvard University Press.

Marsden, M. (2007). 'All-Male Sonic Gatherings, Islamic Reform, and Masculinity in Northern Pakistan.' *American Ethnologist* 34 (3): 473–90.

Marsden, M. (2010). 'A Tour Not So Grand: Mobile Muslims in Northern Pakistan.' In *Islam, Politics, Anthropology*, edited by F. Osella and B. Soares, 54–71. Chichester: Wiley-Blackwell.

Masquelier, A. (2009). 'Lessons from Rubí: Love, Poverty, and the Educational Value of Televised Dramas in Niger.' In *Love in Africa* edited by J. Cole and L.M. Thomas, 205–28. Chicago and London: University of Chicago Press.

McGhee, D. (2008). *The End of Multiculturalism? Terrorism, Interation and Human Rights*. Maidenhead: Open University Press.

McMichael, C. (2002). '"Everywhere Is Allah's Place": Islam and the Everyday Life of Somali Women in Melbourne, Australia.' *Journal of Refugee Studies* 15 (2): 171–88.

Meer, N., and Modood, T. (2009). 'The Multicultural State We're In: Muslims,'Multiculture'and the 'Civic Re-Balancing'of British Multiculturalism.' *Political Studies* 57 (3): 473–97.

Mehta, U. S. (1999). *Liberalism and Empire. A Study in Nineteenth-Century British Liberal Thought*. Chicago: University of Chicago Press.

Mernissi, F. (1996). *Women's Rebellion and Islamic Memory*. London: Zed.

Meyer, B. (2015). 'How to Capture the "Wow". Awe and the Study of Religion. Marett Memorial Lecture.' *Journal of the Royal Anthropological Institute* 22 (1): 7–26.

Mire, H. (2015). 'Who came before the Somali? Part 1.' *The Mandeeq Blog*, Available online: http://themaandeeq.com/who-came-before-the-somali-1/(accessed 7 November 2016).

Miyazaki, H. (2006). 'Economy of Dreams: Hope in Global Capitalism and Its Critiques.' *Cultural Anthropology* 21 (2): 147–72.

Modood, T. (2005). *Multicultural Politics: Racism, Ethnicity, and Muslims in Britain*. Edinburgh: Edinburgh University Press.

Modood, T. (2010). *Still Not Easy Being British: Struggles for a Multicultural Citizenship*. Stoke-on-Trent: Trentham Books Limited.

Mohamed, H. (2003). 'Multiple Challenges, Multiple Struggles: A History of Women's Activism in Canada.' PhD dissertation, Department of History, University of Ottawa.

Moore, H. L., (2007). *The Subject of Anthropology: Gender, Symbolism and Psychoanalysis*. Cambridge: Polity Press.

Moore, H. L. (2011). *Still Life: Hopes, Desires and Satisfactions*. Cambridge: Polity Press.

Moore, H. L., and Vaughan, M. A. (1994). *Cutting Down Trees: Gender, Nutrition, and Agricultural Change in the Northern Province of Zambia, 1890-1990.* Oxford: James Currey.

Navaro-Yashin, Y. (2009). 'Affective Spaces, Melancholic Objects: Ruination and the Production of Anthropological Knowledge.' *Journal of the Royal Anthropological Institute* 15 (1): 1–18.

Nielsen, K. B. (2004). 'Next Stop Britain: The Influence of Transnational Networks on the Secondary Movement of Danish Somalis.' Sussex Centre for Migration Research Working Paper 22, University of Sussex.

O'Toole, T., DeHanas, D. N. and Modood, T. (2012). 'Balancing Tolerance, Security and Muslim Engagement in the United Kingdom: The Impact of the "Prevent" Agenda.' *Critical Studies on Terrorism* 5 (3): 373–89.

Okin, S. M. (1999). 'Is Multiculturalism Bad for Women?' In *Is Multiculturalism Bad for Women?*, edited by S. M. Okin, M. C. Nussbaum, M. Howard, J. Cohen, 7–26. Princeton: Princeton University Press.

Open Society (2014). *Somalis in London.* London: Open Society Foundations.

Ortner, S. B. (2005). 'Subjectivity and Cultural Critique.' *Anthropological Theory* 5 (1): 31–52.

Ortner, S. B. (2016). 'Dark Anthropology and Its Others. Theory since the Eighties.' *HAU: Journal of Ethnographic Theory* 6 (1): 47–73.

Osella, C. (2012). 'Desires under Reform: Contemporary Reconfigurations of Family, Marriage, Love and Gendering in a Transnational South Indian Matrilineal Muslim Community.' *Culture and Religion: An Interdisciplinary Journal* 13 (2):241–265.

Osella, F., and Osella, C. (2008). 'Islamism and Social Reform in Kerala, South India.' *Modern Asian Studies* 42 (2–3): 317–46.

Osella, F., and Soares, B. (2010). 'Islam, Politics, Anthropology.' In *Islam, Politics, Anthropology*, edited by F. Osella and B. Soares, 1–22. Chichester: John Wiley and Sons.

Ossman, S. (2013). *Moving Matters: Paths of Serial Migration.* Stanford: Stanford University Press.

Ozyurek, E. (2006). *Nostalgia for the Modern: State Secularism and Everyday Plitics in Turkey.* Durham and London: Duke University Press.

Parekh, B. C. (2000). *The Future of Multi-Ethnic Britain.* London: Profile Books.

Pedersen, M. H. (2014). *Iraqi Women in Denmark: Ritual Performance and Belonging in Everyday Life.* Manchester: Manchester University Press.

Peek, L. (2005). 'Becoming Muslim: The Development of a Religious Identity.' *Sociology of Religion* 66 (3): 215–42.

Peter, D. F. (2006). 'Individualization and Religious Authority in Western European Islam.' *Islam and Christian–Muslim Relations* 17 (1): 105–18.

Phillips, A. (2007). *Multiculturalism without Culture*. Princeton: Princeton University Press.

Povinelli, E. A. (2006). *The Empire of Love: Toward a Theory of Intimacy, Genealogy, and Carnality*. Durham and London: Duke University Press.

Rights Watch. (2016). *Preventing Education? Human Rights and UK Counter-Terrorism Policy in Schools*. London: Rights Watch UK.

Roy, O. (2004). *Globalized Islam: The Search for a New Ummah*. London: Hurst.

Samatar, A. I. (1988). *Socialist Somalia: Rhetoric and Reality*. London: Zed Books.

Samuel, G. (2011). 'Islamic Piety and Masculinity.' *Contemporary Islam* 5: 309–22.

Schielke, S. (2010a). 'Being Good in Ramadan: Ambivalence, Fragmentation, and the Moral Self in the Lives of Young Egyptians.' In *Islam, Politics, Anthropology*, edited by F. Osella and B. Soares, 23–38. Chichester: Wiley-Blackwell.

Schielke, S. (2010b). 'Second Thoughts About the Anthropology of Islam, or How to Make Sense of Grand Schemes in Everyday Life.' *Working Papers*, Zentrum Modernier Orient, Belin (2).

Schielke, S. (2015). *Egypt in the Future Tense. Hope, Frustration, and Ambivalence before and after 2011*. Bloomington: Indiana University Press.

Shire, W (2012). To be Vulnerable and Fearless: An Interview with Writer Warsan Shire. By Kameelah Janan Rasheed Available online: http://wellandoftenpress.com/reader/to-be-vulnerable-and-fearless-an-interview-with-writer-warsan-shire/ (Accessed 28 August 2018).

Simmel, G. (1971a). 'The Stranger.' In *On Individuality and Social Forms: Selected Writings*, edited by D. N. Levine, 143–9. Chicago: University of Chicago Press.

Simmel, G. (1971b). 'The Metropolis and Mental Life.' In *On Individuality and Social Forms: Selected Writings*, edited by D. N. Levine, 324–39. Chicago: University of Chicago Press.

Simon, G. M. (2009). 'The Soul Freed of Cares? Islamic Prayer, Subjectivity, and the Contradictions of Moral Selfhood in Minangkabau, Indonesia.' *American Ethnologist* 36 (2): 258–75.

Spivak, G. C. (1988). 'Can the Subaltern Speak?' In *Marxism and the Interpretation of Culture*, edited by C. Nelson and L. Grossberg, 271–316. Urbana: University of Illionois Press.

Talle, A. (2008). 'Precarious Identities: Somali Women in Exile.' *Finnish Journal of Ethnicity and Migration* 3 (2): 64–72.

Tarlo, E. (2010). *Visibly Muslim: Fashion, Politics, Faith*. London: Berg.

Taylor, C. (1994). 'The Politics of Recognition.' In *Multiculturalism*, edited by A. Gutmann, 25–73. Princeton: Princeton University Press.

Tiilikainen, M. (2003). 'Somali Women and Daily Islam in the Diaspora.' *Social Compass* 50 (1): 59–69.

Tiilikainen, M. (2005). 'Suffering, Social Memory and Embodiment: Experiences of Somali Refugee Women.' *Pakistan Journal of Women's Studies* 12 (2): 1–16.

Touval, S. (1963). *Somali Nationalism: International Politics and the Drive for Unity in the Horn of Africa*. Cambridge: Harvard University Press.

Valentine, G., and Sporton, D. (2009). 'How Other People See You, It's Like Nothing That's Inside': The Impact of Processes of Disidentification and Disavowal on Young People's Subjectivities.' *Sociology* 43 (4): 735–51.

Valentine, G., Sporton, D., and Nielsen, K. B. (2009). 'Identities and Belonging: A Study of Somali Refugee and Asylum Seekers Living in the UK and Denmark.' *Environment and Planning D: Society and Space* 27 (2): 234–50.

Van Hear, N. (1998). *New Diasporas: The Mass Exodus, Dispersal and Regrouping of Migrant Communities*. London: Routledge

Vertovec, S. (2010). 'Towards Post-Multiculturalism? Changing Communities, Conditions and Contexts of Diversity.' *International Social Science Journal* 61 (199): 83–95.

Vertovec, S., and Wessendorf, S., eds (2010). *The Multiculturalism Backlash: European Discourses, Policies and Practices*. Abingdon: Routledge.

Voll, J. O. (1983). 'Renewal and Reform in Islamic History: Tajdid and Islah.' In *Voices of Resurgent Islam*, edited by J. L. Esposito, 32–47. Oxford: Oxford University Press.

Walls, M. (2014) *A Somali Nation-State: History, Culture and Somaliland's Political Transition*. Pisa, Italy: Ponte Invisibile.

Werbner, P. (2004). *Pilgrims of Love: The Anthropology of a Global Sufi Cult*. London: Hurst Publishers.

Werbner, P. (2009). 'Revisiting the UK Muslim Diasporic Public Sphere at a Time of Terror: From Local (Benign) Invisible Spaces to Seditious Conspiratorial Spaces and the 'Failure of Multiculturalism' Discourse.' *South Asian Diaspora* 1 (1): 19–45.

Yúdice, G. (2003). *The Expediency of Culture: Uses of Culture in the Global Era*: Durham: Duke University Press

Yusuf, C. L. M. (2012). 'Recollection (Gocasho).' In *Poems Maansooyin*. [Translated from the Somali by C. Pollard, S. J. Hussein and M. Xasan Alto, 26–9. London: Poetry Translation Centre.

INDEX

Lightning Source UK Ltd.
Milton Keynes UK
UKHW020414210319
339583UK00006B/21/P